# Reproduction and the Constitution in the United States



*Reproduction and the Constitution in the United States* dissects the forces that shape US conflicts over birth control and abortion.

In 1973, the United States Supreme Court issued a decision in *Roe v. Wade*, a landmark decision that quickly became the most widely recognized case in the country. Examining the roots of ongoing struggles over reproduction in the United States, Mary Ziegler helps readers not only understand the importance of the Supreme Court's iconic decision in *Roe* but also places it in context, illuminating constitutional, political, and economic trends that have remade conflicts over abortion and the law. Written by one of the world's leading scholars in the field, this book synthesizes the latest scholarship and provides an accessible and concise look at:

- Why the United States criminalized abortion and birth control in the nineteenth century.
- Why there has been a stark disconnect between the law of the land and actual practice when it comes to controlling reproduction.
- What *Roe v. Wade* said and how the law and politics of abortion have moved beyond it.

With an up-to-date guide to Further Reading, Who's Who of important figures, and a Glossary of key terms, this book provides a crucial introduction to students of women's history, American history, and legal history.

**Mary Ziegler** is Stearns Weaver Miller Professor at Florida State University College of Law, USA. Previous works include *After Roe: The Lost History of the Abortion Debate* (2015) and *Abortion and the Law in America: Roe v. Wade to the Present* (2020).

# Introduction to the series

History is the narrative constructed by historians from traces left by the past. Historical enquiry is often driven by contemporary issues and, in consequence, historical narratives are constantly reconsidered, reconstructed, and reshaped. The fact that different historians have different perspectives on issues means that there is often controversy and no universally agreed version of past events. *Seminar Studies* was designed to bridge the gap between current research and debate, and the broad, popular general surveys that often date rapidly.

The volumes in the series are written by historians who are not only familiar with the latest research and current debates concerning their topic, but who have themselves contributed to our understanding of the subject. The books are intended to provide the reader with a clear introduction to a major topic in history. They provide both a narrative of events and a critical analysis of contemporary interpretations. They include the kinds of tools generally omitted from specialist monographs: a chronology of events, a glossary of terms, and brief biographies of "who's who." They also include bibliographical essays in order to guide students to the literature on various aspects of the subject. Students and teachers alike will find that the selection of documents will stimulate the discussion and offer insight into the raw materials used by historians in their attempt to understand the past.

Clive Emsley and Gordon Martel
Series Editors

# Reproduction and the Constitution in the United States

Mary Ziegler

Routledge
Taylor & Francis Group
LONDON AND NEW YORK

Cover Image: © Getty Images

First published 2022
by Routledge
2 Park Square, Milton Park, Abingdon, Oxon OX14 4RN

and by Routledge
605 Third Avenue, New York, NY 10158

*Routledge is an imprint of the Taylor & Francis Group, an informa business*



*British Library Cataloguing-in-Publication Data*
A catalog record for this title has been requested

*Library of Congress Cataloging-in-Publication Data*
A catalog record has been requested for this book

ISBN: 978-1-032-10562-8 (hbk)
ISBN: 978-1-032-10250-4 (pbk)
ISBN: 978-1-003-21593-6 (ebk)

DOI: 10.4324/9781003215936

Typeset in Sabon LT Std
by Apex CoVantage, LLC

# Contents

# Chronology

| | |
|---|---|
| 1847 | The American Medical Association is founded. |
| 1848 | |
| *July* | Feminists in Seneca Falls, New York, pass a Declaration of Sentiments demanding rights for women. |
| 1857 | |
| *Winter* | Dr. Horatio Storer and the American Medical Association launch campaign to criminalize abortion throughout pregnancy. |
| 1868 | |
| *July* | Congress ratifies the 14th Amendment, which guarantees due process and equal protection of the laws. |
| 1873 | Comstock Act prohibits providing information about abortion or birth control. |
| 1883 | Sir Francis Galton coins the term "eugenics" to describe strategies to improve "genetic stock." |
| 1890 | Most states criminalize abortion unless two physicians certify that the procedure will save a patient's life. |
| 1907 | Indiana passes the nation's first compulsory eugenic sterilization law. |
| 1916 | |
| *October* | Margaret Sanger helps to found the nation's first birth-control clinic in Brownsville, New York. |
| 1918 | |
| *January* | In *People of the State of New York v. Margaret Sanger*, the New York Court of Appeals upholds Sanger's conviction but reasons that doctors were already exempt from prosecution under the state's ban on birth control. |
| 1921 | |
| *November* | Sanger founds the American Birth Control League to advocate for access to contraception. |
| 1936 | The Second Circuit decides *United States v. One Package of Japanese Pessaries*. |
| 1939 | The Birth Control Federation of America launches its Negro Project. |

| | |
|---|---|
| 1942 | The Birth Control Federation of America takes a new name, the Planned Parenthood Federation of America. |
| 1950s | Many hospitals launch therapeutic hospital committees. |
| 1952 | As the population-control movement grows, Frederick Osborn founds the Population Council. |
| 1959 | The American Law Institute (ALI) introduces a model abortion law. |
| 1960 | The Food and Drug Administration approves the birth control pill. |
| 1963 | Betty Friedan publishes *The Feminine Mystique*. |
| 1965 | The Supreme Court decides *Griswold v. Connecticut*. |
| 1967 | Colorado becomes the first state to pass the ALI bill.<br>The Clergy Consultation Service on Abortion launches an abortion referral service.<br>The National Organization for Women endorses the repeal of all criminal laws on abortion. |
| 1968 | Pope Paul VI issues *Humanae Vitae*, an encyclical on birth control and sexuality.<br>Zero Population Growth, Inc. is founded.<br>The Family Life Division of the National Conference of Catholic Bishops founds the National Right to Life Committee (NRLC). |
| 1969 | The National Association for the Repeal of Abortion Laws (NARAL) begins operations. |
| 1970 | Congress passes Title X of the Public Health Service Act, creating a comprehensive family planning program.<br>New York eliminates all restrictions on abortion. |
| 1971 | The Supreme Court upholds a Washington, DC, abortion regulation in *United States v. Vuitch*. |
| 1972 | The Supreme Court strikes down a Massachusetts contraceptive regulation in *Eisenstadt v. Baird*. |
| 1973 | In *Doe v. Bolton* and *Roe v. Wade*, the Supreme Court recognizes a right to choose abortion. |
| 1974 | The federal government introduces new regulations to prevent involuntary sterilization. |
| 1975 | A Boston jury convicts Dr. Kenneth Edelin of manslaughter for performing an abortion. An appelate court later reverses his conviction. |
| 1976 | Congress passes the Hyde Amendment. |
| 1977 | In *Maher v. Roe* and two other cases, the Supreme Court upholds restrictions on funding for low-income patients seeking abortions. |
| 1979 | The Committee for Abortion Rights and Against Sterilization Abuse forms to demand not only abortion rights but also a broader social justice agenda. |

| | |
|---|---|
| | NARAL launches an effort to brand its movement pro-choice. |
| | The Moral Majority forms and takes a leading role in the Religious Right. |
| 1980 | Ronald Reagan, who runs as a champion of fetal rights, is elected president. |
| | In *Harris v. McRae*, the Supreme Court rejects a challenge to the constitutionality of the Hyde Amendment. |
| 1981 | The Senate confirms Sandra Day O'Connor to the Supreme Court. |
| 1980–1983 | Congress debates the merits of a statute banning abortion and a constitutional amendment allowing, but not requiring, the state to do so. Neither passes. |
| 1982 | The antiabortion Army of God kidnaps abortion provider Hector Zevallos and his wife. |
| 1983 | The Supreme Court strikes down abortion restrictions in *City of Akron v. Akron Center for Reproductive Health*. Sandra Day O'Connor's dissent inspires abortion foes to focus more on the courts. |
| 1986 | In *Thornburgh v. American College of Obstetricians and Gynecologists*, the Court strikes down a Pennsylvania law. The majority in favor of abortion rights shrinks to five justices. |
| | Antonin Scalia is confirmed to the Supreme Court. |
| 1987 | Robert Bork's nomination to the Supreme Court fails. |
| 1988 | Anthony Kennedy is confirmed to the Supreme Court. |
| | George H.W. Bush is elected president. |
| 1988–1994 | Launching massive blockades of abortion clinics, Operation Rescue becomes a household name. |
| 1989 | The Court decides *Webster v. Reproductive Health Services*. |
| 1990 | In *Rust v. Sullivan*, the Court rejects a challenge to the Reagan Administration's family-planning regulations. |
| | The Senate votes to confirm David Souter's Supreme Court nomination. |
| 1991 | Notwithstanding accusations of sexual harassment, Clarence Thomas is narrowly confirmed as a Supreme Court justice. |
| 1992 | The Supreme Court decides *Planned Parenthood v. Casey*. |
| | Bill Clinton is elected president. |
| 1993 | The Supreme Court decides *Bray v. Alexandria Women's Health Clinic*. |
| | An antiabortion extremist murders Dr. David Gunn. |
| | Ruth Bader Ginsburg joins the Supreme Court. |
| | Congress passes the Religious Freedom Restoration Act. |
| 1994 | Congress passes the Freedom of Access to Clinic Entrances (FACE Act). |

| | |
|---|---|
| | An antiabortion extremist murders Dr. John Britton and his bodyguard. |
| | At the International Conference on Population and Development, activists of color launch a new movement for reproductive justice. |
| | Stephen Breyer joins the Supreme Court. |
| 1996 | Fox News Channel launches. |
| 1997 | The Supreme Court decides *Mazurek v. Armstrong.* |
| 1997–1998 | The first forms of emergency contraception come on the market. |
| 1998 | Congress impeaches Bill Clinton, but the Senate ultimately acquits him. |
| 2000 | The Food and Drug Administration approves RU 486 but subjects it to several restrictions. |
| | George W. Bush is elected president. |
| 2002 | Congress passes the Born-Alive Infants Protection Act. |
| 2003 | Congress passes the Partial-Birth Abortion Ban Act. |
| 2005 | John Roberts and Samuel Alito join the Supreme Court. |
| 2007 | The Supreme Court decides *Gonzales v. Carhart.* |
| 2008 | Barack Obama is elected president. |
| 2009 | Conservative Christian leaders put out the *Manhattan Declaration: A Call of Christian Conscience.* |
| | Sonia Sotomayor joins the Supreme Court. |
| 2010 | Congress passes the Affordable Care Act. |
| | Tea Party Republicans take over several state legislatures. |
| | Elena Kagan joins the Supreme Court. |
| 2014 | The Supreme Court decides *Burwell v. Hobby Lobby Stores.* |
| 2015 | The Supreme Court decides *Obergefell v. Hodges.* |
| 2016 | The Supreme Court decides *Whole Woman's Health v. Hellerstedt.* |
| | Donald Trump is elected president. |
| 2017 | Neil Gorsuch joins the Supreme Court. |
| 2018 | Brett Kavanaugh joins the Supreme Court. |
| 2019 | States pass heartbeat bills, banning abortion around the sixth week of pregnancy. |
| 2020 | The Supreme Court decides *June Medical Services v. Russo.* |
| | Amy Coney Barrett joins the Supreme Court. |
| 2021 | The Supreme Court agrees to hear *Dobbs v. Jackson Women's Health Organization*, a case that poses a threat to *Roe v. Wade.* |

# Who's Who

**Alito, Samuel** (1950–) A justice of the Supreme Court, Alito was nominated by George W. Bush. After serving in the Reagan Administration early in his career, Alito went on to become a prosecutor and judge on the Third Circuit Court of Appeals.

**Anthony, Susan B.** (1820–1906) An anti-slavery activist, Anthony became the nation's best-known campaigner for women's suffrage in the latter part of the nineteenth century. Anthony endorsed temperance laws limiting access to alcohol, but her most lasting impact was on the law of women's rights. Arrested and put on trial for trying to vote in 1872, Anthony became one of the most effective advocates for women's suffrage.

**Arkes, Hadley** (1940–) A political scientist and professor, Arkes promoted the idea that the founders of the Constitution had recognized certain implied, natural rights, among them, a right to life for the unborn child. Arkes was also the moving force behind the Born-Alive Infants Protection Act of 2002.

**Atwater, Lee** (1951–1991) A political strategist and Republican Party consultant, Atwater worked for Ronald Reagan and George H.W. Bush, helping to engineer the latter's presidential campaign. Atwater also worried that an association with the pro-life movement would damage the standing of the Republican Party and pushed for the creation of a pro-choice group in the party, Republicans for Choice.

Baird, Bill (1932–) Often referred to as the father of the birth control movement, Baird became involved in the fight to legalize contraception in 1963 after watching a mother of nine die after trying to end her own pregnancy with a coat hanger. The clinical director of EMKO, a contraceptive manufacturer, Baird began lecturing on birth control and abortion and handing out contraceptives, going to prison in five states for doing so. He is perhaps best known for his role in the landmark Supreme Court case on contraception, *Eisenstadt v. Baird.*

**Barrett, Amy Coney** (1972–) The fifth woman to serve on the Supreme Court, Barrett was nominated by Donald Trump in 2020. Barrett was a professor at Notre Dame Law School and an appellate judge before her Supreme Court nomination. Among the justices, she was also unique in having personally been involved in right-to-life politics.

**Beilenson, Anthony** (1932–2017) A Democratic lawmaker from Southern California, Beilenson served both in Congress and the California State Legislature. He authored and fought for California's 1967 abortion bill that made abortion legal in cases of rape, incest, or a risk to physical or mental health.

**Benham, Flip** (1948–) An evangelical Christian minister, Benham became the head of Operation Rescue in 1994. Benham famously helped to baptize Norma McCorvey, the "Roe" of *Roe v. Wade*, and bring her into the right-to-life movement. During his time at Operation Rescue, the issue of violence against abortion providers fragmented and weakened the clinic blockade movement. In 2021, he led a smaller successor of Operation Rescue, Operation Save America.

**Blackmun, Harry** (1908–1999) A justice of the United States Supreme Court from 1970 until 1994, Blackmun began his career as a conservative nominated by Richard Nixon and ended it as one of the Court's most storied liberals. Blackmun was best known for authoring the majority opinion in *Roe v. Wade.*

**Bopp, James Jr.** (1948–) A prominent conservative lawyer, Bopp served as the general counsel for the National Right to Life Committee since the late 1970s. Bopp also played a leading role in the politics of campaign spending, leading legal challenges to campaign-finance reforms and helping Republicans get around existing spending limits. Bopp held several leadership roles in the Republican Party and championed greater influence for conservative interest groups within the party.

**Bork, Robert** (1927–2012) One of the pioneers of the conservative legal movement, Bork, a professor at Yale Law School, served as the United States solicitor general from 1973 to 1977 and went on to serve on the United States Court of Appeals for the DC Circuit. Bork was one of the best known conservative legal theorists, and his unsuccessful Supreme Court nomination changed the way presidents and social movements approached future selections for the High Court.

**Breyer, Stephen** (1938–) Nominated by Bill Clinton to serve on the Supreme Court, Breyer became a justice after working as a prosecutor and an appellate judge. In his time on the Court, Breyer authored several key opinions on abortion, including in *Whole Woman's Health v. Hellerstedt* and *June Medical Services v. Russo.*

**Brind, Joel** (1952–) An endocrinologist at Baruch College, Brind became convinced that abortion increased the risk of breast cancer. A Christian convert and abortion opponent, Brind became the most visible proponent of arguments about the so-called abortion/breast cancer connection, testifying at trials and in state legislatures, publishing research, and promoting restrictive legislation.

**Burger, Warren** (1907–1995) Nominated to the Supreme Court by Richard Nixon, Burger was the Court's fifteenth chief justice, a position he held until 1986. Burger had been a strong critic of the liberal jurisprudence of the Warren Court, but he voted with the majority to recognize a right to choose abortion in *Roe* before that position in 1986 in *Thornburgh v. American College of Obstetricians and Gynecologists*.

**Bush, George H.W.** (1924–2018) The forty-first president of the United States, Bush had a long career in Republican politics, having served as ambassador to the United Nations, the director of central intelligence, a member of Congress, and vice president of the United States. Bush had been a supporter of family planning but moved sharply to the right on abortion to win the presidency.

**Bush, George W.** (1946–) The forty-third president of the United States, Bush led the country during the September 11th terrorist attack, oversaw a costly war in Iraq and Afghanistan, launched a "war on terror," and oversaw the beginnings of an economic recession. Bush signed several federal abortion restrictions into law, the federal Partial-Birth Abortion Ban Act chief among them.

**Buxton, C. Lee** (1904–1969) A gynecologist and medical professor at Yale, Buxton became a birth control activist after moving to Connecticut, a state with restrictive laws. Buxton helped to lobby for changes to the state law and brought several challenges in court, including the landmark case of *Griswold v. Connecticut*.

**Byrn, Robert M.** (1928–2017) A law professor and lawyer, Byrn became one of the leading legal theorists for the right-to-life movement. While working as a law professor at Fordham, Byrn petitioned to be named guardian for all the fetuses scheduled to be aborted in New York after that state amended its law. While his effort ultimately failed, Byrn continued to advise the right-to-life movement on its legal strategy, particularly when it came to amending the Constitution in the aftermath of *Roe*.

**Cano, Sandra (1947/1948?–2014)** Best known as Mary Doe in *Doe v. Bolton*, Cano had to overcome a serious disability, poverty, and abusive relationships. She regretted her involvement in the *Doe* case and later became involved in antiabortion advocacy, including efforts to get her case overturned.

**Carter, Jimmy** (1929–) The thirty-ninth president of the United States, Carter got his start in Georgia politics, holding office as a Democratic state senator and governor before his presidential bid. Carter's presidency coincided with the rise of conservative evangelicals as a political force; Carter's own evangelical faith—and willingness to break with some faith leaders on certain issue—helped inspire conservative Christians to mobilize. After his time in office, Carter became a well-known philanthropist focused on international human rights.

**Cassidy, Harold** (1947–) A New Jersey trial attorney, Cassidy made a name for himself as a criminal defense attorney and a lawyer representing biological parents in adoption and surrogacy matters. A strong opponent of abortion, Cassidy pioneered a strategy centered on the idea that abortion violated rights for women.

**Clinton, Bill** (1946–) The forty-second president of the United States, Clinton was a centrist Democrat and the first pro-choice president since 1973. Clinton survived the failure of his health-care reform proposal and several scandals, including a sexual harassment accusation, and was acquitted in a subsequent impeachment. Nevertheless, he went on to serve two terms.

**Coffee, Linda** (1942–) An American attorney based in Texas, Coffee was best known as one of the attorneys who challenged Texas's abortion ban in *Roe v. Wade.*

**Comstock, Anthony** (1844–1915) An anti-vice crusader, Comstock successfully campaigned for a federal law making it illegal to mail "obscene" material, a category that included most information on anatomy, birth control, and abortion.

**Crutcher, Mark** (1948–)An antiabortion activist based in Texas, Crutcher was the founder of Life Dynamics, Inc., a right-to-life group that taught other abortion foes how to sue abortion providers. Crutcher popularized a tactical plan that used lawsuits to make abortion inaccessible. Later, Crutcher pushed the argument that the movement to legalize abortion was rooted in eugenics and racism.

**Darwin, Charles** (1809–1882) A biologist and naturalist, Darwin was best known for his contributions to the study of evolution. Positing that all living species shared a common ancestor, Darwin published *On the Origin of Species* in 1859. His theory of natural selection, which explained that species with more desirable traits were able to out-reproduce and outcompete their rivals, inspired some eugenic thinking in the late nineteenth and early twentieth centuries.

**Davenport, Charles** (1866–1944) A zoologist and eugenicist, Davenport founded the Eugenic Records Office in Cold Springs Harbor, New York, to study what he claimed were the genetic origins of everything from alcoholism and sexual promiscuity to intelligence. Davenport also published work suggesting that interracial relationships led to the birth of defective children. His scientific racism helped to inspire restrictive immigration policies and compulsory sterilization laws.

**Dennett, Mary Ware** (1872–1947) A suffragist and birth control activist, Dennett lost several children in infancy and experienced a number of life-threatening pregnancies. Following her well-publicized divorce, Dennett became a professional advocate for women's right to vote. She also lobbied for reforms to birth control laws, arguing that more information would protect women like her. In 1915, Dennett co-founded the National Birth Control League. The legal proceedings against her for disseminating contraceptive devices and advice helped lead to an expansion and normalization of birth control in the United States.

**Douglas, William** (1898–1980) A politician and jurist, Douglas began his career working for the presidential administration of Franklin D. Roosevelt. As a member of Supreme Court, Douglas wrote the majority opinion in *Griswold v. Connecticut*, recognizing a right for married people to use contraception.

**Downer, Carol** (1933–) A feminist activist and health care provider, Downer was a pioneer in the feminist women's health movement, which forged a model of care that sought to demystify women's bodies and give women more control over their reproduction. Downer and her colleague, Lorraine Rothman, toured the country showing women how to perform cervical self-exams and how to do one method of early abortion, menstrual extraction. After helping to launch a network of feminist clinics, Downer attended law school and continued to promote the cause of women's liberation.

**Du Bois, W.E.B.** (1868–1963) One of the most important civil-rights activists of his era, Du Bois attended Harvard University and did path-breaking work in sociology, studying how the experience and legacy of slavery affected Black families. In 1910, Du Bois became the head of the National Association for Advancement of Colored People (NAACP) and helped publish the *Crisis*, an NAACP magazine that offered important perspective on racism and civil rights. Du Bois was also an advocate of women's right to vote and supported efforts to expand contraceptive access in the Black community.

**Eagleton, Thomas** (1929–2007) A Democratic Senator and former vice-presidential candidate, Eagleton had an accomplished career in Congress. Having battled depression for much of his life, Eagleton became a leading voice on foreign relations and environmental issues in the Senate, opposing the Vietnam War and championing the Clean Air Act and Clean Water Act. He was also a strong opponent of abortion. Eagleton campaigned to make sure that federal protections against pregnancy discrimination did not cover abortion and co-authored a constitutional amendment banning abortion. After Eagleton left the Senate in 1987, antiabortion Democrats became harder and harder to find.

**Ellis, Havelock** (1859–1939) A psychologist and social reformer, Ellis worked to demystify both heterosexual and homosexual sex. A confidante and lover of Margaret Sanger, Ellis argued that birth control access for women would have eugenic benefits.

**Falwell, Jerry Sr.** (1933–2007) The founding pastor of the Thomas Road Church, a megachurch in Lynchburg, Virginia, Falwell was arguably the nation's best-known televangelist and the face of the Moral Majority, a leading organization in the rise of the Religious Right in the 1970s.

**Ford, Christine Blasey** (1966–) A professor of psychology at Palo Alto University and a research psychologist at Stanford University of Medicine, Ford is best known for accusing Supreme Court Justice Brett Kavanaugh of sexually assaulting her when the two were in high school. Although the Senate ultimately confirmed Kavanaugh, Ford's accusations sparked a national conversation about sexual violence and accountability.

**Ford, Gerald** (1913–2006) The thirty-eighth president of the United States, Ford came to office following the resignation of President Richard Nixon, who was inculpated in the Watergate scandal. Ford had been a star athlete before beginning a career in politics and rising quickly up the ranks of the Republican Party, becoming minority leader in the House of Representatives in 1964. Ford served as Nixon's vice president before the latter's resignation; in office, he tried to sidestep the abortion issue and focus on easing Cold War tensions but lost popularity after he decided to pardon Nixon. He lost his bid for reelection in 1976.

**Friedan, Betty** (1921–2006) A writer and activist, Friedan was one of the central leaders of the women's movement in the 1960s and 1970s. Her 1963 book, *The Feminine Mystique*, proved to be a major catalyst for second-wave feminism in the United States. In 1966, she co-founded the National Organization for Women to pursue a more equal form of citizenship for women. After stepping down from her position as the leader of that organization, Friedan helped to found the National Women's Political Caucus, a group committed to helping women seek elected office. She courted controversy later in life by arguing that the women's movement had become too extreme, especially when it came to advocacy for lesbian rights. She was also a key figure in the fight to legalize abortion, spearheading efforts to get the National Organization for Women to endorse abortion rights and helping to lead the National Association for the Repeal of Abortion Laws.

**Galton, Francis** (1822–1911) A statistician, explorer, and sociologist, Galton helped to launch the eugenics movement. As the cousin of Charles Darwin, Galton took a keen interest in how genetic inheritance affected a wide range of physical and mental traits as well as behaviors. He helped to make eugenics respectable.

**Ginsburg, Ruth Bader** (1933–2020) A groundbreaking civil rights attorney and Supreme Court justice, Ginsburg helped to revolutionize the law of sex discrimination in the United States. As a young attorney at the

American Civil Liberties Union, Ginsburg helped to establish that sex discrimination violated the Fourteenth Amendment of the Constitution. As a Supreme Court justice, Ginsburg wrote key opinions on sex discrimination and reproduction.

**Goldberg, Arthur** (1908–1990) A former Supreme Court justice and ambassador, Goldberg was a heavyweight in liberal politics. After a storied career as a labor lawyer, Goldberg held several positions in the administration of John F. Kennedy, serving as secretary of labor before Lyndon Johnson nominated him to serve on the Supreme Court. Goldberg was a member of the Court for only three years before resigning to become ambassador to the United Nations. Goldberg made a significant impact during his time on the Court and helped to author a major concurrence in *Griswold v. Connecticut* discussing what the right to privacy had to do with birth control.

**Gorsuch, Neil** (1967–) Nominated by Donald Trump to serve on the Supreme Court, Gorsuch was a self-described originalist and textualist judge who worked in private practice and as an appellate judge before becoming a member of the High Court.

**Griswold, Estelle** (1900–1981) An activist for women's rights, Griswold was best known for her role in the famous *Griswold v. Connecticut*, a case expanding access to birth control. Griswold had wanted to be a singer before studying medicine. While working to resettle refugees in the aftermath of the Second World War, she became convinced that more women needed access to birth control to gain control of their lives. She went on to become the head of the Planned Parenthood League of Connecticut and fought to legalize contraception in that state.

**Guttmacher, Alan** (1898–1974) An obstetrician-gynecologist, Guttmacher served as the vice president of the American Eugenics Society and the president of Planned Parenthood. Guttmacher enjoyed great success as an obstetrician-gynecologist. In his medical work, he noticed differing fertility rates of women of different economic backgrounds. This experience convinced him of the importance of expanded contraceptive access. He campaigned to legalize contraception in New York and then across the country. Later, he took a major part in efforts to reform abortion laws. An organization he helped to form, the Guttmacher Institute, now serves as a major source of data on family planning and abortion.

**Harlan, John Marshall II** (1899–1971) A justice of the Supreme Court, Harlan was considered one of the more conservative members of the liberal Warren Court. After a long career as a trial lawyer, Harlan was nominated to the Supreme Court in 1955 by Republican Dwight Eisenhower. He was more reluctant to strike down legislation than some of his colleagues, but he believed that the Constitution protected a number of implied rights, including those related to birth control for married couples.

**Haskell, Martin** (1946–) An abortion provider, Haskell became known for a paper on the procedure dilation and extraction, which antiabortion leaders described as partial-birth abortion.

**Hill, Anita** (1956–) A lawyer and academic, Hill became a national name after accusing Supreme Court nominee Clarence Thomas of sexual harassment.

**Jefferson, Mildred** (1927–2010) A pioneering physician, Jefferson was best known as one of the nation's most charismatic antiabortion activists. Jefferson became the first Black woman to attend Harvard Medical School. She went on to become board certified in surgery and worked as a surgeon and medical school professor at Boston University. She became active in abortion politics in 1970 and served as president of the National Right to Life Committee from 1975 to 1978.

**Jones, Paula** (1966–) A former civil servant in Arkansas, Jones sued former president Bill Clinton for sexual harassment. Jones' suit set off a chain of events that culminated in Clinton's impeachment and ultimate acquittal.

**Kagan, Elena** (1960–) Nominated to the Supreme Court by Barack Obama, Kagan was a former dean of Harvard Law School and solicitor general of the United States.

**Kavanaugh, Brett** (1965–) Nominated to the Supreme Court by Donald Trump, Kavanaugh helped Ken Starr in the investigation of Bill Clinton, served under George W. Bush, and worked as an appellate judge before joining the Supreme Court. Kavanaugh's confirmation inspired a new wave of abortion legislation.

**Kennedy, Anthony** (1936–) Nominated to the Supreme Court by Ronald Reagan, Kennedy tended to vote with his conservative colleagues but often carved out his own path on abortion, co-authoring the join opinion in *Planned Parenthood of Southeastern Pennsylvania v. Casey* and often casting the deciding vote in other abortion cases.

**Kolbert, Kathryn** (1952–) An attorney who worked with the American Civil Liberties Union Reproductive Freedom Project and the Women's Law Project, Kolbert argued the key case, *Planned Parenthood v. Casey*, before the Supreme Court. Kolbert went on to co-found the Center for Reproductive Rights (then, the Center for Reproductive Rights and Policy) and have a national radio program before leading the liberal People for the American Way.

**Lader, Larry** (1909–2006) An author and activist, Lader was a tireless champion of abortion rights. He became interested in abortion while writing a book on Margaret Sanger and went on to write a comprehensive study on abortion that shaped the Supreme Court's decision in *Roe v. Wade*. A leading member of the National Association for the Repeal of Abortion Laws, Lader left that organization in 1976 to pursue a more aggressive approach, challenging the tax-exempt status of the Catholic Church and seeking to bring RU 486 to the United States.

**Lamm, Richard** (1935–) The former governor of Colorado, Lamm prioritized issues related to the environment, overpopulation, and urban sprawl. During his time in the state legislature, Lamm led the effort to reform his state's abortion law, making Colorado the first state in the country to loosen restrictions on abortion.

**Laughlin, Harry** (1880–1943) A former schoolteacher and principal, Laughlin worked with Charles Davenport at the Eugenic Records Office and helped to popularize eugenic policies in Congress and the states. Laughlin helped to draft a "model" compulsory sterilization law that served as a blueprint for many states pursuing eugenic policies, including Virginia, whose law the Supreme Court upheld in 1927.

**Lewinsky, Monica** (1973–) A television personality and anti-bullying activist, Lewinsky became a household name because she had a sexual relationship with President Bill Clinton while Lewinsky worked as a White House intern.

**Limbaugh, Rush** (1951–2021) A conservative radio host, Limbaugh helped to establish rightwing talk radio as a medium. One of the most highly compensated broadcasters in history, Limbaugh had an outsized influence in U.S. politics, helping to launch the careers of Republican politicians who were far further to the right.

**Lohman, Ann Trow (Madame Restell)** (1812–1878) The most notorious abortion provider of the nineteenth century, Madame Restell and her husband provided contraception and abortion services in New York. Due to several criminal trials and sensationalized press coverage, Restell became a symbol of the widespread use of abortion in the nineteenth century.

**Maginnis, Pat** (1928–) A feminist and abortion-rights activist, Maginnis helped to found the Society for Humane Abortion, advocating for the complete repeal of all regulations on abortion. Maginnis also helped women in California find abortion providers in the years before *Roe*.

**McCorvey, Norma** (1947–2017) The "Roe" of *Roe v. Wade*, McCorvey became a symbol for those on both sides of the abortion debate. She had already had two children and put them up for adoption before the *Roe* case. While trying to abort her third pregnancy, McCorvey was put in touch with attorneys Sarah Weddington and Linda Coffee. McCorvey eventually gave birth to that child and put it up for adoption. She went on to work for the pro-choice movement before meeting Flip Benham, a leader of Operation Rescue, converting to Christianity, and joining the antiabortion movement. The sincerity of her conversion—and her true beliefs about abortion—would remain contested years after her death.

**McGovern, George** (1922–2012) A Senator and for presidential candidate, McGovern clawed his way to the Democratic nomination by spotlighting his opposition to the Vietnam War. McGovern had once courted the women's movement but did not support abortion rights during his 1972 campaign, choosing right-to-lifer Thomas Eagleton as his running mate.

**Moore, Hugh** (1887–1972) The president and founder of the Dixie Cup Company, Moore became obsessed with the threat of world overpopulation. He worked with Planned Parenthood and the Association for Voluntary Sterilization before founding his own, more alarmist group, the Population Crisis Committee, in 1965.

**Murdoch, Rupert** (1931–) An Australian-American television mogul, Murdoch owned hundreds of publishing outlets across the globe. Murdoch's News Corporation acquired leading media outlets, including Twentieth Century Fox, Harper Collins, and the *Wall Street Journal*. Murdoch's Fox News Channel became a kingmaker in Republican politics.

**Nixon, Richard** (1913–1994) The thirty-seventh president of the United States, Nixon did not always govern as a conservative, working to normalize relations with China and to expand family planning services in the United States. Avoiding an earlier position on abortion, Nixon did an about-face and proclaimed his opposition to abortion to win over former Democrats during the 1972 race. He left office in disgrace in the aftermath of the Watergate scandal when the press exposed his confederates' efforts to bug the offices of political opponents. Nixon resigned before Congress had a chance to impeach him.

**Obama, Barack** (1961–) The forty-fourth president of the United States, Obama became the first Black American to hold that office. Obama oversaw the passage of the Affordable Care Act, but the rise of the Tea Party, together with racial backlash to his presidency, deepened polarization during his tenure.

**O'Connor, Sandra Day** (1930–) Nominated to the Supreme Court by Ronald Reagan, O'Connor was the first female Supreme Court justice. While O'Connor most often sided with the Court's conservative bloc, she wrote several landmark opinions that frustrated her conservative colleagues, including co-authoring the 1992 joint opinion in *Planned Parenthood of Southeastern Pennsylvania v. Casey*. O'Connor retired from the Court in 2005 and retreated from public life in 2018 following a diagnosis of dementia.

**Osborn, Frederick** (1889–1981) A former general, Osborn played a prominent part in the eugenics and population control movements. After serving in World War II, Osborn returned to a career at Princeton, where he helped to legitimize new ideas about eugenics—especially the importance of encouraging the "right" people to have children. One of the founding members of the American Eugenics Society, Osborn later founded the Population Council and became a vocal advocate for curbing demographic growth.

**Parker, Allan** (1952–) An antiabortion activist former academic and attorney, Parker promoted the argument that abortion damaged women's mental health. The leader of Operation Outcry, an effort to gather the stories of women who regretted their abortions, Parker represented Norma McCorvey, the former Jane Roe, and Sandra Cano, the former Mary Doe, in their efforts to eliminate abortion rights.

**Paul, Alice** (1885–1977) A leading feminist, Paul played a prominent part in securing the right to vote for women. Paul favored a more confrontational approach and prioritized the ratification of a constitutional amendment. Paul's National Women's Party marginalized women of color and suggested that suffrage would not upset the existing racial order in the United States. Following ratification of the Nineteenth Amendment, Paul championed an Equal Rights Amendment that would write sex discrimination out of the federal Constitution. Later in life, Paul saw the fight for an Equal Rights Amendment fail in the 1970s but celebrated when Congress chose to prohibit sex discrimination in federal civil rights law.

**Paul VI, Pope** (1897–1978) The head of the Catholic Church from 1963 to 1978, Pope Paul VI oversaw the end of the Second Vatican Council and implemented several reforms while improving relations with Orthodox and Protestant faith communities. Pope Paul VI's most controversial legacy was the *Humanae Vitae*, a 1968 encyclical that restated the Church's opposition to all forms of artificial birth control.

**Phelan, Lana Clarke** (1921–2010) A feminist activist, Phelan was a key member of the Society for Humane Abortion. Phelan had personal experience with abortion, and she became the organization's leading orator. She and her organization framed abortion as a fundamental right for women before such arguments became common.

**Pitts Hames, Margie** (1933–1994) An Atlanta civil-rights lawyer, Hames was best known for her role in *Doe v. Bolton*, one of the cases that established abortion rights under the United States Constitution. She had been working on a project to eliminate tensions between law enforcement and civil rights protestors before the Bolton case. After, she continued representing abortion clinics in cases on reproductive rights.

**Porter, Janet Folger** (1962–) An antiabortion activist and author, Porter began her career in the mainstream antiabortion movement and helped to pass the nation's first partial-birth-abortion ban in Ohio. Porter then worked for D. James Kennedy, a Religious Right leader, battling civil rights legislation for gays and lesbians. Porter became best known for championing heartbeat bills, laws that criminalized abortion at roughly the sixth week of pregnancy, when doctors could detect fetal cardiac activity.

**Powell, F. Lewis Jr.** (1907–1998) Nominated to the Supreme Court by Richard Nixon, Powell sat on the High Court from 1972–1987. Perhaps best known for his opinion on race-based affirmative action in *Regents of the University of California v. Bakke*, Powell often joined key majority opinions, including in *Roe v. Wade*.

**Reagan, Ronald** (1911–2004) The fortieth president of the United States, Reagan, a hero to the Republican Party, helped to rewrite the rules of Republican politics. Reagan helped to forge a coalition of fiscal and social conservatives. He also cemented the Republican Party's position as the "party of life" and courted right-to-life voters. Reagan also worked to make Supreme Court nominations a rallying point for rightwing voters.

**Reardon, David** (1956–) An engineer and antiabortion activist, Reardon was one of the most prominent proponents of the argument that abortion caused women to suffer something close to post-traumatic stress. He founded the Elliot Institute in 1997 to oversee research into the negative effects of abortion on women and believed that by focusing on the supposed harm done to women, the antiabortion movement could finally make progress in the abortion debate.

**Rehnquist, William** (1924–2005) The former chief justice of the Supreme Court, Rehnquist was nominated to the High Court by Richard Nixon and made chief justice by Ronald Reagan. Before joining the bench, Rehnquist served as a political advisor to conservative stalwart Barry Goldwater and a member of the Nixon Administration. Rehnquist was one of the most outspoken critics of what he regarded as liberal judicial activism.

**Roberts, John** (1955–) The chief justice of the Supreme Court, Roberts was nominated to the High Court by George W. Bush. Before becoming a justice, Roberts served in the Reagan and George H.W. Bush Administrations and staked out a reputation for caring particularly about the institutional legitimacy of the Supreme Court.

**Robertson, Pat** (1930–) An American media mogul and televangelist, Robertson was one of the leaders of the Religious Right. He also spearheaded efforts to defend the interests of conservative Christians in the High Court, helping to found the conservative Regent University and Regent University Law School and the American Center for Law and Justice.

**Rockefeller, John D. III** (1906–1978) A philanthropist and the scion of the Rockefeller dynasty, Rockefeller was also a major donor to population-control and abortion-rights organizations. He helped to lead the Population Council and chaired a commission on population growth chartered by President Nixon. Rockefeller continued to support family planning and abortion-rights organizations later in his career.

**Rockefeller, Nelson** (1908–1979) The longtime Republican governor of New York, Rockefeller also served as vice president under Gerald Ford from 1974 to 1977. Rockefeller was one of the nation's most vocal pro-choice Republicans, and he vetoed a bill that would have reinstated criminal penalties for abortion in New York State.

**Rose, Lila** (1988–) An antiabortion activist and social media influencer, Rose became known as the leader of Live Action, a right-to-life group that posted heavily edited viral videos claiming to expose wrongdoing at Planned Parenthood.

**Sanger, Margaret** (1879–1966) The best-known champion of contraception in the United States, Sanger helped to found the nation's first birth control clinic and campaigned effectively to change the rules governing birth control in the United States. Controversial because of her support for eugenics, Sanger founded organizations that eventually became the Planned Parenthood Federation of America and was involved in several legal cases that expanded contraceptive access.

**Scalia, Antonin** (1936–2016) Nominated to the Supreme Court by Ronald Reagan, Scalia was long the Court's most outspoken conservative and one of the most outspoken critics of the Court's abortion jurisprudence.

**Sotomayor, Sonia** (1954–) Nominated to the Supreme Court by Barack Obama, Sotomayor became the first Latina, the first woman of color, and the third woman to serve on the High Court. Earlier in her career, Sotomayor served as a prosecutor and worked in private practice before working as a district judge and appellate judge.

**Souter, David** (1939–) Nominated to the Supreme Court by George H.W. Bush, Souter had worked as a prosecutor and a state judge before joining the High Court. He played an instrumental role in *Planned Parenthood v. Casey*, the decision saving the right to choose abortion. He retired in 2009 and was replaced by Sonia Sotomayor.

**Starr, Ken** (1946–) A former appellate judge and solicitor general, Starr was best known for overseeing the investigation into President Bill Clinton's failed real estate deal, known as the Whitewater investigation.

**Storer, Horatio** (1830–1922) A pioneering gynecologist, Storer led the campaign to criminalize most abortions in the nineteenth century. One of the first doctors to perform a Cesarean section, Storer argued that abortion murdered a living baby and threatened to overrun the United States with inferior immigrants.

**Taussig, Fred** (1872–1943) A St. Louis obstetrician-gynecologist, Taussig became an outspoken proponent of abortion reform in the 1930s. Taussig recognized growing support for abortion during the Great Depression. Although few in the medical profession heeded his calls for reform in his lifetime, his arguments shaped the later reform movement.

**Thomas, Clarence** (1948–) Nominated to the Supreme Court by George H.W. Bush, Thomas became known for the sexual-harassment scandal surrounding his nomination. Married to a conservative activist, Thomas was the Court's most vocal critic of the *Roe* decision.

**Trías, Helen Rodríguez** (1929–2001) A pediatrician and activist for women's rights, Trías played a leading role in fighting the coerced sterilization of women of color in Puerto Rico and the United States mainland. In the 1980s, Trías did pioneering work on behalf of women of color suffering from HIV/AIDS. She became the first Latina woman to lead the American Public Health Association in 1993.

**Weddington, Sarah** (1945–) An attorney, law professor, and legislator, Weddington was best known for representing Norma McCorvey, Jane Roe, in *Roe v. Wade*. After the *Roe* case, Weddington served three terms in the Texas House of Representatives and worked in the Carter Administration. She remained a vocal advocate for reproductive rights.

**Wells, Ida B.** (1862–1931) A prominent journalist and civil rights activist, Wells was a Black suffragist who played a key role in advocating for the vote for Black women. Wells spearheaded major campaigns against lynching in the South and exposed the racism that sometimes suffused the movement for women's suffrage.

**White, Byron** (1917–2002) Nominated to the Supreme Court by John F. Kennedy, White was a former professional football player, military veteran, and attorney.

**Willke, John** (1925–2015) A physician and antiabortion activist, Willke converted many to the antiabortion cause through graphic slideshows. He served for years as the president of the largest national antiabortion organization, the National Right to Life Committee, before forming his own group, the Life Issues Institute. Willke popularized efforts to argue that abortion harmed women as well as fetal life. He was also known for pushing the theory that rape victims could not get pregnant.

**Woodhull, Victoria** (1838–1927) A notorious suffragist, Woodhull courted controversy by proclaiming her support for "free love," the right to marry, divorce, and bear children without government meddling. Woodhull was among the first women to run a newspaper or a brokerage house on Wall Street. A fierce fighter for women's right to vote, Woodhull also ran for president.

**Yuzpe, Albert A.** (1936–) A Canadian obstetrician-gynecologist, Yuzpe helped to design a method of emergency contraception that would be used to prevent pregnancy in a brief window after sexual intercourse.

# Part I

# Introduction

# Introduction

Most conversations about abortion and the Constitution in the United States begin with *Roe v. Wade*. In that 1973 decision, the US Supreme Court struck down a Texas law allowing abortions only when a patient's life was at risk. In a companion case, *Doe v. Bolton*, the Court invalidated a Georgia statute that made abortion legal only in cases of rape, incest, fetal abnormality, or a threat to patient health—and only when several physicians and a hospital committee signed off first. Seven justices—many of them nominated by Republican presidents—joined a majority opinion that upended the law and politics of abortion.

The Court in *Roe* relied on the idea of a fundamental right to privacy. The text of the Constitution did not say anything about privacy, but several times before, the Court had recognized rights to use birth control, get married, procreate, or raise children. In *Roe*, the Court held that whatever privacy the Constitution protected was broad enough to protect a woman's decision to end a pregnancy. The majority spotlighted the harms that pregnant people would face if forced to continue a pregnancy—the difficulties and dangers of pregnancy, the stigma of unwed motherhood, and even the burdens of childcare.

The Court considered and rejected arguments made by leading opponents of legal abortion. *Roe* reasoned that an unborn child or fetus did not count as a person for constitutional purposes (and therefore did not have a right to equal protection or due process of law). The Court likewise concluded that the government did not have a compelling interest in protecting life from the moment that sperm fertilized an egg. Noting that medical experts, theologians, and philosophers disagreed about when life began, the Court suggested that Texas could not impose its view on everyone else.

The effect of the two decisions was seismic. At the time, the vast majority of states criminalized all or most abortions. Only a handful, including New York, had removed all restrictions. In the aftermath of *Roe*, almost every state had to rewrite its abortion laws.

Before 1973, most abortions happened in hospitals, under the tight supervision of multi-doctor committees that rejected many requests (and worked primarily with middle-class or wealthy patients). After 1973, freestanding abortion clinics opened nationwide. For a time, the abortion rate shot up.

DOI: 10.4324/9781003215936-2

Harry Blackmun, the judge who wrote the *Roe* decision, had hoped that the Court's decision would help to deescalate the abortion conflict. After all, at the time *Roe* came down, proponents and opponents of legal abortion had fought a state-by-state war to determine policy in both legislatures and courts. Blackmun had clipped a newspaper story on a recent Gallup poll suggesting that more than two thirds of Americans believed that the abortion should be left to the woman and her doctor. If most Americans agreed with the result in the *Roe* decision, he thought, then the Supreme Court might help make the conflict less ugly.

Blackmun's hope came to seem extremely naïve. If anything, decades after *Roe*, fights have become even more bitter. After 1973, a movement opposed to legal abortion—already active for the better part of a decade—expanded. The pro-life or antiabortion movement promoted a constitutional amendment that would overturn *Roe*. Over time, abortion foes abandoned this quest in favor of an effort to change the Supreme Court itself. With different people on the High Court, it might be possible to reverse *Roe*.

Ever since 1973, discussions of abortion in the United States have revolved around *Roe*. Any time a vacancy opens on the Supreme Court, members of the Senate quiz a nominee about their views about *Roe*. In many such nominations, the *Roe* decision often looms larger than any other consideration. Many Americans know relatively little about the work of the Supreme Court; the same, of course, is true of those in other countries. Yet *Roe* is uniquely well-recognized. When many think of the US Supreme Court, they think of *Roe*.

*Roe* also helped to reshape party politics in the United States. Before the early 1980s, neither the Democratic nor Republican Parties had staked out a clear position on the abortion issue. By 1980, however, the Republican Party had proclaimed its opposition to both *Roe* and legal abortion, while the Democratic Party favored abortion rights. Abortion became the most visible wedge issue in US politics, helping to convince some Catholics, Mormons, and evangelical Protestants to switch parties.

On occasion, the fate of *Roe* could decide elections, with some voters prioritizing control of the Supreme Court when they went to the polls. Every year, in January, Americans protested or celebrated the *Roe* decision. *Roe* helped to launch a debate about whether there was a right to procreate, a right not to procreate, or a right to life. At the heart of the abortion battle were profound questions about the meaning of equality, autonomy, and personhood in the United States.

Both in the United States and abroad, *Roe* has defined conversations about reproductive health and the American culture wars. And yet our collective fixation on *Roe* obscures as much as it reveals.

This book takes our preoccupation with *Roe* as its starting point, studying both why *Roe* has such a hold on the US abortion dialogue and how fights about reproductive health in the country have moved beyond it. *Roe* primarily framed abortion as a medical matter determined in large part by expert physicians. Almost immediately, however, commentators made

"*Roe*" stand for much more. In addition to reinterpreting *Roe*, politicians, scholars, and social movements created myths about *Roe*'s effects—arguing that *Roe* had created the antiabortion movement, the American Religious Right, or the so-called culture wars over contraception, sex, and religion.

Mythmaking about *Roe* gave it unique symbolic resonance for groups across the US political spectrum. But if we want a real grasp of the history, law, and politics of abortion and contraception in the United States, we have to understand that *Roe* is only part of a much more complex history. Indeed, when Americans talk about *Roe*, they only sometimes mean the 1973 Supreme Court decision. We often talk about *Roe* and miss a complicated story of abortion and the Constitution in America. This book provides an overview of that struggle.

We tend to view *Roe* as the starting point of conflicts about abortion in the United States. In truth, struggles over legal abortion began much earlier. Prior to the late nineteenth century, most states had allowed early abortions, prohibiting the procedure only after quickening, the point at which a doctor could detect fetal movement. In 1858, the American Medical Association, a group for physicians, launched a campaign to criminalize all abortions. This effort was a stunning success: by the end of the nineteenth century, almost every state made abortion a crime from the very beginning of pregnancy.

While abortions continued, few challenged the legal status quo until the 1960s. In 1959, the American Law Institute, an elite group of lawyers, proposed a law allowing abortions in cases of rape, incest, fetal abnormality, or a threat to the patient's health. States began passing laws patterned on the American Law Institute model. Republicans and Democrats found themselves on both sides of the abortion divide.

While reform, as it was called, was popular, a movement formed to fight it. At the beginning, the so-called pro-life movement was predominantly Catholic—and at times, linked opposition to birth control with abortion. Over time, the antiabortion movement severed its formal ties with the Church and reframed its cause as a secular battle for civil rights for the unborn child. Most abortion foes were socially conservative on a variety of issues, and few fought for civil rights for people of color. Nevertheless, the fight for a right to life attracted a more diverse set of activists: small-government conservatives and self-styled liberals who wanted more protections for unwed mothers and pregnant workers, Mormons and Protestants as well as Catholics.

Reformers, for their part, did not feel satisfied with the laws they had championed. In states that passed the American Law Institute's style of law, the abortion rate hardly budged. A new generation of activists described abortion not just as a public health issue but also as a matter of women's liberation—or a tool to curb out-of-control population growth. These advocates demanded the complete repeal of abortion restrictions. Before 1973, the two sides fought to a draw. While some states eliminated all criminal laws on abortion, others rejected repeal and reform. Some courts recognized a privacy right to access abortion, while others protected the government's interest in preserving fetal life.

*Roe* did not start the abortion conflict, and as early as the 1970s, the fight had moved partly beyond *Roe*. At the time, abortion foes fought to amend the US Constitution. Leaders of the movement wanted to define the word "person" to include fetuses or unborn children. If this gambit had succeeded, the Court would have had to give unborn children due process and equal protection. That would have made abortion illegal nationwide. But the constitutional amendment process was onerous. Three-fifths of the House and Senate had to propose the amendment, and three-quarters of the states had to ratify it. At the time, Congress lacked a majority opposed to abortion, much less willing to push an outright ban.

So, the leaders of antiabortion groups like the National Right to Life Committee and Americans United for Life searched for a different way to reduce the abortion rate. These groups began to promote restrictions that would make it harder to access abortion. Laws required patients to get the consent of their husbands or parents. Others imposed a waiting period or required doctors to recite certain statements before performing an abortion. The most influential affected the Medicaid program, a government program that provided health insurance to low-income Americans. In 1976, Congress passed a bill to fund the federal Department of Health, Education, and Welfare. A rider to the bill, the Hyde Amendment, prohibited Medicaid reimbursement for most abortions. States soon introduced Medicaid funding prohibitions of their own.

The antiabortion movement had been active since the 1960s. Much like the abortion-rights movement, abortion foes had long focused on a constitutional right, the right to life from fertilization to natural death. Self-proclaimed pro-lifers pointed to the nation's Declaration of Independence, which recognized a right to life, liberty, and happiness. But the laws of the 1970s did not some seem to advance a right to life. All of the new laws allowed people to get abortions, subject to certain restrictions. Antiabortion leaders argued instead that *Roe v. Wade* permitted a wide range of abortion restrictions. If successful, this argument would make it much easier for states to limit access to abortion. As important, if *Roe* did not stop states from eliminating abortion access, abortion foes believed they would have an easier time arguing later that the Supreme Court should overturn the decision altogether.

The Supreme Court upheld some of these incremental restrictions (including the Hyde Amendment) and thereby began to transform what abortion rights meant in the real world. The Court ushered in a period in which access increasingly depended on a patient's race, income, and zip code.

These cleavages deepened in the 1980s as the Democratic and Republican Parties' positions on abortion diverged. Throughout the 1960s and 1970s, neither party had a clear position on abortion, but by 1980, it was no longer possible to confuse the parties' positions. Ronald Reagan ran as a pro-life president and supported a constitutional amendment banning abortion. His opponent, Jimmy Carter, endorsed *Roe* as the law of the land.

The shifting party politics of abortion changed the pro-choice and pro-life movements. Many abortion opponents had long been profoundly conservative on social and racial issues. But even those who identified as liberal had to realign their priorities when the antiabortion movement came to rely on the GOP. By aligning with the Republican Party, abortion foes could not lobby as effectively for more robust protections for pregnant workers, better access to contraception, or more support for the poor, at least without alienating their political patrons. The antiabortion cause became increasingly identified with the destruction of *Roe* and nothing more.

Throughout the 1980s, abortion foes continued chipping away at *Roe* and hoping that Republican presidents would reshape the Court. By the early 1990s, six conservatives sat on the nation's highest court, and it seemed that abortion rights would not last for long.

After 1992, however, *Roe* no longer defined the law on abortion, but not because the Supreme Court reversed it. The book takes readers through the Court's landmark decision, *Planned Parenthood v. Casey*, which preserved the idea of an abortion right but put in place a new test, the undue-burden standard, that made it much easier for lawmakers to pass abortion regulations. Under *Casey*, a law was unconstitutional only if it had the purpose or effect of creating a substantial obstacle for a person seeking abortion. After *Casey*, the debate turned less on whether the Constitution protected a right to abortion and more on what an "undue burden" meant.

After *Casey*, the pro-choice and pro-life movements battled to define an undue burden. Abortion foes believed that the Court had saved abortion rights because the justices believed that women relied on abortion access to lead more equal lives. To reverse *Casey* and *Roe*, anti-abortion attorneys developed a plan to prove that abortion actually hurt women. The antiabortion movement began with laws like one upheld in *Casey* itself: statutes requiring patients to hear certain information before securing an abortion. Over time, antiabortion lawmakers included more and more controversial statements in informed-consent laws: arguments that abortion increased the risk of breast cancer, suicidal ideation, or post-traumatic stress. Leading medical organizations and published studies refuted these conclusions, but abortion foes maintained that scientific authorities and mainstream media ignored the evidence because of their pro-choice commitments.

In the mid-1990s, fights about the line between science and politics intensified when states began outlawing a procedure that opponents called partial-birth abortion. In the early 1990s, Dr. Martin Haskell gave a paper on a relatively unknown abortion technique. Abortion opponents in Minnesota saw the paper, added line drawings of the procedure, and labeled it partial-birth abortion. By the mid-1990s, Republicans in Congress and the states had begun an initiative to ban the procedure. While supporters of abortion rights insisted that the procedure sometimes best protected patients' health, abortion foes responded that the science on the subject was too uncertain and supplied experts and evidence of their own.

In the mid-1990s, some feminists of color saw struggles over partial-birth abortion as another sign of their movement's mistakes. Since the 1960s, both the pro-choice and pro-life movements had been predominantly white, although prominent people of color had worked for organizations on both sides of the abortion issue.

It was no surprise that women of color had long questioned the strategies pursued by larger pro-choice organizations. Some people of color questioned the historic ties between pro-choice leaders and population-control organizations, which sometimes espoused eugenic and racist aims. Other people of color believed that the pro-choice movement's single-issue agenda—and focus on the idea of self-determination—disserved communities of color. For people confronting racism or poverty, free choice was not a reality but an aspiration. To have the ability to make autonomous decisions about reproduction, activists of color demanded protection from forced sterilization, access to birth control, neonatal, and maternal care, and the means to raise the children. Demands for a more comprehensive approach to reproductive health began before *Roe*, but in the 1990s a more organized movement took shape. Groups like the SisterSong Reproductive Justice Collective coined their approach reproductive justice: a recognition that, for communities of color, reproductive freedom and social justice were interdependent and equally important.

As the reproductive justice movement launched, the Supreme Court weighed in on partial-birth abortion, reinforcing concern about the politicization of science. The Court upheld a federal ban on the procedure. A majority reasoned that Congress could seek to protect women from regretting abortions. As important, the justices reasoned that when a matter was scientifically uncertain, lawmakers had more latitude to regulate. Abortion foes sought to establish that the safety of specific abortion procedures—or of terminating any pregnancy—was scientifically uncertain. In this way, the antiabortion movement could justify new restrictions and build the case for reversing *Roe* and *Casey*.

As antiabortion groups began arguing that much about abortion was scientifically uncertain, new technologies shook up the abortion debate. In the 1980s and 1990s, unplanned pregnancies in the United States remained high, especially among teenagers. Research on new birth control methods stalled in the face of resistance from conservative Christians, pro-life forces, and groups that advocated for parents' rights. Questions about the safety of contraceptives—together with major medical failures involving devices like the Dalkon shield, an intrauterine device, scared off companies that might have invested in birth control research.

The arrival of new contraceptive methods in the 1990s and beyond escalated conflicts about abortion—and the difference between birth control and abortion. Some presented RU 486, a medication used in a two-pill abortion, as a form of birth control. By the time the US government approved RU 486 in the 2000s, hundreds of thousands of European women had already used the drug. New intrauterine devices (IUDs) also arrived on the market. While the Dalkon Shield had caused serious complications in the 1970s, newer models like Mirena (introduced in 2001) and Skyla (introduced in 2013) were safer and more effective.

Some abortion foes insisted that some blocked the implantation of a fertilized egg and therefore counted as an abortifacient. Antiabortion leaders leveled the same accusation against emergency contraception after the US government approved it in 1999. Fights about the difference between birth control and abortion took on new importance after Congress passed President Barack Obama's health-care reform. As part of the law, the federal government mandated that employers provide insurance coverage for most common contraceptives. Some employers resisted, insisting that the mandate violated their religious liberty. Religious employers further insisted that the drugs covered by the mandate actually aborted pregnancies rather than preventing them.

The spread of assisted reproductive technologies also blurred the line between abortion and birth control. By 2010, assisted reproductive technologies had contributed to 1.5 percent of all US births. A common technique, in vitro fertilization, required the creation, storage, and implantation of pre-embryos. Often, to maximize the chances of a successful pregnancy, fertility specialists implanted several embryos and then terminated some of the pregnancies to maximize the chances that one would come to term. This process, called selective reduction, raised concern for abortion foes, as did the destruction of embryos in storage. By the 2010s, Americans no longer only contested the legality of abortion but also what defined abortion in the first place.

After the 2010s, antiabortion absolutists gained more power in their movement. For decades, abortion foes had prioritized an incremental attack on legal abortion. Rather than seeking to criminalize abortion outright or defend a right to life, leading antiabortion groups instead defended more modest laws. These statutes were designed to limit abortion access and help set the stage for an eventual overturning of *Roe*. Abortion foes hoped to hollow out abortion rights until there was nothing left to save. Some abortion foes had always seen this tactical plan as futile, but absolutist forces gradually gained more influence. In the late 1980s and early 1990s, Operation Rescue launched blockades of abortion clinics that produced major news coverage and thousands of arrests. But states passed laws protecting abortion clinics, and Congress introduced the Freedom of Access to Clinic Entrances (FACE) Act. Operation Rescue sympathizers murdered abortion doctors and damaged the credibility of the organization.

Absolutists made another bid for influence in the antiabortion movement in the 2010s and 2020s. Having lost patience with the pace of change, new organizations like Faith2Action proposed laws criminalizing abortion at six weeks when fetal cardiac activity or a heartbeat could be detected. The rise of the Tea Party, a populist movement initially focused on small government, gave Republicans control over most state legislatures. Tea Partiers passed a record number of abortion bills, including some heartbeat bills. More absolute bans became more popular after the 2016 election of Donald Trump. Trump nominated three new justices to the Supreme Court, enough to create a six-to-three conservative majority. Conservative state legislators concluded that it was only a matter of time before the Court overturned *Roe* and *Casey*. As states competed to pass the most restrictive legislation, others imagined what a post-*Roe* United States would look like. Conservative state lawmakers debated whether to allow abortion in cases of rape and incest—or to punish pregnant people for ending their pregnancies. Progressive states allowed nurses and other medical experts to perform abortions and approved telemedicine abortions.

Few could predict what the Supreme Court would do or how the abortion debate would evolve if the Court reversed *Roe*. What was clear was that changes to US abortion law and politics went far beyond anything explained by the 1973 decision. Through legal, political, and cultural shifts, lawmakers and commentators remained preoccupied by the fate of *Roe* itself, long after *Roe*, properly understood, was already gone.

# Part II

# Analysis

# 1 Criminalizing abortion and birth control

Before the 1850s, it would have been hard to imagine that the abortion issue would transform law and politics in the United States. Abortion was certainly in the news from time to time, especially when it came to **Madame Restell.** Born Ann Trow Lohman, Restell was known to the American public as the "wickedest woman in New York." She and her husband operated outside of a gracious brownstone mansion on New York City's Fifth Avenue; both performed abortion surgeries and sold pills that would bring on a miscarriage. Restell was so successful that she attracted imitators. Her fame also drew attention from reporters and, eventually, prosecutors opposed to abortion. When Restell ultimately went on trial for violating New York's state abortion law in 1847, the press had a field day. She became a symbol of how common abortion had become. Reporters suggested that there were thousands just like Restell in cities and small towns across the United States.

Much to Madame Restell's dismay, her name also became a rallying cry for an emerging movement to criminalize virtually all abortions in the United States. In the mid-nineteenth century, after the **American Medical Association** began a campaign to outlaw all abortions, doctors condemned the evils of what they called "Restellism," a synonym for abortion.

Restell's life reflected the dramatic changes to the law of abortion in the United States taking place in the nineteenth century. In the mid-nineteenth century, Restell's work might have been controversial, but newspapers frequently advertised abortion drugs. Doctors made a fortune catering to a growing group of patients seeking abortion. Married, wealthy women sought out her services. So did immigrants who were flooding into the nation's major urban centers from Ireland, Germany, and beyond.

By the end of the nineteenth century, Madame Restell's fortunes had changed significantly. She found a nemesis in **Anthony Comstock,** a military veteran and inspector for the United States Postal Service. Comstock was a conservative Christian who became distressed by what he saw as the sexual looseness of his fellow soldiers during the Civil War. In 1873, he founded the New York Society for the Suppression of Vice and later successfully lobbied Congress to pass the Comstock Act, a statute outlawing the mailing of "obscene" material—a category that encompassed information about birth

DOI: 10.4324/9781003215936-4

control, abortion, sex, and even anatomy. Comstock boasted that he had arrested thousands of people for violating the law and destroyed even more books. In 1878, he approached Madame Restell, posing as a husband looking for a birth control prescription. When she fulfilled his request, Comstock arrested her. The next morning, she committed suicide.

The drama of Comstock and Restell was part of a larger shift in the law and politics of abortion in the United States. Restell profited from widespread interest in abortion in the nineteenth century. While historians dispute whether abortion was legal or morally accepted at the time, there is no question that it was common. By contrast, toward the end of the nineteenth century, moral crusaders like Comstock had transformed the law and practice of birth control and abortion. People still used both, but at considerable personal risk. After all, for decades after the late nineteenth century, someone who had an abortion (or used birth control) was a criminal.

But the gap between demand for abortion and birth control and the law on the books eventually upended the laws that Comstock and his allies put in place. In the context of both abortion and birth control, doctors played a decisive role in unsettling the status quo. In the first half of the twentieth century, lawmakers listened to the Catholic leaders who wanted to preserve existing limits on birth control. In a series of court decisions, however, judges carved out exceptions for contraceptives provided by a physician. These decisions helped to legitimize birth control. Dozens of clinics opened their doors, and big businesses made millions selling condoms and diaphragms.

Doctors also helped to destabilize abortion laws. Physicians had led the fight to criminalize abortion in the late nineteenth century, and in the 1940s and 1950s obstetricians and gynecologists set up hospital committees to lower the number of procedures performed. But the more influence these "therapeutic committees" gained, the more Americans saw abortion as a medical as well as moral issue. And if abortion was a medical matter, there was no reason that doctors could not fight against criminal abortion laws instead of for them. By the middle of the twentieth century, that is exactly what happened.

***

Before the mid-nineteenth century, it is hard to get a firm grip on what abortion practice looked like in the United States. What is clear is that Americans always had abortions. In the 1600s and 1700s, women tried to end pregnancies by using herbs, doing vigorous exercises, or inserting sharp implements into their uteruses. These methods were not especially effective and often proved quite dangerous. Few Americans discussed abortion openly.

Law on the topic was even murkier. From the colonial era to the mid-nineteenth century, American jurisprudence to varying degrees embraced the **quickening doctrine.** Under this rule, abortions were legal prior to the point when a patient could feel fetal movement—usually, around the fourth month of pregnancy.

Prior to quickening, the doctrine treated abortions as a regulation of menstruation, not a criminal act. But historians debate the extent to which state law adopted the quickening doctrine—and the degree to which Americans saw abortion as acceptable early in pregnancy. Some argue that the quickening rule set the standard in the United States for some time. They believe that most Americans had few qualms about abortion, at least early in pregnancy. These historians suggest that lawmakers primarily worried about abortion drugs or surgeries because they occasionally killed the women seeking them, but not because they ended pregnancies. This account makes some sense. For years, in the nineteenth century, abortions were common, even among the nation's elites. Most laws that did mention abortion did so only after quickening—or treated certain abortifacient drugs (correctly) as poisons.

Other historians dispute this account. They suggest that adoption of the quickening doctrine was not as widespread as many believe. They emphasize evidence that Americans were sometimes punished harshly for abortion—and proof that some believed that it was wrong to intentionally end a pregnancy, regardless of whether there were any legal consequences for doing so.

Whoever is right, by the mid-nineteenth century, leading American doctors believed that abortion had become far too common, especially among wealthier, white families. At the time, physicians were hard at work distinguishing themselves from midwives and practitioners of alternative medicine. Early in the nineteenth century, the medical profession was poorly regulated and delivered inconsistent care. Many physicians had not attended medical school and knew little about how the human body worked. Unsurprisingly, then, physicians faced serious competition from midwives, who sometimes delivered safer and more compassionate care.

So-called regular physicians responded by trying to professionalize medicine and explain what set their services apart. **Dr. Horatio Storer**, a Boston-born, Harvard educated physician, saw abortion as a point of differentiation. Storer argued that only regular physicians had the expertise to recognize that a child in the womb was a person from the moment of fertilization [**Doc. 1**]. And in Storer's view, only regular physicians had the moral compass to understand that abortion was wrong, no matter how profitable the practice was.

Storer's father, himself a prominent doctor, had spoken out against abortion, and Horatio intended to pick up where his father left off. Founded in 1847, the organization he helped to lead, the American Medical Association (AMA), led the effort to criminalize earlier abortions in the United States. Storer primarily emphasized arguments about fetal rights. As Storer saw it, the quickening doctrine did not make sense because human life began much earlier—when sperm fertilized an egg. Storer defined abortion as murder, plain and simple. Doctors had superior knowledge about the nature of life in the womb, he argued, and abortion should be against the law.

But the AMA did not rely only on arguments about the rights and humanity of fetuses or unborn children. Storer also tapped into anti-immigrant racism. In the mid-1800s, large numbers of immigrants from Ireland, Germany, and China entered the United States. Immigrants came for many reasons: some sought out cheap farmland; artisans and skilled workers applied for places in the nation's new factories. Some fled famine or poverty, looking for a job in the busy mines, factories, and infrastructure projects that sprang up across the country. Some even hoped to strike gold in the California goldrush. Storer thought that these immigrants were having too many children. By contrast, he believed that the "better sort" of women, white, "Anglo-Saxon," and relatively wealthy, wanted smaller families and used abortion to accomplish that goal. He urged these women to remember that the nation's future depended on their "loins."

Storer was no champion of the women's movement. In the nineteenth century, a mostly white, middle-class group of women with experience fighting for the abolition of slavery or the prohibition of alcohol began calling for women's rights. In 1848, over 300 men and women attended a conference on women's rights in Seneca Falls, New York, where they adopted the ***Declaration of Sentiments***. The declaration criticized rules that prevented married women from owning property, voting, serving on juries, or testifying in court. Black feminists like **Ida B. Wells** were often marginalized in the early women's movement, but they fought for rights for women as well as civil rights for people of color. Those at the forefront of efforts to criminalize abortion and birth control also opposed the women's movement. Anthony Comstock was an outspoken opponent of giving women the vote. Horatio Storer blamed new-fangled ideas about women's role for the spread of abortions.

Historians contest what so-called **first-wave feminists** actually thought about abortion. Some argue that **Susan B. Anthony**, one of the biggest names in the movement for women's suffrage, equated abortion and infanticide. **Victoria Woodhull**, a feminist who embraced the idea of **free love** and once ran for president, criticized abortion. But few feminists endorsed laws criminalizing abortion. Indeed, some campaigned for what they called **voluntary motherhood**, women's ability to control when their husbands had sexual access to them—and their right to space their children.

Whatever feminists thought about abortion, Storer's argument clearly struck a nerve with the conservative Christians who supported Anthony Comstock. Anti-vice activists like Comstock worried primarily about the corruption of young men, who could get addicted to pornography, patronize prostitutes, and contract venereal disease. Storer, by contrast, primarily browbeat white, upper-class women who did not want large families. Storer and Comstock certainly maintained different public images as well. While Comstock portrayed himself as a soldier warring against sin and sex,

Storer framed even his most moralistic arguments as the work of a dispassionate man of science.

But in the late nineteenth century, both men had tremendous success in changing the law. The Comstock Act produced thousands of arrests and prosecutions. The AMA's campaign also had far-reaching effects. By the end of the nineteenth century, most states had criminalized abortion unless a patient's life was at risk. There were some unanswered questions: for example, which medical conditions would make it life-threatening to continue a pregnancy? Should the law punish patients as well as doctors? For the most part, however, the legal status quo seemed settled. Abortion was a crime, and the laws of the United States condemned it.

The actual practice of abortion was another story. In the late nineteenth century, some observers estimated that doctors performed over 2 million abortions a year—many more than women received in the late 1990s. A late nineteenth-century exposé by the *Chicago Times* identified dozens of doctors in the city who were willing to either perform an abortion or refer patients to someone who would.

Doctors proved willing to risk criminal consequences partly because prosecutions were so rare. For the most part, from the late nineteenth century into the early decades of the twentieth century, prosecutors pursued charges against abortion doctors only when a woman died. Convictions were as rare as prosecutions: one study found that less than a quarter of defendants in abortion cases were found guilty.

To stand a chance of success, prosecutors often had to rely on **dying declarations**. Generally, in court, prosecutors could not rely on **hearsay**, statements made by witnesses who were not in court and thus were not available for cross-examination. Hearsay rules reflected a belief that witnesses who could not be cross-examined would lie without consequences. On the theory that someone would tell the truth before dying, the law made an exception for a witness's dying words.

Dying women with no choice of survival were badgered into giving the names of anyone who participated in an abortion, including former lovers. Some state laws, including one passed in New York, treated women as a guilty party, even though prosecutors did not pursue charges against them.

In the early twentieth century, fear of criminal consequences made illegal abortions even more dangerous. At the time, many women died in childbirth—at a rate of nearly 800 per 100,000 in 1920. Obstetrics—considered an unglamorous field—did not attract the best doctors, and physicians performing abortions or other surgical procedures rarely took the proper steps to sanitize equipment. Fear of public exposure caused some women battling infections to delay seeking medical care, making the odds of survival even more remote.

In the early twentieth century, abortion-related mortality did not inspire anyone to challenge abortion laws. The same was not true of birth control. In the 1910s, **Margaret Sanger** began distributing information about contraceptives—and political arguments about the benefits of small families. Sanger was one of eleven children and had been studying nursing when she met her first husband, William, and eventually moved to New York. The Sangers initially took an interest in **Socialist** politics, believing that capitalism in the United States was devastating workers and their families. The Sangers' politics reflected the upheaval of the early twentieth century. In the 1910s, massive income inequality sparked periodic uprisings by workers.

Margaret Sanger began writing columns on sex education and birth control for the working-class women that Socialists tried to reach. After becoming estranged from her husband, she focused her energies more fully on birth control and sex education. In 1914, she began publishing ***The Woman Rebel***, where she openly discussed ways that women could prevent pregnancy. When she faced charges for violating the Comstock Act, she went into exile in England, where she became a lover and disciple of **Havelock Ellis**, a progressive sex researcher who thought that if women had more choice over whom they married or when they reproduced, their children would be better, stronger, and smarter. Havelock Ellis was a self-described eugenicist, and Sanger followed in his footsteps.

In 1883, **Sir Francis Galton**, a geneticist and the cousin of the famous **Charles Darwin**, a naturalist who pioneered a theory of evolution, coined the term "**eugenics**," a word that literally meant well-born. Darwin had developed a theory of **natural selection** whereby genes that conferred a reproductive or survival advantage became more common. Galton sought to apply this theory to weed out people's undesirable genetic traits. At first, Galton focused on positive eugenics, designed to convince those with "desirable" traits to have more children. But other eugenicists began searching for strategies to stop so-called defectives from reproducing.

With funding from major foundations and wealthy philanthropists, biologist **Charles Davenport** founded the Eugenics Record Office (ERO) to study eugenics. Davenport grew up in a religious Protestant family in Connecticut and went on to become a zoologist. Together with **Harry Laughlin**, a former school superintendent fascinated by animal breeding, Davenport circulated voluntary questionnaires and sent teams of researchers to interview circus performers, convicted criminals, and those at state institutions for the disabled, the mentally ill, and the poor. The ERO argued that everything from sexual promiscuity to alcoholism had a genetic basis.

The ERO and other eugenic organizations had a major impact on US law and policy. Laughlin took a particular interest in immigration. The years between 1850 and 1920 counted as a kind of golden age for mass migration in the United States, with many pouring in from Southern and Eastern Europe as well as Canada and Latin America. By 1910, 22 percent of the American labor force was foreign-born, and the numbers reached far higher outside the American South. Opponents of immigration maintained that the new arrivals would never assimilate into US society. Laughlin brought a veneer of scientific expertise to these arguments.

Relying on the work of the ERO, he marshalled data to support a restrictive immigration law that imposed annual quotas based on the national origin of those entering the United States. While Laughlin argued that all immigrants were genetically unfit, he suggested that recent arrivals were the most likely to be defective. His statements helped to shape the **Immigration Act of 1924**, which heavily limited all immigration and favored entrants from Northern and Western Europe, giving them 86 percent of the total available slots.

Davenport and Laughlin also strongly supported **compulsory sterilization laws**. In 1907, Indiana became the first state to pass such a bill. More than 30 others soon followed suit. Before World War I, these laws disproportionately affected low-income women (and some men), particularly immigrants from Southern and Eastern Europe. At least before the 1940s, Black and Latinx patients often lacked access to state-run health care, which shielded them from the worst eugenic abuses (later sterilization regimes in the mainland United States and Puerto Rico targeted women of color). Those in state-run institutions, or those receiving welfare, were more likely to be sterilized.

The Supreme Court ultimately rejected constitutional challenges to the new sterilization laws in *Buck v. Bell* [**Doc. 3**]. Carrie Buck, a woman in a state institution in Virginia, was scheduled to be sterilized because the state had designated her a mental defective (Buck's IQ was in the normal range, but her family was poor, and Virginia authorities viewed her as sexually promiscuous). Buck sued and challenged the constitutionality of Virginia's law. The Supreme Court rejected her argument, reasoning that Virginia had put in place more than enough safeguards before sterilizations took place. The Court emphasized the importance of the state's interest in preventing the nation from being swamped by defectives.

After returning from England, Margaret Sanger used eugenic ideas to advocate for the legalization of birth control devices and information about them. In 1916, she founded the nation's first birth control clinic in Brownsville, New York, but promptly faced criminal charges. Her trial, sentence, hunger strike, and subsequent force feeding attracted the support of sympathetic donors.

Sanger's legal troubles also ultimately paved the way for broader access to birth control. In ***People of the State of New York v. Margaret Sanger***, a Brooklyn judge convicted Sanger and two co-defendants for violating New York criminal law. However, the judge interpreted the law to allow physicians to operate such a clinic. After her release from prison, Sanger founded the **American Birth Control League**, an advocacy group that eschewed the radical politics of Sanger's earlier years in favor of the arguments that, because all children had a right to be wanted, all women should have access to contraception [**Doc. 2**]. In the early 1920s, Sanger also took advantage of the loophole created by *People v. Sanger* and opened a series of physician-run clinics.

Sanger framed birth control partly as a matter of rights for women. While many birth controllers like Sanger and **Mary Ware Dennett** saw birth control as a way for women to space their children and have more control of their own lives, most feminists in the 1910s and 1920s did not sign on to the birth control fight. At the time, first-wave feminists focused on winning the vote for women and sought a constitutional amendment to do so. While supporting what they called voluntary motherhood, many leading suffragists believed that a sexually conservative message would play better with voters and legislators.

Even after the **Nineteenth Amendment** became part of the Constitution, suffragists did not back calls for the legalization of birth control. Some prioritized laws designed to protect working women, such as laws that limited the number of hours they could work. Others, like prominent former suffragist **Alice Paul**, the head of the National Woman Suffrage Association, fought for an Equal Rights Amendment to the Constitution, which would prohibit discrimination on the basis of sex. The birth control movement would not enjoy the support of leading feminists for years.

At first, Sanger's bid to win over eugenicists likewise came up short. Like Davenport and Laughlin, Sanger argued that social undesirables should not reproduce. But she parted ways with most mainstream eugenicists when it came to voluntary birth control—or even women's sexuality. Davenport, Laughlin, and other leading eugenicists argued that sexually "promiscuous" women were almost necessarily unfit or "feeble-minded." By contrast, Sanger thought that there was nothing wrong with women being interested in sex. She saw birth control access as a way for women to "develop and advance in life"—as well as a way to "better the race." She posited that if women had smaller families, mothers would do a better job raising their children. Sanger believed that better parenting would prevent some of the social ills that eugenicists described.

Eugenicists initially rejected Sanger's overtures and mocked the idea of voluntary birth control. Activists like Laughlin and Davenport wanted nothing to do with Sanger. After all, some in respectable society still saw her as a radical or even a criminal. As important, most eugenicists argued that "defectives" could not be trusted to make their own decisions about birth control.

Nevertheless, Sanger's birth control movement grew in the 1920s. Although many laws against contraception were still on the books, enforcement was spotty. Dozens of clinics opened across the United States. Open discussion of birth control became far more commonplace (and positive). Certain churches, particularly those that embraced modernism or the social activism, began framing birth control as a eugenic priority. The Catholic Church stood out as the leading opponent of legal birth control. Catholic groups like the Knights of Columbus and the Catholic Social Welfare League mobilized to block discussion of birth control at live events or on the radio. Catholics also fought successfully to preserve existing laws against contraceptives.

Ironically, Sanger and her Catholic opponents seemed to agree about the need to preserve criminal laws on abortion. Sanger argued that abortion was unquestionably wrong, but she maintained that abortion became almost inevitable when Americans lacked access to appropriate methods of contraception. By contrast, Catholic anti-contraception advocates insisted that both birth control and abortion reflected dangerous and immoral attitudes about sexuality and the family.

No matter how much anyone denounced abortion, the number of procedures performed in the United States continued to climb. The Great Depression led the US fertility rate to fall to a then-low of 2.1 children per woman in 1936. A profound economic downturn began after a 1929 stock market crash wiped out millions of investors. Consumer spending and investment cratered in the next several years, and failing companies laid off scores of workers. By 1933, approximately 15 million Americans were unemployed.

As more Americans delayed marriage or struggled to make ends meet, demand for abortion skyrocketed. Some practitioners began specializing in abortion services. Middle-class or wealthy women, most of them white, had an easier time finding reliable abortion services in the 1930s. Meanwhile, poor women of color were more likely to induce their own abortions and face serious complications. Maternal mortality numbers improved in the 1930s as physicians took steps to prevent sepsis in surgical patients. Nevertheless, with so many hospitalized after post-abortion complications, it was much harder for physicians to avoid the fact that abortions were taking place—and often.

The Depression also increased demand for birth control. While the Comstock Act prohibited the shipment of contraceptives across state lines, sales of condoms and diaphragms spiked, and companies like Trojan and Ramses made handsome profits. Buoyed by public interest in birth control, Sanger lobbied Congress to legalize it. A Catholic-led opposition contended that birth control devices were unsafe and would unleash a tidal wave of sexual promiscuity. The opposition prevailed: the Comstock Act remained in place. Nevertheless, increasing demand, together with support from an increasingly profitable contraceptive industry, made a difference.

So did several legal decisions. In 1930, in *Youngs Rubber Corporation v. C.I. Lee & Co.*, a condom manufacturer claimed that a competitor had infringed the trademark of one of its contraceptive brands. The other company argued that the trademark was unenforceable because the birth control business was illegal. The Second Circuit Court of Appeals rejected this argument.

Seeking to build on this victory, Margaret Sanger ordered a diaphragm from Japan in 1932 and had it mailed to a physician. This purchase violated the Comstock Act, and the diaphragm was confiscated and destroyed. Sanger and her allies argued that purchases by doctors should be exempt from the act, and a trial court agreed. The Second Circuit Court of Appeals affirmed this outcome in 1936 in *United States v. One Package of Japanese Pessaries*.

The *One Package* decision made it far harder for states to eliminate access to birth control; as long as a physician acted as a middleman, contraception got much easier to obtain. By 1938, contraceptive manufacturers were making hundreds of millions of dollars in profits. Women—who accounted for more than 80 percent of contraceptive sales—often relied on diaphragms and contraceptive foam, but condoms were also a big business, with some vending machines in men's restrooms.

Sanger and her allies tried to change the law too. In 1938, a coalition formed the Birth Control Federation of America (BCFA). As one of their first initiatives, BCFA staffers tackled the issue of birth control in the Black community. In 1929, Sanger had opened a clinic in Harlem, New York, at the invitation of James Hubert, a Black social worker. The effort received support from some leading civil-rights proponents, including **W.E.B. Du Bois**. The BCFA took on a more ambitious project with the launch of the **Negro Project** in 1939. The Negro Project worked to open birth control clinics in Black communities, primarily across the American South. The Negro Project's founders also sought to get the buy-in of Black community leaders, like ministers, who could increase Black families' willingness to use birth control.

The Negro Project shone a light on the complex politics of birth control in communities of color. On the one hand, civil-rights leaders like Du Bois—who believed that people of color wanted and needed better contraceptive access—supported the effort. But the Negro Project also unquestionably reflected the ongoing influence of racism and eugenics on the birth control movement and the broader society.

The eugenics movement itself was very different by the 1940s. Two decades earlier, many educated Americans had embraced eugenics, supported compulsory sterilization, and even entered their children in "better baby" contests. By the late 1930s, however, eugenicists like Davenport had lost some of their professional standing, and researchers had begun to question eugenicists' data and conclusions. After the **Nazi Party** took power in Germany and began waging war in other countries, many Americans saw a striking resemblance between Hitler's sterilization policies and the ones in place in the United States.

But eugenic impulses very much survived in the birth control movement. The founders of the Negro Project officially worked to address problems within the Black community, but quite clearly, the project focused on reducing the Black birth rate across the board. While the project did not coerce anyone to use birth control, the white physicians leading it often held deeply racist attitudes about the communities they served, and some spoke openly about the desirability of sterilizing women of color.

Racism notwithstanding, some volunteers for the Negro Project had some genuine concern about the connection between poverty and access to birth control. Sanger believed that communities of color had been denied meaningful access to contraception *because of* racism. Nevertheless, the biases of many of those leading the Negro Project ensured that it would do little to help anyone.

The Negro Project aside, the birth control movement continued to grow in the 1940s. By 1942, the BCFA became the **Planned Parenthood Federation of America**, a group that reframed birth control as family planning. In the 1940s, during and after World War II, the country entered a pronatalist phase, where having large, traditional families was seen as a patriotic duty. To adapt to this new cultural climate, Planned Parenthood retooled its message to appeal to women seeking to improve their marriages or do a better job raising their children.

While birth control became more accepted in the 1940s, pronatalism fueled a much more aggressive crackdown on abortion. While prosecutors had previously targeted those who had killed their patients, dragnets in the 1940s and 1950s swept much further. What many viewed as respectable doctors began facing serious charges. Women—who had had rarely engaged with the criminal justice system—now had to testify against abortion providers in open court and risk public shame.

The new crackdown on abortion inspired doctors to do more to self-regulate. Many hospitals formed **therapeutic abortion committees**, groups of obstetrician-gynecologists that had to sign off before an abortion could take place. In theory, these committees could authorize abortions only when a patient's life was at risk. In practice, the committees sought to protect physicians from criminal liability (and civil lawsuits) by keeping the number of abortions low (and providing a rigorous justification for any procedure that was performed). As important, the committees once again made these abortions the domain of obstetric experts rather than midwives or family doctors. In their early operation, the committees achieved their aim: abortion rates at most hospitals plummeted.

But the new status quo on abortion would not last for long. A new movement around reproduction, the **population control movement**, gained considerable influence after World War II. Many prominent population controllers were refugees from the earlier eugenic movement. Leading funders of that movement, including the **Rockefeller Foundation**, led by **John D. Rockefeller III**, a philanthropist from one of the nation's most prominent families, poured money into efforts to curb demographic growth in the 1940s and 1950s. **Frederick Osborn**, a prominent eugenicist, founded the **Population Council** in 1952 to research strategies to lower birth rates at home and abroad.

At first, Rockefeller and his allies focused mostly on funding contraceptive research and training field staff to work in fertility control programs abroad. But as the 1950s progressed, population controllers began lobbying the federal government to fund programs for international and (eventually) domestic family planning. Well-funded and politically connected, population controllers pressured lawmakers to expand family planning;

eventually, some population controllers would push for the legalization of abortion as well.

Despite the pronatalism of the 1940s and 1950s, demand for abortion hardly faded. More Americans were having sex and children out of marriage. But unwed motherhood was not just more common; it was more stigmatized. White, unwed mothers, pressured to put their children up for adoption, were forced into maternity homes designed to preserve their own reputations for morality and chastity. Black unwed mothers, especially those on welfare programs such as Aid to Dependent Families with Children, faced new limitations on their benefits or even criminal charges for having additional children. The more stigma surrounded unwed motherhood, the more some demanded access to family planning and abortion.

Therapeutic abortion committees, which set out to shore up the status quo, eventually caused it to shatter. Some hospitals began authorizing abortions when women were suicidal. In theory, there was nothing surprising about this—if a patient would kill herself if she were denied an abortion, an abortion could be lifesaving. But the spread of mental health indications for abortion exposed new disagreements about how the law of abortion should work.

Catholics had long been among the fiercest opponents of legal abortion. For example, in the 1930s, **Dr. Fred Taussig**, a gynecologist and professor at Washington University School of Medicine, wrote a book calling for the legalization of abortion. Catholic physicians were Taussig's most outspoken critics. The Catholic Church had long condemned birth control and abortion, portraying both as a threat to marriage, the traditional family, and the moral teachings of the church. And in the 1950s, it was Catholic physicians who offered the most trenchant critiques of the therapeutic abortion committees. These doctors pointed to the spread of mental-health indications as evidence that the therapeutic committees had failed to reduce the abortion rate.

Other physicians saw the matter in radically different terms. **Dr. Alan Guttmacher**, a prominent obstetrician-gynecologist, estimated that only a small fraction of the abortions performed at his hospital were lifesaving. Guttmacher served as the director of obstetrics and gynecology at Mt. Sinai Hospital in New York, and he had long worked to expand access to birth control in New York. He also served as the vice president of the American Eugenics Society. When it came to therapeutic abortions, Guttmacher was uncomfortable with the widespread use of mental-health indications. But unlike his Catholic colleagues, Guttmacher insisted that the problem was with the law. By the early 1960s, he began to argue that the time had come to repeal the nation's abortion laws.

The fight over abortion repeal would revolutionize US law and politics in the decades to come. When Madame Restell met an inglorious end, many, including Anthony Comstock, felt she deserved it. In 1915, Comstock passed away, no doubt convinced that the war against abortion and birth control was won. While Margaret Sanger fought vigorously to distinguish birth control and abortion, eugenicists—who enjoyed significant influence over political leaders and the public health establishment—sometimes rejected both.

Over time, birth control came to enjoy much greater social support. In the 1930s, condom companies raked in cash. Many Americans used contraception, and large faith communities endorsed it. Planned Parenthood became a respectable, well-funded family planning organization. When it came to abortion, by contrast, police raided clinics and sent physicians to prison. The law of birth control and abortion diverged as well. While decisions like *One Packet* facilitated the spread of birth control clinics, abortion remained a crime.

Ultimately, however, the forces that led to the loosening of the laws on birth control changed the law of abortion too. Ever since Horatio Storer had led the American Medical Association in fighting to criminalize abortions, doctors had determined when abortion was acceptable (or legal). Even when law enforcement officers arrested abortion providers, medical experts still weighed in about whether a procedure was lifesaving. Later, therapeutic hospital committees served as gatekeepers, deciding which patients could end their pregnancies. But as Alan Guttmacher recognized, giving doctors so much power could destabilize the law of abortion just as it had the law of birth control. In the 1960s, physicians like Guttmacher decided that abortion laws no longer reflected the best medical practices. The conflict they helped touch off would help to reshape US politics.

# 2 The reform battle and the right to privacy

In 1965, the United States Supreme Court issued a decision that was closely watched by Dr. Alan Guttmacher and his colleagues at the **Association for the Study of Abortion** (ASA). Founded the year before to advocate for the reform of abortion laws, ASA was a small, elite group based in New York City—a symbol of the emerging fight to legalize abortion. While many Americans were taking the **birth control pill** and talking openly about sex outside of marriage, abortion often remained taboo. The push to change abortion laws, it seemed, primarily appealed to a small group of highly educated, very liberal activists in the nation's largest cities.

But the United States was changing, not least when it came to abortion and birth control. Earlier in the twentieth century, Margaret Sanger had gone to prison for distributing contraceptives. By 1965, the Supreme Court was considering whether the Constitution gave married couples a right to use birth control. Changes to the rules on abortion would not be far behind.

The Supreme Court's big new birth control case, ***Griswold v. Connecticut*** [**Doc. 4**], involved a Connecticut law that criminalized married couples' use of contraception. The law was rarely enforced, but that was true of a variety of statutes criminalizing "morals crimes," such as sex before marriage. For the leaders of the Planned Parenthood League of Connecticut, enforcement of the law was almost beside the point. Leaders of the group wanted to establish that access to birth control was a fundamental right.

By the mid-1960s, Planned Parenthood's goal would not have seemed far-fetched. Many Americans were certainly open about their contraceptive use by the time the Court agreed to hear *Griswold.* At the start of the decade, the Food and Drug Administration (FDA) approved a birth control pill that would prevent pregnancy, fulfilling a dream of Margaret Sanger's. Earlier methods, such as contraceptive foam or diaphragms, were relatively unreliable or required a willing partner.

In the late 1950s, large-scale studies of the pill's safety and efficacy began in Puerto Rico, which already had a broad network of birth-control clinics. In Puerto Rico, large numbers of test subjects complained about side effects or dropped out (at the time, the pill had far more progestin and estrogen than do contemporary formulations).

DOI: 10.4324/9781003215936-5

Nevertheless, when the FDA approved the pill, demand for it stateside was immediate. In the decades to come, the United States—a country that had treated birth control as both criminal and obscene—became one of the world's leading consumers of contraception.

The pill helped set off what commentators called the **sexual revolution**. It was not that Americans had just started having sex outside of marriage. Indeed, between 1941 and 1953, the rate of single motherhood more than doubled. Nevertheless, in the 1960s, more Americans openly discussed their changing sexual habits and birth control use. As the population control movement gained power, older Americans in both political parties saw access to family planning as a political imperative. In earlier decades, population controllers, who had primarily focused on international birth rates, took aim at demographic growth in the United States. By then, organizations like Planned Parenthood, which called itself Planned Parenthood-World Population, began receiving significant bipartisan support.

If birth controllers had reason for optimism when it came to popular opinion, legal changes also boosted their mood. By the 1960s, most states had legalized some forms of contraception but still prohibited advertising it. Connecticut's law, which prohibited married couples from using birth control, was the only one of its kind. A local Planned Parenthood affiliate had tried challenging it in the early 1960s, and the case got all the way to the Supreme Court. But in 1961, in *Poe v. Ullman*, the Court held that because no one ever enforced Connecticut's contraception law, there was no case or controversy for the Court to resolve.

The Planned Parenthood League of Connecticut set out to create one. **Estelle Griswold** of Planned Parenthood and **C. Lee Buxton** of Yale Medical School opened a small clinic next to the state Planned Parenthood office. Married women immediately called the clinic seeking advice on birth control—all of them violating the state law. Of course, for Griswold and Buxton, that was the point.

When the case again reached the Supreme Court, the justices handed down a seven-to-two opinion invalidating Connecticut's law. Writing the majority, **Justice William Douglas** held that the Constitution protected more rights than the ones spelled out in its text. He reasoned that the Constitution had penumbras—that is, the text implied the existence of other rights, including the right to privacy. The Constitution guaranteed individuals the freedom of association and prohibited unreasonable searches and seizures by the police. Douglas reasoned that, together, these constitutional provisions implied the existence of a right to be left alone—one broad enough to protect married couples' decision to use birth control. Douglas emphasized the historical importance accorded to marriage, an institution of unique value that he stressed was older than the **Bill of Rights**. **Justice Arthur Goldberg** wrote a **concurring opinion**, providing an alternative justification for the result. Goldberg relied on the **Ninth Amendment** of the Constitution, which stated: "The enumeration in the Constitution, of certain rights, shall not be construed to deny or disparage others retained by the people." In Goldberg's view, the Ninth Amendment protected rights beyond those spelled out in the text of the Constitution. He concluded that the right to marital privacy was of "similar order and magnitude" as the protections outlined in the Constitution.

In his own concurring opinion, **Justice John Marshall Harlan II** relied on the Due Process Clause of the Fourteenth Amendment. Congress had first introduced the Fourteenth Amendment in the aftermath of the US Civil War. In the Thirteenth, Fourteenth, and Fifteenth Amendments, the Constitution ended slavery, extended voting rights to free people of color, and guaranteed **equal protection of the law** and **due process of law**.

In the late nineteenth century, attorneys had relied on part of the Fourteenth Amendment, the **Privileges and Immunities Clause**, when arguing that the Constitution protected rights beyond those spelled out in the text. That provision stated: "the citizens of each state shall be entitled to all the privileges and immunities of the citizens of the several states." Many believed that "privileges and immunities" included implied fundamental rights. But in 1873, in the ***Slaughterhouse Cases***, the Supreme Court rejected that interpretation. Ever since, the Court had periodically reasoned that the Due Process Clause protected certain rights "implicit in the concept of ordered liberty." Harlan believed marital privacy to be one of those rights.

The two **dissenting** justices acknowledged that Connecticut's law seemed stupid and unnecessary. But they saw no constitutional basis for invalidating it and argued that the Court had substituted its policy preferences for the law.

In the immediate aftermath of *Griswold*, many court watchers wondered what the opinion augured for individual use of birth control. Was *Griswold* really about the importance of marriage? Or would the Supreme Court also find that individuals had a privacy right to use contraception?

The federal government certainly threw its weight behind birth control programs. By 1966, 30 states had established family planning programs. Amendments to the Child Health Act and the Aid to Families with Dependent Children program required that funds be set aside for family planning. In 1970, with strong bipartisan support, **Title X of the Public Health Service Act** sailed through Congress. Title X created a comprehensive, federal family planning program—what some called Congress's "blank check for birth control."

The sexual revolution, the spread of the birth control pill, and the *Griswold* decision all emboldened advocates of abortion reform. Advocates like Alan Guttmacher believed that opposition to birth control and abortion came from the same place: superstition, religion, and outmoded stereotypes about women. If laws against birth control fell, Guttmacher and his colleagues believed that the abortion debate would likewise break in their favor.

In the 1960s, the Association for the Study of Abortion and other reformers rallied around a reform proposal by the **American Law Institute** (ALI), an elite research and advocacy group (the final version of the ALI's Model Penal Code on abortion was completed in 1960). The ALI argued that states should legalize abortion in cases of rape, incest, certain fetal abnormalities, and threats to patient health. The last category was the easiest to justify: some doctors in therapeutic abortion committees had complained that criminal laws prevented them from delivering the best care for their patients. When it came to the remaining proposals, ALI leaders argued that doctors were in revolt against criminal abortion laws. By adopting the ALI proposal, states would simply be codifying what the medical profession was already doing.

In 1967, Colorado became the first state to pass the ALI proposal. Others, including Georgia and California, soon followed. Support for abortion reform did not at first break down along partisan lines. **Richard Lamm**, a Democrat, was the moving force behind Colorado's law. **Anthony Beilenson**, another liberal, led the effort in California. But in both states, Republicans as well as Democrats supported the push. Republican governors, including future conservative leader **Ronald Reagan**, signed ALI bills into law.

Abortion reformers like Beilensen, Lamm, and Guttmacher managed to win over politicians in both parties partly because they portrayed abortion as a public health crisis. **Larry Lader**, a prominent author and reform proponent, stressed that thousands of women died each year in botched criminal abortions. The reality of abortion in the United States was complex. In the 1960s, estimates of the number of annual illegal abortions varied from roughly 200,000 to 1.2 million. In the nineteenth century, many of those who had abortions had been white, married, and relatively wealthy. In the 1960s, by contrast, low-income pregnant people of color made up a disproportionate number of those seeking illegal abortions—and were far more likely to suffer complications. In the decades immediately before *Roe*, the total number of deaths per year attributed to illegal abortion had fallen below 200, but Lader and his colleagues believed that each death was unnecessary.

Early opponents of reform, many of them with ties to the Catholic Church, ridiculed the idea that the ALI bill was lifesaving. As abortion foes saw it, the ALI authorized murder—the killing of unborn children when a pregnant person's life was not at risk. Opposition to abortion was not new in the 1960s, but abortion foes had not done much to organize their efforts until the ALI bill topped the nation's agenda. Some Catholic opponents of abortion reform repeated familiar arguments about the connection between birth control, abortion, and promiscuity. Indeed, as recently as 1968, **Pope Paul VI** issued an encyclical, ***Humanae Vitae***, that restated the church's opposition to artificial birth control and reaffirmed traditional teachings on the sanctity of life. The church had long framed abortion as one more threat to the sanctity of marriage and parenthood.

But in states like California, antiabortion lawyers and local activists began experimenting with different arguments. Many Americans were using the pill. Many, even Catholics, did not abide by the teachings laid out in *Humanae Vitae*. Besides, tying abortion to contraception branded the former a "Catholic issue" in the eyes of some Protestants, some of whom still derided the influence of "Rome" on US politics.

Some abortion foes thought that the time had come for a new strategy: instead of emphasizing moral norms or religious beliefs, insisting that legal abortion violated the rights of the unborn child. Catholic lawyers pioneered such arguments in the mid-1960s, but they soon became far more widespread. Many groups opposed to abortion picked names that referred to the "right to life" mentioned in the US Declaration of Independence, suggesting that abortion reform robbed unborn children of their most sacred right.

Members of the emerging right-to-life movement rejected the ALI in its entirety. Some abortion foes accepted the need for the procedure when a patient's life was at risk. After all, one adult could kill another if she were acting in self-defense. But no one could legally take a person's life because of a rape or a health threat or potential disability. For right-to-lifers, unborn children were rights-holding persons. The ALI bill struck them not as a sensible compromise but as a rejection of fetal personhood.

In the short term, right-to-lifers seemed to come up short. States in the North and South passed the ALI bill. Liberals and conservatives endorsed it. Reform laws seemed to be under consideration everywhere. And yet wherever the ALI bill was in effect, the abortion rate barely budged. Both California and Colorado performed well under 1,000 procedures the year after implementing the ALI bill; almost no one from out of state received an abortion in either state. The ALI bill might have looked like a promising compromise to many legislators. What it was not was a law that would fundamentally change how abortion worked in the United States.

The reasons that ALI bills had such a modest impact were easy to see. Reform laws often required women to convince their personal physicians of the need for an abortion, then win over several doctors and a hospital committee. The whole process was expensive. The patients who managed to run the gauntlet set by ALI laws tended to have a family physician advocating for them. Just as the case before the ALI, these patients tended to be white and relatively well to do. Most people seeking abortions lacked the money or connections to navigate the ALI process.

Some patients found their way to doctors who performed illegal abortions but adhered to relatively high standards. Others traveled to Mexico. Others still used drugs or sharp instruments to try to end pregnancies on their own. Feminists sought to offer patients a safer alternative. The Chicago Women's Liberation Union, a feminist group founded in 1969, launched an underground abortion service, **Jane Collective**, that helped patients find safe abortion services or terminate their own pregnancies. At first, Jane had hired a doctor to help patients, but feminists in the organization soon learned to perform the procedure themselves. Started in 1967 by a group of 21 rabbis and Protestant ministers, the **Clergy Counseling Service**, also provided abortion referrals, both inside and outside the United States. **Carol Downer**, a feminist in California, popularized the idea of **menstrual extraction**, a technique for early abortions that women could perform themselves, and ran a referral service of her own.

But the kind of services offered by Jane or the Clergy Counseling Service were at best a stopgap for feminists seeking the complete repeal of criminal laws. **Repeal** caught on partly because new activists had joined the movement to change abortion laws. Feminists had been involved in the movement from the beginning. In California, for example, **Pat Maginnis** and **Lana Clarke Phelan** had helped patients find abortions or induce their own in the early 1960s. Maginnis had seen the mistreatment of abortion patients in a military hospital and become active on the issue. Phelan had survived an illegal abortion. The two activists suggested that women had a right to abortion, full stop.

More feminists took up the cause in the later 1960s when **second-wave feminism** exploded onto the national political scene in that decade. The first wave of feminism had focused on issues like voting and protecting women workers from dangerous workplaces. Second-wave feminists had a different focus: rooting out sex stereotypes that hurt both men and women. Many saw the start of second-wave feminism as 1963, the year that **Betty Friedan** had published a book entitled ***The Feminine Mystique.***

A graduate of Smith College, Friedan was highly educated, but like many of her classmates, she set those ambitions aside to focus on homemaking. Friedan found this experience empty and alienating. When she surveyed her former classmates, she found that many homemakers experienced similar feelings of frustration and sadness. Friedan later argued that many men *and* women felt trapped by the roles assigned to them. *The Feminine Mystique* came out the same year that a commission convened by President John F. Kennedy issued a report on discrimination against women. The women's movement was quickly becoming a major topic of conversation.

Second-wave feminists tackled issues from sex stereotypes in the media to discrimination at work and at school; others fought for new laws on marital rape and family planning. By the late 1960s, leading feminists also took on the abortion issue. The **National Organization for Women** (NOW), Friedan's group, endorsed the repeal of all abortion regulations in 1967. Some members of NOW opposed legalizing abortions, while others worried that signing onto the repeal cause would damage the organization's reputation. But generally, NOW leaders framed abortion as a civil right for women—and argued that women, not men, should set the course of the struggle. Other feminist groups soon followed NOW into the abortion wars. The Women's National Abortion Action Campaign (WONAAC), a socialist feminist group, organized in 1971 to campaign for the full repeal of criminal abortion restrictions. Feminists also convinced the leaders of groups like the **American Civil Liberties Union** to fight against criminal abortion laws.

Feminists drew on the idea of a right to privacy articulated in *Griswold*, but Friedan and her colleagues also saw abortion as a question of equality for women. If only (cisgender) women got pregnant, and if these women were the ones who did most childcare, then abortion laws affected women's right to pursue a career or an education. Some feminists also argued that abortion bans reflected outdated ideas about women belonging in the home.

Some population controllers also began endorsing the repeal of abortion restrictions. Of course, the population control and abortion-rights movements were always different from one another, and some large population control organizations stayed silent on the abortion issue. For example, the **Association for Voluntary Sterilization** (**AVS**), a group with roots in the eugenics movement, advocated voluntary sterilization as a family planning technique.

AVS had begun as a group advocating compulsory sterilization of so-called "defectives," but after World War II it dropped its explicit embrace of eugenics in favor of praising population control. AVS leaders had long celebrated sterilization, and when the abortion-rights movement picked up steam, AVS leaders did not change their focus.

Neither did the **Population Crisis Committee**, a group launched by **Hugh Moore**, the founder of the Dixie Cup Company, in 1963. The Population Crisis Committee took a more alarmist approach to what the eccentric Moore viewed as a demographic ticking time bomb [**Doc. 5**]. But Moore did not always think that *voluntary* population control of any kind would work and hardly embraced a right to abortion. Neither did the Population Council, a group then headed by the patrician John D. Rockefeller III. The Population Council primarily presented itself as a research organization. Rockefeller and his allies had built close relationships with leading politicians in both parties. Taking on the abortion issue seemed likely to create unnecessary divisions in the Population Council's growing coalition.

Besides, some population controllers had little in common with those pursuing abortion reform. The population control movement was still home to some who had led the eugenics fight in the early twentieth century. Other population controllers worried primarily about the **Cold War.** Arguing that poverty and food insecurity made people vulnerable to Communist doctrines, these advocates argued that overpopulation would push some countries into the orbit of the Soviet Union.

Nevertheless, Rockefeller became a major donor to the abortion-rights cause. Other population controllers were more direct about their support for legal abortion. Founded in 1968, **Zero Population Growth, Inc.** (**ZPG**), spread rapidly on college campuses. ZPG attracted people concerned about the environment or even women's rights. Even Hugh Moore tried to tap into growing environmentalist sentiment, sponsoring the first **Earth Day** celebration in 1970. ZPG endorsed the repeal of abortion laws as a weapon in the war against overpopulation. Some population controllers worked in the movement to legalize abortion. Even feminist organizations like NOW used population control rhetoric in their own advocacy.

Family planning organizations, Planned Parenthood chief among them, also signed on to the repeal movement. In earlier decades, Margaret Sanger had always denounced abortion, but in 1968, Planned Parenthood-World Population endorsed its legalization. Alan Guttmacher, a vocal advocate of legalization, had become one of the organization's leaders.

Single-issue pro-repeal organizations also launched. The **National Association for the Repeal of Abortion Laws** (**NARAL**) began operating in 1969. NARAL brought together many of the most prominent reformers, including Betty Friedan and Larry Lader, who contested how the fight to legalize abortion should be framed. Activists like Lader sometimes favored arguments believed to have the widest appeal, especially those involving population control. Friedan worried that NARAL made women's rights seem like a shameful secret.

There were practical reasons to be concerned about population control arguments too. Feminists feared that population rhetoric would alienate people of color. New federally funded family planning clinics were often located in communities of color. States with a long history of racism seemed strangely enthusiastic about family planning programs, even if they otherwise provided few benefits to people of color. Some racist politicians openly celebrated the idea of using birth control to eliminate Black babies. Some population controllers, like Hugh Moore, made racist statements linking overpopulation to the "ghetto" and celebrating the idea that population control would lower welfare expenses or illegitimacy rates. At times, civil rights activists accused population controllers of seeking to create a **Black genocide**—trying to prevent Black people from being born rather than supporting them.

The reality of the family planning programs of the 1960s and early 1970s was more complex. Many Black women used family planning clinics, describing them as liberating (and as offering better service than other health resources available to people of color). Nevertheless, by linking their cause to population control, groups like NARAL made it harder to win over people of color.

More sustained opposition came from the right-to-life movement. In the late 1960s, Catholic leaders concluded that it was both necessary and possible to expand the antiabortion movement beyond its Catholic origins. In 1968, the Family Life Division of the National Conference of Catholic Bishops founded the **National Right to Life Committee** (**NRLC**), a secular group committed to defending fetal rights and criminal abortion laws. A young, left-leaning priest, James McHugh, wanted to separate the abortion and birth control issues. NRLC also sought to coordinate the work of effective state organizations that were already in the field. States like Minnesota and New York were home to effective antiabortion organizations that knew how to lobby state lawmakers. Many of these activists had experience in fights against pornography or contraception. Indeed, the antiabortion movement at times drew members from existing socially conservative Catholic, Mormon, and other faith networks.

Nevertheless, by the late 1960s, the movement had positioned itself as a struggle for civil rights. Groups like NRLC compared abortion to slavery and racial segregation. Just as the United States had denied the humanity of Black Americans, abortion foes reasoned, abortion denied the personhood and most basic rights of unborn children. This argument had a political dimension: by moving away from religious arguments, abortion foes could attract a broader, more diverse following. But antiabortion arguments had a legal aim as well. While supporters of abortion rights insisted that the Constitution may protect a right to abortion access, abortion opponents responded that legalizing the procedure was unconstitutional.

To make this argument, abortion foes relied on the Fourteenth Amendment of the Constitution. That amendment stated that all "persons born or naturalized in the United States" counted as citizens. The Fourteenth Amendment then guaranteed "persons" equal protection and due process of the law. Abortion foes insisted that the drafters of the Fourteenth Amendment intended to include unborn children in the category of "persons." This meant that fetuses enjoyed rights to due process and equal protection of the law. Some antiabortion lawyers argued that before an abortion could constitutionally take place, a judge would have to appoint a guardian to speak on behalf of an unborn child and hold a hearing [**Doc. 6**]. Other antiabortion lawyers asserted that legalizing abortion violated the Equal Protection Clause—discriminatorily allowing the killing of persons based on their age and position in the womb.

By focusing on arguments about a right to life, the antiabortion movement did attract a broader group of supporters. Self-identified liberals joined antiabortion organizations; so did a larger number of non-Catholics. Some abortion foes spoke for a vision of liberalism that centered on a broad welfare state for the poor and more protections for the vulnerable, a category these abortion foes defined to include not only fetuses but also women, disabled persons, and the poor. Some even supported broader access to contraception or stronger laws against discrimination against pregnant workers.

Nevertheless, historians contest the extent to which the antiabortion movement was ever aligned with the political left. While linking their fight to the civil rights movement, very few abortion foes actually campaigned for equal treatment for people of color. Indeed, antiabortion leaders maintained that abortion was worse than slavery or the **Holocaust**. Right-to-lifers positioned fetuses, many of them white, as the ultimate victims of discrimination in the United States. The movement did attract some Black leaders. **Dr. Mildred Jefferson**, the first Black graduate of Harvard Medical School, held a leadership role NRLC. Nevertheless, the antiabortion movement, like the abortion-rights movement, remained predominantly white.

The rise of the repeal movement had not made either side any more willing to compromise. If anything, the abortion conflict had already become extremely polarized: in state legislatures, in presidential elections, and in the courts. In the wake of *Griswold*, some abortion-rights attorneys wanted to press their advantage. Some agreed to represent doctors accused of violating criminal abortion laws. Dr. Leon Belous, a prominent California physician, faced criminal charges after helping a desperate couple find an abortion provider. During a raid, police officers found an abortion doctor's log proving that Belous had referred him several abortion patients. Rather than proclaiming his innocence, Belous argued that California's abortion regulations violated the same kind of right to privacy recognized in *Griswold*—the autonomy of individuals to make vital decisions about their own lives. In 1969, in *People v. Belous*, the California Supreme Court agreed. Cases like *Belous* emboldened abortion-rights supporters to challenge more regulations in court.

Battles became heated in state legislatures as well. In 1970, New York passed the most liberal abortion law in the nation. Constance Cook, a liberal Republican, proposed eliminating all the restrictions on abortion in the state. Antiabortion resistance to the bill was relatively weak, partly because Catholic leaders in New York had not expected the bill to pass. After New York repealed all of its restrictions on abortion before the twenty-fourth week of pregnancy, the state quickly became a magnet for people looking to end a pregnancy. In the first 15 months after New York passed its law, doctors performed over 200,000 abortions. Because there was no residency requirement, over 60 percent of patients came from out of state. In 1970, Hawaii also repealed its abortion laws. Republicans and Democrats supported legalization, and opposition to the move had been poorly organized and did not fully take shape until the last minute.

The New York and Hawaii legislation sparked a more intense organizing effort from the antiabortion movement. Rather than only speaking about rights in the abstract, leading abortion foes in the states wanted to zero in on the details of how abortions actually worked. Abortion techniques themselves were in flux. Prior to the early 1970s, most abortion techniques were risky and often required a hospital stay. Then, for earlier abortions, providers began adopting **vacuum aspiration abortion**, a technique that involved the dilation of the cervix, the insertion of a tube, and the vacuuming of the contents of the uterus. The techniques used in later abortions varied. Traditionally, doctors would perform abortions by **hysterotomy**, a procedure somewhat resembling a Cesarean section, requiring an incision in the uterus to remove fetal remains. Other techniques included **saline abortions**, wherein a doctor removed the amniotic fluid and injected a saline solution that would induce a miscarriage. Some abortion doctors used **prostaglandins**, a type of fatty acid that regulates uterine activity, to induce contractions. Abortion opponents began acquiring images of abortion procedures and aborted fetuses. They believed that showing Americans what abortions looked like would change their minds.

**Dr. John Willke**, a prominent antiabortion activist, traveled the country with a slideshow of a vacuum aspiration abortion. Willke, like Dr. Mildred Jefferson, became one of the first right-to-life celebrities; he and his wife had already made a name for themselves in early decades as Catholic sex educators. But his slideshows soon became one of the right-to-life movement's most powerful tools for converting viewers. Like many of his colleagues, Willke believed that most Americans would oppose abortion if they just understood what it was.

Abortion-rights supporters contended that these fetal images were misleading and manipulative. There was no way to verify whether the images Willke used depicted aborted fetuses rather than miscarriages. And he did not just display images of abortion; he described the pain and fear experienced by unborn children—without evidence to support it. But images of life in the womb had tremendous emotional resonance. Abortion-rights supporters responded with images of women who had died during botched abortions. The coat hanger—an implement sometimes used for ending pregnancies—became a symbol of the fight to legalize abortion.

Nevertheless, slideshows helped abortion foes recruit new supporters, particularly among **evangelical Protestants**. In the early 1970s, it was primarily Northern evangelicals who began speaking out against the procedure. Southern evangelicals still felt uncomfortable with elective abortions but also felt ill at ease aligning with what they saw as a Catholic pro-life movement. Mormons, Orthodox Jews, and other religious conservatives found fetal images to be proof of the unborn child's right to life. In the mid-1960s, states had passed ALI bills with little effective resistance from a weak and heavily Catholic antiabortion movement. By the early 1970s, the antiabortion movement was molding itself into a political force.

The more divisive the abortion issue seemed, the more unstable the party politics of abortion became. Before 1972, there were prominent Republicans in favor of legalizing abortion, including **Nelson Rockefeller**, the governor of New York and a scion of the Rockefeller dynasty. Other Republicans spoke out against abortion. Democrats could be found on either side of the issue as well.

The Republican president, **Richard Nixon**, a supporter of population control, had tried to stay away from the abortion issue, believing it would divide and weaken his party. He had chartered a commission to study population control and asked John D. Rockefeller III, a prominent donor to abortion-rights organizations, to lead the effort. The Nixon Administration oversaw a major expansion of federal family planning programs and required military bases to perform abortions for military members and their families.

But when the time came for Nixon to run for reelection, the president began to view the politics of abortion in a different light. When Senator Ed Muskie, one of the Democrats seeking that party's presidential nomination, made headlines by discussing the "sanctity of life" and denouncing legal abortion, Nixon did not want to lose conservative Catholic voters to any Democratic competitor. So, in the leadup to the 1972 race, Nixon proclaimed himself to be opposed to "abortion on demand," changed the administration's policy on abortion on military bases, and condemned the Rockefeller Commission when its report on population control endorsed the legalization of abortion [**Doc. 7**].

When **George McGovern**, a South Dakota Senator known for his opposition to the **Vietnam War**, emerged from a crowded Democratic primary, Nixon played up his supposed support for abortion. Nixon routinely accused his opponent of endorsing "the three As," "acid, abortion, and amnesty"—that was, access to **LSD** and illegal drugs, legal abortion, and protection for those who avoided the **draft** for the conflict in Vietnam. By the middle of 1972, Nixon and his staffers viewed abortion as a **wedge issue**—a way to mobilize socially conservative voters who might, for economic reasons, have otherwise voted for a Democrat.

The irony was that McGovern was no supporter of abortion rights, even if he had flirted with the idea. Feminists had organized to lobby McGovern and influence the Democratic platform. The women's movement had gained some influence over the party. But Nixon's about-face intimidated McGovern, who backed away from his earlier position and chose one of the most outspoken opponents of abortion in Congress, Missouri Senator **Thomas Eagleton**, to be his running mate.

If abortion opponents felt emboldened by the 1972 presidential election, the abortion wars in the states appeared to have been fought to a stalemate. That year, abortion reformers asked Michigan voters to consider a referendum that would legalize abortion in the first 20 weeks of pregnancy. North Dakota considered a referendum based the ALI model. Abortion foes managed to defeat both proposals. Abortion foes even had some success in pushing New York to reinstate criminal abortion restrictions. It was only Governor Nelson Rockefeller's decision to veto the new criminal restrictions that saved abortion repeal in New York.

Nevertheless, it was hardly clear that pro-lifers were winning. States across the country had passed the ALI bill, which abortion foes rejected for ignoring fetal rights and fetal personhood. Repeal was still on the agenda in other jurisdictions. Polls showed that large majorities of Americans believed that the abortion decision should be left to a patient and her doctor.

The picture was equally murky in the courts. Some state and federal courts rejected challenges to abortion laws, while others recognized a right to end a pregnancy. In Georgia, in a case called ***Doe v. Bolton***, attorney **Margie Pitts Hames** challenged a law patterned loosely on the ALI model. In July 1970, a district court held that the law violated the right to privacy recognized in *Griswold*. Georgia appealed the case directly to the Supreme Court.

Another major case, ***Roe v. Wade***, came from Texas. Attorneys **Sarah Weddington** and **Linda Coffee** represented **Norma McCorvey**, a 21-year-old woman pregnant with her third child. Weddington and Coffee challenged the constitutionality of a Texas law that allowed abortions only when a patient's life was at risk. A three-judge panel unanimously held that Texas's law violated the constitutional right to privacy, and the Supreme Court agreed to hear the case.

The US Supreme Court first heard **oral argument** in *Roe* in December 1971. **Harry Blackmun**, the justice assigned to write the **majority opinion**, initially planned to hold that Texas's law was unconstitutionally vague—that is, most doctors would not know which procedures would be deemed to be lifesaving. As a result, doctors could face criminal punishment without a fair opportunity to know what was and was not allowed.

Blackmun's vagueness argument mirrored one made in ***United States v. Vuitch***, a case decided by the Supreme Court a year earlier [**Doc. 8**]. *Vuitch* involved a Washington, DC, abortion ordinance allowing abortions only when the life or health of a woman was at risk. Dr. Milan Vuitch, a doctor who routinely performed illegal abortions, was charged with violating the law and challenged its constitutionality. His attorneys argued that the law was unconstitutionally vague, but the Supreme Court had disagreed. The *Vuitch* Court interpreted the ordinance to permit abortions in cases of a threat to physical or mental health. Interpreted in this way, the ordinance was constitutional.

Blackmun planned to expand on the logic of *Vuitch*. He thought that doctors would not know ahead of time when an abortion would be deemed to be life-saving. But some of the liberal Court's members, including William Douglas, the author of *Griswold*, wanted a further-reaching ruling. The Court eventually had to schedule *Roe* for reargument in the fall of 1972.

In the meantime, the Court was set to decide a challenge to a Massachusetts contraception law in ***Eisenstadt v. Baird*** [**Doc. 9**]. That case began when **Bill Baird**, a self-proclaimed contraceptive crusader, headlined an event on a Massachusetts college campus where he spoke about birth control and distributed contraceptive foam to attendees. The problem was that Massachusetts law allowed unmarried people access to contraception only for the purpose of preventing sexually transmitted diseases. Only married people could use contraception for the purpose of birth control. Baird had violated the law, and he knew it. Facing criminal charges, Baird challenged the constitutionality of the Massachusetts statute. A district court sustained Baird's conviction in 1969, but an appellate court reversed it, and the Supreme Court agreed to take the appeal.

In March 1972, the Supreme Court struck down the Massachusetts law. The seven-to-two majority opinion relied on the Equal Protection Clause of the Fourteenth Amendment. When the law treated people differently based on their race or sex, the courts closely scrutinized it. In *Eisenstadt*, the state treated people differently depending on whether they were married or single and justified its law as a way to protect people against dangerous contraceptive drugs, a measure to block birth control, and a strategy to cut down on sex outside of marriage. The Supreme Court did not find any of these justifications convincing. When it came to illicit sex, Massachusetts did criminalize **fornication** but treated it as a misdemeanor. The Court did not believe that lawmakers would want to punish someone for a minor offense by forcing them to continue a pregnancy. *Eisenstadt* reasoned that the health justification did not make sense either. If birth control drugs were dangerous, the state would have no reason to protect single people while endangering married ones. Finally, *Eisenstadt* concluded that the state had no interest whatsoever in preventing people from using contraception. Whatever privacy right the Constitution protected, the Court reasoned, it had to apply equally to married and unmarried people. And whatever the right to privacy meant, it was broad enough to encompass an individual's decision about whether to have a child.

Bill Baird felt that history was about to be made. His case seemed to be only the beginning of much bigger changes. After all, the Supreme Court was set to hear *Roe v. Wade* and *Doe v. Bolton* once again. **Robert Byrn**, an antiabortion professor at Fordham Law, was not that worried about *Roe*. Earlier that year, he had asked a New York court to name him the guardian of all the unborn children scheduled to be aborted in New York hospitals. He succeeded, at least in the short term. Eventually, a New York appellate court reversed the decision to let Byrn serve as a guardian and to recognize fetal personhood [**Doc. 6**]. Byrn nevertheless believed that his case proved a point: the courts were not predictably supportive of abortion rights. Besides, for Byrn, there was reason to be optimistic about the Supreme Court. Richard Nixon spent much of 1972 reminding the public how much he opposed legal abortion. Four of his justices sat on the High Court.

Baird and Byrn did not agree about what the future held for the law of abortion and contraception, but they saw eye to eye on one thing: the Constitution would be key to the future of the conflict. For much of the twentieth century, it seemed that doctors would set the course of the conflict. Doctors had fought to criminalize abortions in the late nineteenth century. Then, physicians had created hospital committees that tightly regulated abortion care. It was doctors who led the reform movement of the mid-twentieth century, and physicians like Mildred Jefferson and John Willke had led the opposition to reform. But by 1972, few saw abortion in the United States as a medical question and nothing more. Religion, morality, feminism, racial politics, and constitutional wrangling all cast a shadow over the debate. And increasingly, the fate of the US abortion conflict would be determined not in doctors' offices but in courtrooms. As Byrn and Baird understood, fights about abortion in the United States would no longer be about what medical professionals believed. Instead, the debate would turn on party politics—and what the Constitution had to say about reproduction.

# 3 The fight for *Roe v. Wade*

In January 1973, Harry Blackmun delivered an opinion in *Roe v. Wade* [**Doc. 10**] that would become one of the most notorious in US constitutional law. Richard Nixon had recently nominated both Blackmun and his childhood friend, **Warren Burger**, to the Court. Nixon presented the two as conservatives concerned with law and order; the two were so similar that commentators called them the "Minnesota Twins." But in the winter of 1973, Blackmun wrote one of the Supreme Court decisions many would most associate with the liberal federal judiciary.

Over the last summer, Blackmun had spent time researching abortion at the library of the Mayo Clinic, an elite medical facility in his native Minnesota. This medical research shaped the *Roe* decision. Blackmun began by noting how profoundly divisive the abortion issue had already become. In a seven-to-two majority opinion, Blackmun mentioned everything from racism to population control to religion in surveying the roots of the nation's abortion conflict. Nevertheless, he hoped that *Roe* would help to lead the nation out of this dilemma. If the Court resolved the abortion issue "by constitutional measurement, free of emotion and of predilection," then perhaps the conflict might not be as intense.

The Court began by addressing whether anyone had the right to challenge Texas's law in the first place. Norma McCorvey (the real name of Jane Roe) had already given birth by the time the case arrived at the High Court. Arguably, there was no need to resolve the case anymore. Other plaintiffs similarly might have lacked standing to bring a case. But the Court concluded that McCorvey's suit was not moot; the constitutional questions raised in *Roe* would not go away simply because Norma McCorvey was no longer pregnant: other people would inevitably seek out abortions, possibly including McCorvey herself.

Blackmun turned next to a medical history of abortion. He recognized that the Hippocratic Oath, a vow taken by doctors, seemed to treat abortions as nonethical. Nevertheless, *Roe* described medical hostility to abortion as recent and contested—not part of a longstanding national tradition. Blackmun argued that, for centuries, the English common law had allowed abortion before quickening, and state law had followed suit. Then, according to Blackmun, the American Medical Association had led the charge

DOI: 10.4324/9781003215936-6

to criminalize abortion in the nineteenth century, but in 1970 the AMA no longer backed strong criminal prohibitions. Neither did the American Public Health Association, another professional group for doctors, nor the American Bar Association, the nation's leading professional group for lawyers. To Blackmun, all of this elite support suggested that opposition to abortion was recent and shallow, not a cornerstone of American constitutional tradition.

The Court concluded that the constitutional right to privacy was broad enough to encompass a woman's decision to terminate her pregnancy in consultation with her doctor. The majority noted that the abortion decision resembled a network of other key choices involving procreation, parenting, and marriage that were already afforded constitutional protections. As *Roe* framed it, the abortion decision was particularly consequential. Pregnancy created physical discomfort and health risks. Childrearing could also tax a parent's health and welfare. So could the stigma surrounding unwed motherhood.

Antiabortion lawyers had insisted that a right to life trumped any privacy right to abortion. The Court first considered the argument that an unborn child was a rights-holding person under the Fourteenth Amendment. If the Court did recognize fetal personhood, then the case for a right to abortion would "collapse," given that the Constitution would protect a fetal right to life. Ultimately, however, the Court rejected an argument for fetal personhood. Canvassing the text, *Roe* concluded that, throughout the Constitution, the word "person" applied only after birth, not before, and there was no reason to believe that Congress had intended anything different when writing the Fourteenth Amendment. Blackmun further noted that abortion was less heavily regulated at the time Congress introduced the Fourteenth Amendment, making it less likely that the provision's authors intended the word person to apply before birth.

Texas responded that states had a compelling interest in protecting life from the moment that an egg was fertilized—and that this interest justified criminal abortion bans, even if there was a privacy right to abortion. *Roe* surveyed medical, theological, and philosophical opinion on when life began. Concluding that leading experts could not reach any consensus on when life began, the Court reasoned that Texas could not write its views into law.

The Court reasoned instead that the state's interest in protecting life became compelling only at **viability**, the point at which survival was possible outside the womb. In 1973, fetal viability occurred between the twenty-fourth and twenty-eighth week of pregnancy. Only after viability could the state prohibit abortion to protect fetal life. In the first trimester of pregnancy (the first 12 weeks), *Roe* suggested that most abortion restrictions would be unconstitutional (the Court made an exception for laws that required all abortions to be performed by a licensed physician). In the second trimester, states could regulate abortion, but only to advance patient health. *Roe*'s new rule was known as the **trimester framework**.

At the same time, the Court resolved *Doe v. Bolton*, the Georgia case involving a law somewhat like the ALI model. The Court concluded that, under the trimester framework, Georgia's law also violated the Constitution. The Court further clarified what doctors and patients should evaluate when considering what would protect patient health: age as well as a wide array of "physical, emotional, psychological, [and] familial factors."

Only two justices dissented. **William Rehnquist** stressed that at the time the Fourteenth Amendment went into effect, most states criminalized abortion. As Rehnquist saw it, there was no reason to think that the authors of the Fourteenth Amendment would have recognized a right to abortion when at the time, most states made the procedure a crime. Rehnquist's dissent also accused the Court of making things up as it went along. Rather than consulting only the Constitution's text or history, Rehnquist argued, the Court had acted more like a legislature.

Only a handful of states had repealed all of their abortion restrictions before 1973. *Roe* invalidated the vast majority of abortion laws then on the books. The decision also sparked a flurry of criticism from legal experts, including some who agreed with the result in the case. For example, John Hart Ely, a professor at Yale, criticized *Roe* for inventing a constitutional right out of whole cloth without relying on the text or history of the Constitution (or any other conventional constitutional methodology).

Abortion-rights supporters in groups like NARAL (which renamed itself the National Abortion Rights Action League) felt that the Supreme Court had more or less put an end to legal struggles around abortion, but access to the procedure was another matter entirely. For the most part, before 1973, abortions took place in hospitals. The procedures were expensive and hard to get. In some parts of the South and Midwest, there were very few abortion providers at all.

NARAL and other abortion-rights organizations set out to change that. While lobbying hospitals and doctors' offices to perform abortions, abortion-rights supporters also sponsored a network of freestanding abortion clinics that would specialize in performing the procedure (many also provided family planning and other medical services). Feminist health centers ensured that women, not men, would provide care and that patients would receive education about their sexual and reproductive health. Some Planned Parenthood affiliates performed abortions; entrepreneurs and doctors opened their own facilities. With the spread of abortion clinics, the nature of abortion care changed significantly. In 1973, 81 percent of abortions were linked to hospitals. By 1980, that number had dipped to 59 percent. In the same period, the number of abortions performed each year more than doubled.

The abortion industry went through growing pains. Concerns about subpar care and even criminal liability for doctors spurred the professionalization of abortion care. Frances Kissling and other advocates brought together two existing provider groups to form the **National Abortion Federation (NAF)** in 1977. NAF would set professional standards and provide education on best practices for abortion providers.

Professionalization became even more important after abortion opponents intensified their campaign to recriminalize the procedure. Leading antiabortion organizations like National Right to Life Committee got their start before *Roe*. So did **Americans United for Life**, an organization that originally focused on public relations. For the most part, however, the most powerful antiabortion groups had operated at the state level.

After *Roe*, antiabortion groups put together a more comprehensive national effort. Most rallied around a constitutional amendment that would ban abortions by defining an unborn child or fetus as a rights-holding person. Some members of Congress sponsored constitutional amendments in Congress, but abortion opponents had no interest in a compromise measure, no matter how likely it was to pass. Some lawmakers, for example, suggested it would be easier to pass a constitutional amendment that allowed states to criminalize abortion but did not require them to do so. Antiabortion leaders almost universally rejected this proposal. Viewing abortion as murder, right-to-lifers saw anything short of an outright ban as unprincipled.

But amending the Constitution was not easy. Antiabortion leaders recognized the need for a stopgap strategy to limit access while the constitutional amendment unfolded and pushed laws requiring patients to get the consent of their parents or spouses before getting an abortion. Other laws imposed waiting periods or required patients to listen to a state-written script. Still others focused on the federal Medicaid program, which provided free or low-cost services for low-income Americans.

Right-to-lifers took a keener interest in incremental abortion restrictions after a Massachusetts jury convicted Dr. Kenneth Edelin of manslaughter. Edelin, a Black obstetrician-gynecologist, provided services to a primarily low-income community of color in the Boston metro. He got in trouble after performing an abortion by hysterotomy, a procedure used later in pregnancy whereby a physician performed a uterine incision, removed a fetus, and completed an abortion. Witnesses disputed what happened next. Prosecutors claimed that after the hysterotomy, a child was born alive and breathing before Edelin killed it. Edelin maintained that the fetus could not have survived and died as a result of the hysterotomy. Prosecutors charged with Edelin with manslaughter and accused him of infanticide, and in 1975, a jury convicted him. Although Edelin's conviction was ultimately overturned on appeal, his criminal ordeal was eye-opening for antiabortion leaders. Prosecutors had not said that there was a right to life or that *Roe* was not the law. Instead, prosecutors had said that a jury could legally convict Edelin even if there *was* a right to abortion. If the Supreme Court would not reverse *Roe v. Wade*, and if Congress could not pass a constitutional amendment, the *Edelin* case taught antiabortion activists that they could still limit access to abortion.

Antiabortion leaders had arguably their most significant post-*Roe* victory the following year when Congress passed the **Hyde Amendment**. Representative Henry Hyde, a Republican from Illinois, added a provision to a bill funding the federal Department of Health, Education, and Welfare that prohibited Medicaid reimbursement for most abortions; the Medicaid program covered certain healthcare costs for low-income Americans, and the Hyde Amendment had a substantial impact on the abortion rate because the population relying on abortion services had changed after *Roe*. Before *Roe*, only relatively wealthy, generally white patients could navigate the maze of requirements governing legal abortions. After *Roe*, those seeking abortions were more likely to be young, poor, unmarried, people of color. Limiting access for the poor promised to force a major decline in the abortion rate.

The Hyde Amendment also exposed a weakness of the abortion-rights movement. Some abortion-rights lawmakers had voted for the funding bill containing the Hyde Amendment because they believed that the Supreme Court would find it unconstitutional. Even after the Hyde Amendment passed, abortion-rights groups struggled to motivate donors and grassroots activists when the spotlight was on abortion funding. For decades, the abortion-rights movement would prioritize initiatives that affected wealthier patients while sometimes sidelining the concerns of low-income people and communities of color. The Hyde Amendment battle also showed that abortion-rights supporters at times relied too heavily on the courts.

Feminists of color had worked in larger organizations like Planned Parenthood, but in the later 1970s, people of color sometimes broke away to found their own organizations. The most divisive issue at the time was forced sterilization. For several decades, population control groups—some of them with connections to the eugenics movement—had campaigned for easier access to sterilization. But in 1973 and 1974, the press reported on widespread **sterilization abuse**. Perhaps the best-known story involved the Relf sisters, Katie, Minnie Lee, and Mary Alice, all of whom were under the age of 18. Doctors had sterilized Minnie Lee and Mary Alice without their parents' knowledge. Katie received several forms of contraception (one of them experimental and not approved by the government) without her parents' consent. The American Civil Liberties Union brought suit on the Relfs' behalf, but their experience was tragically common: sterilization abuse was particularly common among women from Puerto Rico, Black women living in the South, and Native Americans.

In 1974, the Department of Health, Education, and Welfare proposed new regulations designed to guarantee informed consent to sterilization. Some socialist feminists and feminists of color endorsed the regulations, and activists like **Helen Rodríguez Trías** formed the **Committee to End Sterilization Abuse (CESA)** to champion the idea of informed consent. But larger abortion-rights groups did not universally back the new rules on sterilization abuse. Some members of groups like NARAL or Planned Parenthood still had ties to the population control movement and may have sympathized with doctors performing involuntary sterilizations. For the most part, however, groups like NARAL and Planned Parenthood worried that sterilization regulations would open the door to abortion restrictions. If the government could mandate informed consent for sterilization, then states would claim the power to regulate abortion too.

The Hyde Amendment deepened the divide between groups like CESA and the larger abortion-rights organizations. Socialist feminists and feminists of color believed that the broader movement had not done enough to fight the Hyde Amendment, either before or after it passed. As important, feminists like Rodrígues-Trías saw this as a symptom of a bigger problem: the abortion-rights movement was run by white people and primarily addressed their concerns.

Feminists of color hoped to shape party politics on abortion. In 1976, however, neither party had fully staked out a position on the issue. **Jimmy Carter**, the candidate who emerged from the Democratic primary, opposed a constitutional amendment banning abortion but also saw no problem with the Hyde Amendment. Carter favored what he called alternatives to abortion, like bumping up funding for birth control or neonatal care.

His competitor, **Gerald Ford**, likewise took a muddy position. Ford had been Richard Nixon's vice president, but in 1973 a scandal forced Nixon to resign. Nixon operatives had broken into Democratic Party headquarters to gather intelligence. An investigation into what became known as the **Watergate** scandal led to the conviction of several high-ranking Nixon Administration officials and forced the president to resign. Nixon had promoted his antiabortion views, but Ford was far more circumspect. A rough-and-tumble primary fight with Ronald Reagan, the former movie star who had been governor of California, forced Ford to the right on abortion. Reagan had proclaimed his support for a constitutional abortion ban and won the heart of conservatives. But even under pressure from Reagan, Ford (whose wife was an outspoken supporter of abortion rights) only endorsed a provision allowing states to criminalize abortion—a move condemned by most antiabortion leaders. For the most part, Ford and Carter preferred not to say anything about abortion at all.

Despite Ford and Carter's reluctance, antiabortion leaders began to invest more in influencing national elections. Dr. John Willke, the doctor who became famous for antiabortion sideshows, argued that a constitutional amendment would never pass unless different politicians took office. Pro-life groups began forming **political action committees**, groups that would raise and spend money to elect sympathetic candidates.

These antiabortion organizations got a boost when the Supreme Court upheld a major abortion restriction, a Connecticut Medicaid regulation that allowed Medicaid reimbursement only for medically necessary abortions. In 1977, in **Maher v. Roe** [**Doc. 11**], the Court made clear that the Constitution did not guarantee access to abortion funding. As the Court interpreted it, the US Constitution guaranteed only negative rights—freedom from the government rather than any support from the authorities. Instead, a Planned Parenthood affiliate argued that if the state chose to fund any reproductive services, like childbirth, the state also had to cover abortion, which was a fundamental right.

In *Maher*, the Supreme Court disagreed. The Court saw Connecticut's law as completely different from the one struck down in *Roe*. In *Roe*, Texas had created an obstacle to patients seeking abortion. Connecticut, by contrast, did not create the hurdle facing patients. It was poverty, not the law, that made it impossible for some women to get abortions. The state could still favor childbirth over abortion, and the Constitution guaranteed only the freedom to make a decision about abortion, not the ability to actually get one.

*Maher* sparked the interest of antiabortion lawyers in a much more ambitious litigation campaign. Americans United for Life transitioned from working on public relations to prioritizing work in the courtroom, defending regulations claimed to be consistent with *Roe*, all while hollowing out the very idea of an abortion right. The emptier the right to choose became, the easier it would be later on to convince the Supreme Court to get rid of *Roe* altogether.

But focusing on more incremental abortion restrictions required a different strategy. Often, abortion foes had insisted that an unborn child had a right to life. These arguments did not make much sense when abortion foes were defending a law that required doctors to use one procedure or another, or simply required a patient to wait. None of these laws treated abortion as murder. So, instead of talking about fetal personhood, abortion foes instead argued that specific restrictions were good for patients, their families, and the country. They insisted that regulations would preserve marriages, help teenagers from going down the wrong path, save taxpayers' money, and protect patients from regretting their decision to end a pregnancy. More and more, antiabortion groups began focusing on claims about what abortion in America was really like—and whether abortion harmed pregnant people and their communities.

Abortion-rights groups became increasingly concerned that the Supreme Court had abandoned them, especially after the Supreme Court upheld the Hyde Amendment in **Harris v. McRae**. The Hyde Amendment was technically different from the law upheld in *Maher*: the Hyde Amendment defunded all abortions, including those deemed medically necessary. To the Supreme Court, however, this distinction made no difference. The federal government had not made women poor, and it was poverty, not any law, that made the poor unable to afford abortions once the Hyde Amendment was in effect.

The 1980 presidential election was also a wakeup call for the abortion-rights movement. For the first time, both antiabortion and abortion-rights groups had invested significant amounts of money in the campaign for the White House. National Right to Life started its own political action committee. Life Amendment PAC, another antiabortion political action committee, claimed to have cost several Democratic incumbents their seats in 1978 and pledged to do even better in 1980. Abortion-rights groups mobilized to match their opponents' efforts. To do so, activists like Karen Mulhauser, the executive director of NARAL, pioneered a new approach to advocacy. Rather than just relying on *Roe*, NARAL would emphasize the importance of keeping the government out of core reproductive decisions. Leaders of the group recognized that right-to-lifers had made many

Americans uncomfortable with the details of abortion. As freestanding clinics opened across the country, antiabortion pickets spread. So did images of aborted children. Abortion itself was becoming taboo. So, rather than talking about the abortion procedure, NARAL sought out a strategy with a broader appeal. The group settled on the idea of choice, suggesting that the issue was not abortion per se but the freedom to decide. NARAL and its allies began describing themselves as pro-choice.

The pro-choice framing seemed to resonate with Americans who would not have embraced feminism or the civil-rights movement. But it further alienated feminists of color and their socialist feminist allies. The idea of a freedom to choose seemed empty to low-income people who needed support from the government to afford birth control or abortions, safe housing, or the means to raise the children they wanted. In 1979, when NARAL embraced the pro-choice label, feminists of color and socialist feminists launched the Committee for Abortion Rights and Against Sterilization Abuse (CARASA), a group that would treat abortion as part of a more comprehensive **reproductive justice** agenda, which advanced a broad social justice agenda along with calls for reproductive rights. CARASA did not last long: misunderstandings between white members and people of color hobbled the organization. Nevertheless, CARASA delivered a powerful reminder of the fact that the post-*Roe* abortion-rights movement did not connect with all of the communities it hoped to serve.

Arguments about a right to choose also failed to slow down GOP nominee Ronald Reagan. The race had pitted Reagan, the runner up in the 1976 primary, against incumbent Jimmy Carter. Carter faced obvious headwinds: high rates of inflation and unemployment, together with high gas prices, created widespread fear and frustration. Reagan's sunny personality and pledges of low taxes had a strong appeal. Reagan also used the abortion issue to his advantage. Prior to 1980, neither party had taken a clear or consistent position on abortion. There were prominent pro-life Democrats and big-name pro-choice Republicans. Many politicians, like Gerald Ford and Jimmy Carter, saw the abortion issue as a trap. Abortion was controversial, they believed, and no matter what a politician said, it would anger some voters.

Reagan had come to view the abortion issue in a completely different light. Since the **Great Depression**, the Democratic Party had held together a coalition of voters that included labor unions, religious minorities like Jews and Catholics, blue-collar workers looking for higher wages and better working conditions, people of color, farmers, rural white Southerners, and urban intellectuals. Reagan believed that he could use the abortion issue to dismantle this coalition. Catholics and evangelical Protestants in the South and Midwest were more likely to oppose unrestricted abortion access. By making the GOP the "Party of Life," Reagan could convince some voters to switch parties.

Reagan's plan looked especially promising because the religious composition of the antiabortion movement was changing in the late 1970s. While other groups had joined the movement before *Roe*, the antiabortion movement had remained predominantly Catholic in the early 1970s. Some northern evangelicals had denounced what they called "abortion on demand" before *Roe*, but the Southern Baptist Convention, a larger evangelical denomination, had not taken a stand. By the late 1970s, however, leading evangelicals made opposition to abortion a cornerstone of their burgeoning political activity. The Southern Baptist Convention had spoken out against unrestricted abortion access but still backed some degree of access to legal abortion throughout the 1970s. In 1980, however, Larry Lewis, a St. Louis pastor, pushed a resolution denouncing all abortions and committing the Southern Baptists to fighting *Roe*. His proposed resolution passed.

Republican Party veterans saw the Southern Baptists and other faith groups as an untapped source of political power. In the mid-1970s, some operatives created what they called the **New Right**, a group of movement conservatives that sought to push the Republican Party to the right. Paul Weyrich, one architect of the New Right, had experience working with Colorado Republican Gordon Allott; he went on to create a conservative PAC, a rightwing think tank, and the American Legislative Exchange Council, an organization that sent conservative state lawmakers blueprints of bills to pass. Richard Viguerie, another New Right leader, built a direct-mail empire.

These activists grew frustrated with what they saw as the dominance of liberal Republicans in their party. Weyrich, Viguerie, and their colleagues created a phalanx of political action committees and lobbying organizations. Weyrich also wanted to mobilize Christian conservative voters to strengthen the party andmake it more conservative. Weyrich helped convince **Jerry Falwell**, a Virginia televangelist, to start the **Moral Majority** [**Doc. 12**], an organization designed to get conservative evangelical Protestants to the polls. Evangelicals had already been politically active, but by 1980 Weyrich hoped to make them into a political force. The so-called **Religious Right** built up an impressive war chest and offered Ronald Reagan yet another reason to emphasize his opposition to abortion.

Partly because of the influence of the Religious Right, the Republican Party took a more strongly antiabortion position. The GOP platform endorsed a constitutional amendment and the selection of federal judges who subscribed to **originalism**, an interpretive method that relied on the original intentions of the authors of a constitutional text or the original public meaning of the text (at the time, many originalists took the position that *Roe* was wrongly decided). Antiabortion lawyers were elated.

The results of the 1980 election were just as exciting for abortion opponents. Reagan carried 44 states and won the popular vote by a nearly 9 percent margin. Republicans, many of them sponsored by the New Right, took control by the houses of Congress. It seemed that there may be enough votes to pass a fetal-protective constitutional amendment.

The 1980 election also helped to shift the course of the abortion conflict. When it came to party affiliation, the antiabortion movement had long been divided. Many held conservative views about the family and sexuality, but on other issues the movement was divided. Some abortion foes favored expanded family planning programs, believing that if more people prevented unwanted pregnancies, there would be less demand for abortions. Others insisted that widespread access to birth control had created a contraceptive mentality—people had sex for pleasure and saw abortion as a way to avoid the natural consequences of that act. Some abortion foes embraced a racially tinged vision of small government and opposed new protections against employment discrimination. Others favored prohibitions of pregnancy discrimination at work. For a time, these political tensions had been pushed to the side by a movement that tried to win support from both sides of the aisle.

But political party realignment changed the calculus made by abortion foes. Aligning with the New Right and Religious Right promised resources and political support to a badly struggling antiabortion movement. These financial struggles were significant: even the National Right to Life Committee, the nation's largest pro-life group, was badly in debt in the late 1970s. Partnering with the Religious Right seemed to offer stability. And when the GOP came out strongly in favor of a constitutional amendment criminalizing abortion, antiabortion voters began to move permanently into the Republican camp. This shift empowered antiabortion leaders who already embraced the politics of the New Right.

The 1980 election also helped to firm up the pro-choice identity of the Democratic Party. Some members of the New Deal coalition, including union leaders, farmers, and blue-collar voters, did not consistently support abortion rights. But by 1980, more feminists and people of color had gained seats on important Democratic committees and pushed the party to more fully embrace the idea of reproductive rights.

After 1980, it seemed possible that the United States would reinstate criminal abortion bans. But when antiabortion leaders counted likely votes in Congress, there were not enough for the nationwide criminalization of abortion. Senator Jesse Helms, a North Carolinian known for his fierce defense of racial segregation, proposed the Human Life Bill, a federal statute defining an unborn child as a rights-holding person (and effectively banning abortion). Antiabortion skeptics questioned the soundness of Helms' strategy. After all, abortion-rights supporters could challenge the constitutionality of the Human Life Bill in court, and more likely than not, they would win. Congress did have some power to enforce the Fourteenth Amendment: Section Five of the Fourteenth Amendment explicitly assigned Congress some enforcement power. But the Supreme Court had put strict limits on Congress's power. Lawmakers could remedy violations of rights already identified by the Supreme Court but could not redefine which rights were protected. The Human Life Bill almost unquestionably did just that. *Roe* had rejected the argument that unborn children were rights-holding persons. Even within the antiabortion movement, some leaders believed the Human Life Bill to be a waste of time.

Some rallied behind an alternative proposed by Utah Republican Senator Orrin Hatch. Hatch revived the idea of a constitutional amendment allowing, but not requiring, the states to ban abortion. Such a provision would get rid of *Roe*. As important, it stood a chance of getting through Congress. Nevertheless, some antiabortion absolutists denounced the Hatch Amendment because it did not ban any abortions. Absolutists argued that by passing it, Republicans could claim to oppose abortion without accomplishing anything.

While the fight over the Hatch and Helms' proposal ratcheted up, Ronald Reagan nominated his first justice to the Supreme Court. On the campaign trail, Reagan had hinted that he would pick a woman to sit on the High Court. He fulfilled that promise by selecting **Sandra Day O'Connor**, a judge and former legislator from Arizona. Antiabortion leaders could not hide their disgust. Rumors ran rampant that O'Connor had supported abortion rights while she served in the Arizona legislature. Antiabortion leaders cajoled and threatened Reagan. Others outright protested the nomination. Reagan found himself in a bind. He could not guarantee that O'Connor would vote to overturn *Roe* without delegitimizing her nomination. As important, on the campaign trail, Reagan had often pledged to depoliticize the Court. He argued that a liberal judiciary had demolished the distinction between policy-making and legal interpretation, engaging in a kind of judicial activism that damaged American democracy. Reagan could not easily promise that O'Connor would vote for certain policy outcomes without seeming to embrace judicial activism himself.

In the short term, abortion foes' anger about O'Connor hardly seemed to matter. During her confirmation hearing, O'Connor did face questions about whether *Roe* was rightly decided—a first for a Supreme Court nominee. Nevertheless, there was never a serious threat to her confirmation, and the Senate unanimously voted to confirm her. While O'Connor's nomination was never in doubt, abortion foes' anger about her nomination foreshadowed a change to future Supreme Court nominations. The Reagan Administration would have to find a way to placate religious conservatives and abortion foes without abandoning its arguments about judicial activism.

For abortion foes, the news seemed to go from bad to worse. After O'Connor took her seat on the bench, the fight over the Hatch Amendment and the Human Life Bill dissolved into a civil war. Over the course of three years, neither proposal gained the votes to pass—partly, because antiabortion lawmakers and activists themselves were so divided. When the Hatch Amendment finally came up for a vote, it failed. Even the Reagan Administration began to distance itself from abortion foes' constitutional proposals.

The defeat of the Human Life Bill and the Hatch Amendment created an existential crisis for the antiabortion movement. Ever since 1973, the movement's sole aim had been the ratification of a constitutional amendment criminalizing abortion. For the time being, it seemed impossible to ratify an antiabortion amendment (or even come close). Pro-lifers had to find a new strategy for their movement and a new justification for its reliance on the GOP.

An upcoming Supreme Court decision supplied the antiabortion movement with a new way forward. In 1983, the Court heard a challenge to an ordinance from Akron, Ohio, a Rust Belt city that rarely made headlines. The leading lights of the antiabortion had written a law that was designed to serve as a model for restrictions across the country, and Akron had passed it. Antiabortion leaders were particularly pleased with the informed-consent provision of the law, which stated that abortion increased the risk of infertility and psychological distress—all statements that were highly contested or supported by little scientific evidence. Abortion-rights attorneys challenged the constitutionality of the Akron law, and by 1983 the case had reached the Supreme Court.

The Reagan Administration submitted a friend of the court brief requesting that the Court reverse *Roe*. The brief offered the administration a chance to test out new political and legal strategies when it came to *Roe*. Administration lawyers stressed that a wide variety of academics had criticized the soundness of the original *Roe* decision. Republicans could label *Roe* the ultimate example of judicial activism. Doing so would signal that the administration wanted to get rid of *Roe*—and would give future Supreme Court nominees a way to talk about the 1973 decision without taking a position on abortion.

In 1983, the Reagan Administration's bid to reverse *Roe v. Wade* failed in **City of Akron v. Akron Center for Reproductive Health**. Abortion opponents could easily have been dismayed. After all, a few years earlier, the Court had upheld the Hyde Amendment. Some believed that the justices would back away from protecting abortion rights. In *Akron*, however, the Court struck down the challenged ordinance by a six-to-three margin. The majority let it be known that *Roe* was still good law. For abortion foes, the Akron decision was much more heartening than many would have imagined. Antiabortion leaders zeroed in on a dissenting opinion written by their former nemesis, Sandra Day O'Connor. O'Connor and two of her colleagues would have upheld the Akron statute. But more important, O'Connor seemed ready to rethink the *Roe* decision entirely. She complained that *Roe* required state legislators to become medical experts, aware of the latest obstetric techniques and the changing technology that made viability possible earlier in pregnancy. As O'Connor saw it, the trimester framework was broken. She proposed a new rule for abortion cases: all restrictions would be constitutional unless they created "a severe and absolute obstacle" to patients seeking abortion.

Most of the Court's members did not find O'Connor's reasoning convincing. But as abortion foes saw it, the Akron case proved that picking Republican presidents, and nominating different people to the Supreme Court, could work. Reagan had run on his opposition to abortion and promised to change the Court. O'Connor's vote in the Akron case showed that conservative presidents could make good on that promise.

After the Akron decision, Americans United for Life, which had become the epicenter for abortion foes' legal strategy, proposed an alternative to the constitutional amendment that had obsessed the antiabortion movement since 1973. Instead of changing the text of the Constitution, the antiabortion movement could change who sat on the Supreme Court. Eventually, different justices could overrule *Roe v. Wade*. Laws like the Hyde Amendment took on a different purpose. At one point, antiabortion lawyers had viewed these laws as a temporary solution. But after the Akron case, antiabortion leaders proposed restrictions with an eye to narrowing abortion rights and setting up a later decision undoing those rights altogether.

Some antiabortion extremists were not satisfied by the prospect of changing the Supreme Court. Starting in the early 1980s, violent attacks on abortion clinics spiked. In 1982, antiabortion terrorists formed a group called the Army of God. Shortly thereafter, militants from the group kidnapped Dr. Hector Zevallos and his wife and held them hostage before eventually releasing them. Several other clinics were invaded, vandalized, or firebombed. The threat of antiabortion violence would only intensify in the decades to come.

Most antiabortion leaders, however, recognized the need to pick apart abortion rights one piece at a time. In the mid-1980s, leading pro-life groups did so by trying to establish legal protection and popular sympathy for fetal life, even outside the abortion context. Clarke Forsythe of Americans United for Life led efforts to change state criminal laws to treat fetuses or unborn children as victims in homicide cases not involving abortion. Leading antiabortion groups also fought for laws banning lawsuits for wrongful birth or wrongful life, brought when medical negligence led to unplanned pregnancies. Abortion foes also took their case to the media, building discomfort with new abortion techniques. In the second trimester and beyond, many abortion providers had adopted **dilation and evacuation**, a technique that tended to be safer and more comfortable for patients, but also potentially more disturbing to providers and the general public. Dilation and evacuation required a doctor to dilate the cervix and remove fetal remains piece by piece. It became more widely used at a time when more Americans were exposed to ultrasound images of life in the womb.

As ultrasound and other fetal images spread, abortion foes hammered home their views about the nature of fetal life. In 1984, NRLC promoted *The Silent Scream*, a film claimed to depict the pain caused by a real abortion. Dr. Bernard Nathanson, a former abortion-rights leader who had joined the antiabortion movement, narrated the film. *The Silent Scream* was a media sensation.

When it came to the fate of *Roe*, projects like *The Silent Scream* and laws like those on fetal homicide were designed to make *Roe v. Wade* into an outlier. If popular culture recognized fetal personhood, and if other areas of laws did the same, abortion rights would look more and more incongruous. And the more of an outlier *Roe* became, the easier it might be to ask the justices to overturn it later on.

Antiabortion lawyers continued experimenting with incremental restrictions while waiting for Reagan to change the Court. It did not seem like the wait would be that long. In 1986, the Court issued another abortion decision, **Thornburgh v. American College of Obstetricians and Gynecologists**. Again, the Court invalidated an abortion law, this time from Pennsylvania. But only five justices voted that the law was unconstitutional. Four dissented—and suggested that the *Roe* decision went too far in protecting abortion rights. Even Warren Burger, a judge who had originally joined the *Roe* opinion, looked ready to rethink his decision. Then, in 1987, another justice who had joined *Roe*, **Lewis Powell**, announced his retirement. If Reagan replaced Powell with someone opposed to *Roe*, there would be enough votes to undo abortion rights.

As Powell's replacement, Reagan chose **Robert Bork**, a judge who had served in the Nixon Administration and taught at Yale Law School [**Doc. 13**]. Bork was also one of the most outspoken proponents of originalism—and one of the most vocal critics of the *Roe* decision. Partly because Bork made no secret of his conservatism, opposition to his nomination was unusually strong. A coalition of 100 progressive groups, including civil rights groups, unions, and feminist organizations, pledged to block the nomination. The politicization of the Supreme Court nomination process had begun years before. But Bork's nomination was an unprecedented event. The Southern Baptist Convention lobbied for Bork's confirmation. Television ads pushed for and against the nominee. Advocacy groups poured millions of dollars into the fight. Democrats, most of whom disliked Bork's policy positions, controlled the Senate, but Bork did himself no favors when he stood by some of his more controversial positions during his Senate testimony. The Senate rejected his confirmation, but Bork's selection still struck many as a turning point. If enough judges like Bork sat on the bench, interpretation of the Constitution would be revolutionized, not least when it came to abortion.

Reagan soon succeeded in replacing Powell with **Anthony Kennedy**, a judge without Bork's paper trail and conservative credentials. By that time, Reagan had already picked William Rehnquist, one of the dissenters in *Roe*, as a new chief justice to replace Warren Burger and added **Antonin Scalia**, a judge who shared Bork's approach to the Constitution, to the Court. Many expected *Roe* to be a gone in a matter of years.

The Reagan Administration tried to leave its mark on birth control policy as well. In the early 1980s, the number of teenagers having abortions had reached a new high, although the teen pregnancy rate as a whole had declined in the previous decade. Religious Right leaders argued that widespread birth control and sex education in schools were the problem, not the solution. These groups pressed for expanded legal rights for parents, and the Reagan Administration tried to cater to their demands. The administration slashed funding for federal family planning programs and proposed a regulation that many would call the squeal rule, which required any facility receiving federal family planning money to notify the parents of a teenager prescribed birth control within ten days. Religious conservatives defended the measure as a bulwark against the erosion of parental rights—and a step toward lowering teen pregnancy rates. Skeptics argued that the squeal rule could cause adolescent pregnancy rates to rise.

Courts ultimately invalidated the squeal rule, but controversy about birth control raged on. Injured patients filed lawsuits against the manufacturers of **intrauterine devices** (IUDs). The Dalkon Shield, an IUD that dominated the market in the early 1970s, dramatically increased the risk of pelvic inflammatory disease, a condition that could cause sterility, sepsis, and even death. In the mid-1980s, other studies suggested that common IUDs, especially plastic models, could cause infertility. The fear of more lawsuits put the brakes on the research or marketing of new contraceptive products. Feminist advocates for women's health closely scrutinized any new form of birth control put on the market. Sterilization remained the most common form of contraception. Rates of abortion remained higher than in most industrialized nations. So did rates of unplanned pregnancy, especially among teenagers. The number of adolescent pregnancies began to climb in the late 1980s and did not decrease for some time.

In 1988, the Reagan Administration put family planning back in the news after introducing new Title X regulations that dealt directly with abortion. The so-called gag rule did not allow doctors at clinics receiving Title X money to counsel patients about abortion or refer them to anyone who performed the procedure, even when patients asked them to. The rule also required a strict physical separation between facilities that received Title X money and those performing abortions. Family planning organizations challenged the constitutionality of the new regulation, arguing that it violated doctors' rights to freedom of speech and patients' abortion rights. Antiabortion leaders responded that the regulations simply recognized that abortion was not a method of birth control.

In 1990, the High Court sided with the Reagan Administration and upheld the disputed regulations. The majority reasoned that the gag rule did not compromise doctors' freedom of speech because the regulations communicated the government's message, and the government itself was entitled to the freedom to express its own views. More good news for right-to-lifers followed the gag rule decision. **George H.W. Bush**, the Republican who won the race for the White House in 1988, placed two new justices on the Court. **David Souter**, a New Hampshire native without a long political record, joined the Court, as did **Clarence Thomas**, a regular on the conservative legal lecture circuit. The end of *Roe* seemed to be just a matter of time.

In the early 1990s, the abortion debate in the United States seemed more focused than ever on the fate of *Roe*. Breathless press coverage discussed when and how the Court would most likely reverse the 1973 decision. States experimented with a wide range of strategies and restrictions to convince the Court.

But scratch the surface, and it was clear that the 1973 decision alone no longer set the terms of the debate. When feminists mentioned *Roe*, they linked it to ideas about equality and autonomy that went well beyond anything in the original decision. Right-to-lifers seeking to reverse the decision equated it with judicial activism and the politicization of the judiciary. True, both parties made *Roe* a central election issue; in the leadup to the 1992 race, both the Democratic and Republican frontrunners vowed to change the Court and set the course of abortion jurisprudence, but *Roe* garnered so much attention in part because it had come to stand for so many different things.

# 4 *Planned Parenthood v. Casey* and undue burdens

In 1991, the Supreme Court agreed to hear its most important abortion decision since *Roe v. Wade*. **Planned Parenthood of Southeastern Pennsylvania v. Casey** [**Doc. 14**] concerned a Pennsylvania law mandating that minors involve their parents and married women notify their husbands. Patients had to listen to an informed-consent script and wait 24 hours before terminating a pregnancy. In itself, there seemed to be nothing special about the Pennsylvania law. States had been passing similar statutes for decades. And there were much more extreme laws that the Court could have taken up, such as an outright ban, as introduced in Guam. But many knew that *Casey* was about much more. Right-to-lifers were asking the Court to reverse *Roe*.

As it readied for a post-*Roe* America, the antiabortion movement itself looked different. Single-issue organizations like the National Right to Life Committee and Americans United for Life had dominated the movement in the 1980s. But many more evangelical Protestants were entering the pro-life movement in the 1980s. Some of these activists joined established antiabortion groups, but others founded their own. Religious Right groups like the Moral Majority had declined in the 1980s, but by the early 1990s new ones had taken their place. Focus on the Family, a fundamentalist Christian group founded by televangelist James Dobson in 1977, took a more active role in abortion law and politics in the 1990s. So did the Family Research Council, a lobbying organization affiliated with Focus on the Family. Televangelist **Pat Robertson**, the face of the multi-million dollar *Christian Broadcasting Network*, also launched his own organization, a public interest law firm, the **American Center for Law and Justice**, to litigate cases about abortion and the freedom of speech and religion of conservative Christians.

The new evangelical pro-lifers were primed to mount a challenge to *Roe*. They promoted a broader program that included opposition to rights for gays and lesbians. In the 1980s and early 1990s, the **HIV-AIDS crisis**, together with a string of hate crimes, brought new attention to discrimination against gays and lesbians. Evangelical organizations, which opposed homosexuality, had mobilized to defeat civil rights protections, which they argued gave special protection to gays and lesbians and discriminated against Christians who disapproved of homosexuality. Religious Right leaders eagerly awaited the day that the Court overturned *Roe*.

DOI: 10.4324/9781003215936-7

The Republican Bush Administration was far less enthusiastic about the prospect of *Roe* being overturned. Bush had won the race for the White House in 1988 after moving to the right on abortion. Indeed, he had beaten Pat Robertson, who had mounted a longshot presidential campaign of his own. But to rid himself of Robertson, Bush had taken stronger and stronger stands against abortion. Earlier in his career, Bush had supported population control policies, particularly, an expansion of family planning programs. His wife Barbara was openly pro-choice. When he ran for president in 1980, Bush had opposed a constitutional amendment banning abortion. But to secure the GOP nomination in 1988, Bush had changed his tune. He had pledged an end to *Roe*, and now that goal seemed reachable.

When Ronald Reagan left office, there were already five conservatives on the High Court. After 1988, Bush placed new conservative justices on the bench with the help of the **Federalist Society**. Founded by a group of conservative law students in the early 1980s, the Federalist Society billed itself as a debating society that brought fresh (conservative) ideas about the law to judges, lawyers, and law students. By the early 1990s, it had created an impressive professional network for conservatives seeking membership in the legal elite. As part of this process, when Republican presidents were in office, the Federalist Society vetted nominees for the Supreme Court, suggesting those who expected to adopt a particular interpretive method on the bench.

With the help of the Federalist Society, Bush had the opportunity to pick two new justices. David Souter, a former state supreme court judge, was famously soft-spoken, but like all of Bush's picks, Souter seemed likely to reverse *Roe*. Clarence Thomas, a former head of the Equal Employment Opportunity Commission and a circuit court judge, was far more outspoken, but it was his personal conduct that jeopardized his nomination. A former subordinate, **Anita Hill**, accused Thomas of sexually harassing her while she worked at the Equal Employment Opportunity Commission. Several other women stood ready to back Hill's account, but the Senate Judiciary Committee put a stop to testimony, and by a razor-thin margin Thomas was confirmed.

Thomas and Souter joined four justices nominated or elevated by Ronald Reagan: William Rehnquist, Antonin Scalia, Anthony Kennedy, and Sandra Day O'Connor. In a series of recent decisions on the abortion rights of minors, the Court had seemingly applied a lenient standard to and then upheld abortion restrictions. At times, the Court's conservative members had openly criticized *Roe* as an illogical and untenable decision. It seemed inevitable that the Court's conservative majority would roll back abortion rights.

Few, however, expected the Supreme Court to criminalize abortion nationwide. True, in the 1970s, abortion foes had advocated for the recognition of a right to life for fetuses or unborn children. In the early 1990s, groups like National Right to Life Committee still ultimately wanted to see all abortions criminalized, saw the right to life as fundamental, and believed that abortion was murder. But reversing *Roe* would not require the Court to ban abortion by recognizing the personhood of the unborn child. Instead, the Court could simply say that the Constitution said nothing about abortion—and that states could ban abortions if they chose.

This was the preferred outcome for most conservative attorneys and Republican leaders, who often favored originalism, an interpretive theory based on the intentions of the framers or the original public meaning of the constitutional text. Starting with Richard Nixon, Republican presidents had railed against what they saw as an activist federal judiciary. Labeling *Roe* an activist decision was smart politics. Republicans who disagreed about the abortion issue shared disdain for the liberal Supreme Court.

Originalists argued that *Roe* was wrongly decided because the framers of the Fourteenth Amendment would not have recognized an abortion right. After all, in the late nineteenth century, most states were criminalizing abortions. The authors of the Fourteenth Amendment would not have recognized a right to abortion when most states were making it a crime. But for the most part, originalists suggested that the authors of the Fourteenth Amendment simply had not been thinking about abortion at all. Like most of the constitutional provisions introduced after the Civil War, the Fourteenth Amendment seemed primarily focused on the rights of free people of color. That meant, most originalists reasoned, that there was no right to life or right to abortion. The likely outcome of a decision reversing *Roe* would be that states would be free to criminalize abortion but would have no obligation to do so.

Antiabortion briefs, including one from the Bush Administration, made this argument. They contended that *Roe* was an antidemocratic decision—one that took the abortion issue away from the American people and forced the views of the judiciary onto the country. Reversing *Roe*, right-to-lifers argued, would be good for US democracy. Antiabortion briefs further claimed that *Roe* had distorted other areas of the law. *Roe*, they argued, had warped a range of rules on everything from when personhood began to who had the standing to sue.

Bush suggested that the right thing to do was to let the states decide for themselves about abortion. But, in practice, the president had no interest in seeing *Roe* overturned. Opposition to *Roe* had been an excellent way for Republican politicians to get out the vote and raise money. As important, Bush was deathly afraid of what would happen if the Court *did* overturn *Roe*.

For years, Republican presidents had supported a constitutional amendment banning abortion, at least on paper, but fully expected not to do anything about this supposed commitment. Even the largest Republican majorities in Congress had been unable to pass a constitutional amendment, and any sweeping statute that did pass fell in the Supreme Court. But if the Court was no longer an obstacle, there would be nothing stopping Republicans from banning abortion outright, at least in some states. Bush thought that voters would punish his party for pursuing an abortion ban, but right-to-lifers would never be content with allowing some states to continue legal abortions. Bush felt that the reversal of *Roe* would put him in a politically impossible position.

Bush was not the only one in the Republican Party having second thoughts about aligning so closely with the pro-life movement. In 1989, **Lee Atwater**, the mastermind behind Bush's political campaigns, encouraged Ann Stone to found an organization for pro-choice Republicans, **Republicans for Choice**. Atwater thought that younger, upwardly mobile Republicans—and especially women—would be alienated by a GOP linked to the demise of abortion rights.

Pro-choice groups expected to lose in *Casey* but hoped that Bush would pay the price. **Kathryn Kolbert** and Linda Wharton, the lawyers who had originally questioned the constitutionality of the Pennsylvania law, corresponded with members of a tight-knit coalition that included a variety of feminist and pro-choice organizations, and all of their leaders believed that the courts would protect abortion rights for much longer. If the courts were against them, pro-choice leaders believed that they had the support of voters. Kolbert and Wharton strategized about how best to get the Court to admit that it had eliminated abortion rights and avoid a highly technical ruling that few Americans would understand. More transparency, Wharton and Kolbert believed, would mean a bigger political backlash in the 1992 election. If anger about the overruling of *Roe* was intense enough, then Democrats might win control of the White House and the Congress and pass a federal law protecting abortion rights.

Groups like the American Civil Liberties Union and the Planned Parenthood still made the best case they could for saving *Roe*. They emphasized that *Roe* relied on privacy rights that protected everything from marriage to parental rights. If the Court unraveled abortion rights, other protected liberties might soon follow. Kolbert and Wharton likewise stressed what women had gained by virtue of abortion access. By having the right to decide when to have a child, women had gained the ability to participate more fully in US society; people with the ability to decide when or whether to have a child were better able to have a child or pursue an education.

It seemed for a time that Anthony Kennedy, Ronald Reagan's final Supreme Court nominee, would vote to reverse *Roe*. But when the Supreme Court handed down a decision in *Casey* in June 1992, everyone was in for a surprise. *Casey* was a **plurality decision**—there was no majority for parts of the opinion. Nevertheless, the bottom line was a shock: a majority agreed to save abortion rights. Justices Souter, O'Connor, and Kennedy wrote an opinion, joined by Harry Blackmun and John Paul Stevens, declining the invitation to reverse *Roe*.

The opinion began by noting that the abortion decision resembled other crucial choices about sexuality and the family that the Court had protected: choices about parenting, procreation, and marriage. If the Constitution gave people autonomy to make crucial, intimate life decisions, then abortion certainly belonged on the list. *Casey* also suggested that abortion rights had something to do with equality for women; the consequences of the decision to become a parent were too serious to force any woman to assume a role that she did not want.

The *Casey* opinion also analyzed **stare decisis**, a body of rules used to determine whether to overturn a prior decision. As the membership of the Court changed, new justices naturally had a different take on what the Constitution meant. As a matter of institutional integrity, the Court hesitated to reverse prior precedents simply because they were wrong—usually, there had to be some additional factor militating in favor of reversal.

The *Casey* opinion concluded there was no such justification for overturning *Roe*. It was not **unworkable**—even if it was controversial, there was nothing that made abortion rights particularly hard for judges to understand or apply. *Casey* further reasoned that neither the law nor the reality on the ground had changed in ways that made *Roe* obsolete.

Courts were often more reluctant to overturn decisions when people had planned their lives around the legal status quo; for example, those writing contracts or making business arrangements had to plan in advance and rely on the rules in place. Pennsylvania argued that there were no reliance interests in the abortion context: many women seeking an abortion did not plan to be pregnant. The *Casey* Court nevertheless found that many profoundly relied on *Roe* in organizing their lives. Sexually active women pursuing an education or career assumed that they would have the option of terminating a pregnancy. *Casey* reasoned that, in this way, *Roe* had helped women (and other people who could become pregnant) to lead more equal lives.

But for all that *Casey* reinforced the importance of abortion rights, the plurality significantly weakened the rules protecting them. *Roe* had applied a trimester framework, which invalidated most abortion restrictions in the first trimester and honored the government's interest in protecting fetal life only after fetal viability.

*Casey* retained viability as the point at which states could outlaw abortion outright. But the plurality suggested that the government's interest in protecting life must exist throughout pregnancy, not only at its later stages. *Casey* described the *Roe* framework as unduly rigid and rejected it in favor of a new rule: **the undue burden test**. Abortion regulations would be unconstitutional only if they had the purpose or effect of creating a substantial obstacle for people seeking abortions. The plurality made clear that states could not deprive patients of having the final say on whether to continue a pregnancy, but other regulations, particularly those designed to inform a patient's decision, would be constitutional.

The *Casey* opinion easily upheld most of the challenged restrictions under this new test, with only the state's spousal notification regulation proving to be an exception. Pennsylvania obligated married women to inform their husbands before ending a pregnancy. There were several exceptions for women who were victims of **domestic violence**. Kolbert and Wharton insisted that the exceptions did not go far enough. Pennsylvania disagreed—and stressed that the regulation would burden very few women because most would tell their husbands (or face no serious consequences if the state forced them to do so).

The plurality found the absolute number of domestic violence victims to be irrelevant. What mattered, *Casey* suggested, was how the law impacted those whose lives were changed—in this case, victims of domestic violence. For these women, a notification requirement would function like an outright ban: women would not put their health or safety at risk to fulfill a notification requirement.

*Casey* also stated that spousal notification requirements reflected old-fashioned and offensive ideas about marriage. In the nineteenth century, married women had lost their ability to own property, make wages, sign contracts, serve on juries, and much more. *Casey* reasoned that Pennsylvania made similar assumptions about married women's capacity for making wise, independent decisions. As the plurality framed it, this view of marriage could not endure under the Court's current interpretation of the Constitution.

But *Casey* offered a very different idea about equality for women in evaluating an informed-consent requirement. Pennsylvania required patients to hear certain information before receiving an abortion, including details of fetal development, the availability of adoption, and the rules governing child support. Prior to 1992, the Court had struck down several such laws, reasoning that they patronized and intimidated people who had already made up their minds. *Casey* concluded instead that Pennsylvania's restriction served an important interest: preventing people from regretting the decision to abort. The Court had long reasoned that states regulating abortion had an important interest in protecting women's health. *Casey* stressed that the government could also protect women from the consequences of bad choices.

Justice William Rehnquist's dissent repeated arguments that the right to abortion had no basis in the text or history of the Constitution. Rehnquist also stressed that conventional stare decisis analysis supported the reversal of *Roe*.

He took issue with *Casey*'s unwillingness to overturn *Roe* "under fire." The Court worried that reversing *Roe* under political pressure would irreparably damage the Court's political standing; people would perceive the Court as weak and willing to bend to the demands of well-organized minorities and movements. Rehnquist fired back that if the Court had followed a similar approach, the justices would never have found racial segregation in public schools to be unconstitutional. As Rehnquist saw it, the Court had a duty to revisit decisions that were plainly wrong, and *Casey* failed to discharge that duty.

In his own dissent, Antonin Scalia argued that *Roe* itself was destroying the Court's legitimacy. Scalia wrote that promising legislative compromises had been available before *Roe*. But *Roe* destroyed those middle-ground solutions and polarized the nation's politics and Supreme Court nominations.

He predicted that the abortion wars would rage on as long as the Court "continued to recognize a right to abortion."

Scalia was right that the abortion conflict was far more polarized than had been the case in 1973. But pinning all the responsibility on the Supreme Court made little sense. Political party realignment, the changing composition of the pro-choice and pro-life movements, the evolution of new birth control and abortion methods, the rise of **negative partisanship**—all these factors had contributed to the polarization of abortion politics. Nevertheless, Scalia tapped into a compelling new argument for reversing *Roe*. Going forward, abortion foes would argue that *Roe* should be overturned not only because it was wrong but because it was socially destructive.

At first, *Casey* seemed to be a decision that would not make anyone happy. The Bush Administration scrambled to put together a response to a decision that many voters found hard to understand. Abortion foes felt devastated by an unexpected loss, and some donors withdrew funding. Abortion-rights supporters recognized that the undue-burden test opened the door to a wide range of new abortion restrictions.

In truth, *Casey* offered both pro-choice and pro-life leaders reason for optimism. Pro-choice leaders celebrated not only the fact that the Court had saved abortion rights but also that *Casey* had invoked equality for women as well as privacy. Since at least the mid-1980s, feminist scholars, including **Ruth Bader Ginsburg,** had joined a chorus criticizing the reasoning of the original *Roe* decision. The text and history of the Constitution said nothing about a right to abortion or a right to privacy. Ginsburg believed that the Court would have been better off if it had rooted the right to abortion in the Equal Protection Clause of the Fourteenth Amendment. Because only **cisgender** women could get pregnant, abortion restrictions had an impact on them quite different from that on cisgender men. Moreover, some state laws arguably reflected stereotypes about the proper roles of men and women. *Casey* did not explicitly rely on the Equal Protection Clause. Nevertheless, the Court had discussed concerns about equality for women. It seemed possible that abortion rights would soon have a sounder foundation than had been the case in *Roe*.

Abortion foes likewise had reason to be upbeat. Harry Blackmun, the author of *Roe*, certainly recognized this. Blackmun did not join much of the *Casey* plurality, seeing the opinion as a retreat from strong protection for abortion rights. Blackmun was certainly right that the undue burden test gave states more leeway to regulate abortion. And *Casey* gave pro-life legislators a blueprint for the kind of restriction to pass. Abortion foes took note of the plurality's language about post-abortion regret. Antiabortion leaders rushed to write their own informed-consent laws, many of them more ambitious than the one of which *Casey* approved.

In the aftermath of *Casey*, however, many antiabortion activists—some of them already frustrated by the pace of change—felt they had no choice but to radicalize. **Bill Clinton**, the former governor of Arkansas, ran for office as a new kind of Democrat, unafraid to cut welfare programs or balance the budget. He was also unabashedly pro-choice and vowed to use a *Roe*-based litmus test to select nominees for the High Court. Bush had veered to the right on abortion to fend off a primary challenge from Pat Buchanan, a firebrand populist and political commentator. Bush also faced off against Ross Perot, a wealthy businessman who mounted an unusually successful third party run. Clinton was the most strongly pro-choice president to take office since the Court decided *Roe* in 1973. He quickly rolled back the Bush Administration's policies on international family planning and pledged to undo the Hyde Amendment, a prohibition on Medicaid reimbursement for abortion.

With Clinton in office and *Casey* defining the law on abortion, some antiabortion activists felt that legal and political efforts to change abortion law had definitively failed. In 1993, Michael Griffin, an antiabortion extremist, murdered abortion provider Dr. David Gunn in Pensacola, Florida. In the aftermath of Gunn's murder, Paul Hill, another extremist, vocally defended the killing of abortion providers on talk shows and in print. Then, in 1994, Hill murdered another doctor, Dr. John Britton, and his bodyguard, in Pensacola. Hill and Gunn's murders came in the aftermath of a series of fire bombings and acid attacks against abortion clinics.

This escalation of violence energized lawmakers seeking more meaningful protection for abortion clinics, staff, and patients. Some states had already begun implementing their own strategies. Some introduced **bubble zone laws** preventing protestors from approaching patients, staff, or clinics within a certain distance. The National Organization for Women (NOW) relied on federal racketeering law, arguing that clinic blockaders and antiabortion proponents of violence engaged in a criminal conspiracy.

NOW further argued that clinic blockaders engaged in a plot against women. In Washington, DC, Operation Rescue had announced plans to blockade several area clinics. NOW went to court and got an order preventing the blockades from going forward. To get their order, NOW lawyers relied on the federal **Ku Klux Klan Act**, a civil rights statute dating from the years after the Civil War. The Supreme Court had interpreted the Ku Klux Klan Act to prohibit conspiracies to deprive protected groups, like racial minorities, of exercising a protected right. NOW asserted that Operation Rescue had conspired to deny women their rights to abortion and contraception. In 1993, in **Bray v. Alexandria Women's Health Clinic**, the Supreme Court rejected this argument. In the majority opinion, Antonin Scalia argued that antiabortion protestors did not target women as a group; there were many reasons that people condemned abortion beyond hostility to women.

*Bray* gave a boost to those who believed that new legislation was needed to protect clinic entrances. In 1994, Congress passed the **Freedom of Access to Clinic Entrances Act** (**FACE Act**), which prohibited anyone from using force or violence (or threatening either one) against people seeking or providing reproductive health services. Fines for first time offenders could run as high as $100,000. Rather than slaps on the wrist, repeat offenders could face even higher fines and years in prison. The FACE Act devastated an already-struggling clinic blockade movement. Some members of Operation Rescue had seen the murders committed by Paul Hill and Michael Griffin as justified. The issue of violence divided blockaders. Moreover, all but the hardest core activists thought twice before facing the kind of consequences authorized by FACE.

Abortion foes fought back against the new laws protecting clinics, contending that these statutes violated their freedoms of speech. In **Madsen v. Women's Health Center** (1994), a group of antiabortion protestors argued against the constitutionality of a judicial order permanently blocking protests outside a clinic in Melbourne, Florida. Protestors argued that the order discriminated based on their pro-life viewpoint—and unfairly prevented them from spreading their message. In a series of decisions over the next several decades, the Supreme Court continued redrawing the lines when it came to permissible clinic-protective laws. Abortion opponents even brought a series of unsuccessful challenges to the FACE Act, but in real terms the clinic-blockade movement seemed to be in terminal decline.

Pro-choice groups responded by pursuing a proactive agenda for the first time in decades. Groups like NARAL and Planned Parenthood pushed for the repeal of the Hyde Amendment and the passage of the **Freedom of Choice Act**, a federal statute enshrining abortion rights in the law (and blocking the passage of most state abortion laws).

Pro-choice groups also took a keen interest in the health care bill that Bill Clinton had promised on the campaign trail. Clinton proposed a reform that would entitle patients to medical treatment and preventative services, including for preexisting conditions. At first, the bill seemed to have far-reaching support; the question seemed to be what the bill would cover, not whether it would pass. Pro-choice groups fought for the exclusion of abortion in the universal coverage that Clinton promoted. Pro-choice leaders noted that since many private insurers already covered abortion, there was no reason for a federal program not to do the same. Antiabortion leaders insisted that abortion was not a health service but a moral issue. The leadership of Planned Parenthood pushed affiliates to act as primary health care providers rather than focusing so exclusively on reproductive health care. Members of Planned Parenthood revolted, insisting that abortion rights were uniquely important and deserved to be the group's priority.

Clinton's fight for health care reform fizzled in the face of opposition from the American Medical Association, insurers, and the Republican Party. But pro-choice leaders did not drop the idea of abortion being a valuable health service, especially because of a growing shortage of abortion doctors. Most abortion providers active in the 1990s had begun practicing in the years immediately after *Roe* and were quickly nearing retirement, and new doctors were rarely stepping up to fill the gap. Many obstetric and gynecological programs did not train physicians in how to perform abortions; those with proper training often wanted to avoid the protests, threats, and civil lawsuits facing abortion doctors. Antiabortion groups also did their best to sue any doctor who did perform abortions. **Mark Crutcher** of Life Dynamics, an antiabortion group, sent around a playbook about how to sue abortion doctors. Lawsuits became so common that it was hard for many abortion providers to get **malpractice insurance.**

While Planned Parenthood lobbied to expand abortion training in medical schools, pro-choice feminists began looking for a way to make abortions available outside of clinics. In the mid-1980s, physicians had developed a pill, mifepristone (also known as **RU 486**) that could be used to terminate a pregnancy. In Europe, doctors had used RU 486 ever since, working it into a two-drug protocol that also included misoprostol. While mifepristone works by blocking progesterone, a hormone key to the continuation of healthy pregnancies, misoprostol induced labor. While patients in the United States could get misoprostol to treat other conditions, RU 486 had never been available in the United States (antiabortion groups threatened to organize a boycott of any drug company that imported or manufactured it). The George H.W. Bush Administration blocked it from being imported. Feminists hoped that pill-based abortions would allow patients to make decisions in the privacy of their own homes rather than at a clinic.

The Food and Drug Administration would not approve RU 486 until 2000. But in the meantime, framing abortion as a health service resonated with feminists of color looking to create a different approach to reproductive rights. The 1994 International Conference on Population and Development in Cairo proved to be a touchstone for the creation of what proponents called a reproductive justice movement. Earlier conferences had focused on curbing international population growth through the use of family planning. The Cairo conference turned out to be a turning point for similar family-planning meetings; rather than just including government actors, the event also invited citizen groups and called for a broader program covering reproductive health.

Shortly before the Cairo conference, a group of women of color gathered at an event hosted by the Illinois Pro-Choice Coalition and *Ms. Magazine*. Those at the meeting hoped to craft a response to the Clinton health-care plan and offered a trenchant criticism of it, entitled "Black Women on Universal Health Care Reform." Signatories called for a fight for reproductive justice, a new agenda that combined concern about reproductive rights with social justice. The feminists of color at the event asserted that the mainstream pro-choice movement had primarily catered to the needs of white, middle-class women by prioritizing efforts to keep abortion legal. This single-issue, pro-choice framework ignored the ways that people of color and some **transgender** men struggled to access abortion even when it was legal.

But the criticism of the pro-choice movement went further. Reproductive justice advocates maintained that, by putting so much emphasis on saving abortion rights, groups like Planned Parenthood and NARAL had ignored other issues that deprived people of color of a meaningful say over their reproductive lives. Reproductive justice advocates still demanded protection from sterilization abuse and the coerced use of long-acting contraceptives. Reproductive justice also required access to lead-free drinking water, protection from police brutality, access to safe housing and a living wage, and maternal and neonatal health care. In 1997, some of the signatories of "Black Women on Universal Health Care Reform" formed a new coalition to fight for reproductive justice, the **SisterSong Reproductive Justice Collective.**

It seemed that the pro-choice movement was finally in an enviable position. Reproductive justice organizers worked to mobilize a larger and more diverse group of people supporting abortion rights. The Supreme Court seemed unwilling to reverse *Roe*, and pro-choice leaders had allies in the federal government. Clinton even nominated several new members of the Supreme Court; Ruth Bader Ginsburg, an accomplished feminist attorney, joined the Court in 1993. During her time at the American Civil Liberties Union, Ginsburg had argued several key sex discrimination cases before the Supreme Court, helping to establish that the Equal Protection Clause of the Fourteenth Amendment covered sex as well as race discrimination. Ginsburg had also helped to pioneer key arguments for abortion rights and established a Reproductive Rights Project at the ACLU. The following year, Clinton added another judge, **Stephen Breyer**, to the Supreme Court.

But the pro-choice movement's advantage faded before long. Although Clinton had pledged to undo the Hyde Amendment, Congress rebuffed him. Meanwhile, antiabortion leaders regrouped. Some launched **crisis pregnancy centers** (CPCs), facilities designed to discourage patients from having abortions. After Hawaii repealed all of its abortion restrictions in 1967, Robert Pearson founded the first crisis pregnancy center in that state. Before *Roe*, a larger network of CPCs spread from Canada after the founding of Birthright by Louise Summerhill. Alternatives to Abortion, another CPC network, opened its doors in 1971. The Christian Action Council, an evangelical Protestant antiabortion organization, opened its first CPC in 1980.

After *Casey*, however, many more abortion foes invested in the CPC movement. The Christian Action Council redirected all of its energies to CPCs, renaming itself Care Net. Alternatives to Abortion also expanded under the new name Heartbeat International. CPCs, many of which were explicitly faith-based, often discussed abortion in explicitly religious terms, but many also provided pregnancy tests and some supportive services, such as diapers and other essentials. Over time, some CPCs also began performing ultrasounds.

Evangelical organizations grew wealthier and more cohesive after *Casey*, and many mobilized after a group of same-sex couples sought to get married in Hawaii. Like most states at the time, Hawaii defined marriage as being between one man and one woman. The couples argued that Hawaii's restrictions violated the state's constitution. In 1993, the Hawaii Supreme Court agreed, although the state legislature eventually reinstated the old law. The idea of same-sex marriage panicked evangelicals and other socially conservative Christians, who worried that because of the **Full Faith and Credit Clause** of the Constitution, all states would have to recognize same-sex marriage if one state chose to do so. Conservative Christians successfully lobbied for state and federal defense of marriage acts, laws defining marriage as between one man and one woman. Bill Clinton, a Democrat, even signed the federal Defense of Marriage Act into law. A new organization, the **Alliance Defense Fund** (ADF), formed to train and bankroll litigation by socially conservative Christian lawyers—including cases on same-sex marriage and abortion. ADF also tried to beef up conscience protections for doctors and pharmacists who did not want to be involved with either abortion or contraception.

Established antiabortion groups also found a way forward after the disappointments of the early 1990s. With Ronald Reagan and George H.W. Bush in the White House, many antiabortion leaders had at times lost sight of the fact that the movement's real strength was in state legislatures. Once Bill Clinton took office, abortion foes invested even more in getting state laws passed.

Groups like Americans United for Life promoted laws intended to prove that abortion hurt women too. In advancing this kind of strategy, established antiabortion groups shone a spotlight on existing support groups for women who had come to regret their abortions such as Women Exploited by Abortion and American Victims of Abortion. These support groups had existed for some time, but national antiabortion groups had mostly focused on defending fetal rights rather than addressing the concerns of women.

By the mid-1990s, the antiabortion movement put a much greater emphasis on arguments that abortion hurt women. **David Reardon**, an antiabortion activist and engineer, believed that if he could prove that abortion caused women trauma, then he could end the abortion wars. He founded the Elliot Institute to conduct research on abortion and argued that the procedure caused women to suffer from a condition like post-traumatic stress disorder. Reardon published studies claiming that many women who chose abortion were coerced to do so by lovers, husbands, and parents.

Later, peer-reviewed research would find that abortion itself did not cause many of the symptoms that Reardon claimed, at least for women who wanted to have abortions and did not suffer from preexisting mental conditions. But within the antiabortion movement, Reardon's arguments became even more widespread. National Right to Life Committee and other major antiabortion groups highlighted claims about post-abortion trauma—and argued that the medical establishment ignored the truth because the pro-choice movement pulled the strings behind the scenes.

Other antiabortion researchers argued that there was a connection between abortion and breast cancer. **Joel Brind**, an endocrinologist at Baruch College, became the most vocal proponent of these arguments. Some early research suggested that abortion increased the risk of breast cancer, but later, more comprehensive studies suggested that there was no connection. Nevertheless, Brind warned that a coverup was in the works;

the public health establishment was so committed to saving abortion rights that doctors were willing to bury evidence. Brind also insisted that if there was even a possibility that abortion was dangerous, patients had a right to know about it.

At first, after *Casey*, antiabortion groups pushed the kind of informed-consent law upheld in the 1992 decision. But over time, abortion foes began favoring state laws that wove in some of the claims made by Brind and Reardon. Groups like AUL recognized that scientists had cast doubt on some of the premises of the new informed-consent laws. AUL nevertheless thought that its new woman-protective strategy was essential. First, even women who wanted to end their pregnancies might hesitate if they thought that their own health would be at risk. As important, *Casey* had saved abortion rights partly because the Court believed that women relied on abortion access to lead more equal lives. But if abortion actually made women sick, there might be no rationale for saving abortion rights in the future.

AUL leaders also developed a powerful response to scientists' doubts about their claims. Groups like AUL borrowed from a tactical plan that had already fueled campaigns against legislation or other steps to address **climate change**. In the 1990s, for the first time, scientists expressed grave concern that human activity, especially the burning of fossil fuels, had caused global warming. With climate change would come more extreme temperatures, rising sea levels, more droughts, heat waves, and other extreme weather events, and even the extinction of certain species. Some lawmakers had proposed measures to curb the emission of greenhouse gasses. But global warming skeptics contended that evidence for human-produced climate change was too weak to justify bold action, especially if the government inconvenienced people or cost them their jobs.

While rarely involving themselves in global warming politics, right-to-lifers sometimes pursued a parallel strategy. Leading abortion foes insisted that there was genuine uncertainty about whether abortion was safe for women. And they contended that if there were any doubts about safety, legislators should have the liberty to close clinics and protect women from their own decisions.

The new antiabortion strategy got a boost after the 1994 midterm election. Republicans took over the House of Representatives for the first time in decades. The new GOP lawmakers did not initially prioritize the abortion issue, but groups like NRLC began preparing for another federal legislative push to restrict abortion.

In Congress, and in the states, abortion foes decided to focus not on laws that would do the most to eliminate abortion but instead prioritized laws with the broadest popular appeal. Some abortion foes pushed targeted regulations of abortion providers (**TRAP laws**), which required abortion clinics to undergo costly and sometimes difficult upgrades, some of which served no obvious health purpose, and many of which forced clinics to close, especially small, independent operators.

Other antiabortion groups focused on abortion later in pregnancy, recognizing that, as pregnancy continued, more and more people became uncomfortable with the procedure. In the later 1990s, antiabortion leaders proposed a ban on a single, relatively rare abortion procedure that right-to-lifers called partial-birth abortion. This campaign would politicize medical research and raise new questions about how Americans following the abortion debate could distinguish science and spin.

In a sense, these laws were all intended to chip away at *Roe*, limit access, and lay the groundwork for the eventual reversal of *Roe*. But fights over *Roe* spilled over into broader conflicts about whether abortion benefitted women or harmed them—and what equality, dignity, or happiness for women really meant.

# 5 The politics of science

In 2007, after more than a decade of fighting, the Supreme Court upheld a ban on a procedure that abortion foes called **partial-birth abortion**. The procedure had existed for some time, but abortion opponents first got wind of it in the early 1990s. Doctors performing the procedure, often called **dilation and extraction**, removed fetal remains in one pass rather than in multiple steps, as with dilation and evacuation, a far more common procedure. Antiabortion leaders believed that the procedure closely resembled infanticide and proposed laws banning it.

Dilation and extraction was not a new procedure in the 1990s. Dr. James McMahon, one of the few abortion providers to perform the procedure as late as six months into pregnancy, had developed dilation and extraction in earlier decades to reduce risk to patients. Since the 1970s, dilation and evacuation had been the abortion procedure of choice for procedures performed after the first trimester. But dilation and evacuation required doctors to make multiple passes with a sharp instrument, which increased the risk of damage to the uterus.

McMahon's endorsement aside, dilation and extraction was not widely used, and **Dr. Martin Haskell**, an abortion provider in Ohio, thought that it might benefit certain patients. He gave a talk about the procedure at the national abortion conference run by the National Abortion Federation in 1993. There was nothing extraordinary about Haskell's paper—doctors routinely discussed abortion methods at events like the one he attended—but a copy leaked, and antiabortion activists in Minnesota read Haskell's work. They did line drawings of the procedure, which they dubbed partial-birth abortion.

At the time, these images served mostly to derail the federal Freedom of Choice Act (FOCA). Before *Casey*, FOCA had been the primary push of pro-choice leaders, most of whom expected the Court to reverse *Roe*. FOCA would codify a right to choose abortion. Antiabortion leaders pointed to images of partial-birth abortion and claimed that FOCA would make that procedure common and available across the country. FOCA was not going anywhere because the coalition supporting it had fragmented. Some moderate Democrats were unwilling to support a bill unless it allowed for restrictions on abortion funding and parental involvement. Some progressives,

DOI: 10.4324/9781003215936-8

especially feminists of color, thought this was a gutless compromise that once sold out low-income people of color. With pro-choice activists hopelessly divided, FOCA was dead in the water.

Antiabortion leaders believed that their arguments about partial-birth abortion had doomed the federal pro-choice legislation. In 1994, after Republicans secured a majority in Congress, National Right to Life Committee promoted a bill criminalizing partial-birth abortion. From a public-relations standpoint, pro-choice groups did not want to focus on procedures performed later in pregnancy and instead emphasized that the federal bill (like state laws patterned on it) had no health exception. Abortion providers maintained that there were some patients whose safety or fertility would be adversely affected if a doctor performed another procedure rather than dilation and extraction. Moreover, as abortion-rights leaders saw it, *Casey* and *Roe* gave patients the right to choose not only to end a pregnancy but to have a procedure that best protected their health.

At first, antiabortion leaders hardly wanted to discuss the ins and outs of including a health exception because they knew that dwelling on the details of a particular procedure would make Americans uncomfortable with all abortions. Right-to-lifers cared particularly about influencing the generation of Americans born after *Roe* came down. Older Americans could remember a time when most states criminalized abortion and had formed their opinion based on that experience; it seemed possible that the views of younger Americans would be more malleable. Right-to-lifers wanted Americans to think about partial-birth abortion when anyone mentioned a right to choose.

Clearly, however, the fight about a health exception to the federal ban was not going anywhere. Representative Charles Canady, a Republican from Florida, had introduced a federal ban without a health exception, and in 1995, Congress passed it. But Democrat Bill Clinton **vetoed** the bill because it lacked a health exception, and Republicans lacked the votes in the Senate to override Clinton's veto by the required two-thirds majority. Clinton vetoed another such proposal in 1996.

Abortion-rights supporters hoped that women would not have to rely on surgical procedures much longer, at least earlier in pregnancy. In 1996, a drug company filed a request with the Food and Drug Administration for recognition of RU 486. Clinical trials of the drug began shortly thereafter.

The Supreme Court partly dashed these hopes in 1997 in a case called ***Mazurek v. Armstrong***. That case began in 1995 when Montana passed a law requiring that all abortions be performed by a licensed physician. A group of pro-choice leaders immediately challenged the constitutionality of the bill. Montana was a large and sparsely populated state, and prior to 1995 a physician's assistant had been performing a significant number of the state's abortions. Pro-choice lawyers from the **Center for Reproductive Rights (then known as the Center for Reproductive Law and Policy)**, a pro-choice public interest firm, argued that Montana's law created an undue burden under *Casey*. The Center stressed that Montana's law had no real health benefit—there was no evidence that physicians had a better safety record than physician assistants when it came to performing abortions—and, in truth, Montana had set out explicitly to burden abortion access.

In 1997, by a six-to-three margin, the Supreme Court rejected the challenge to Montana's law. Even in the *Roe* case itself, the Court had reasoned that states could require that all abortions be performed by a licensed physician. Montana had not anything any different. The Court also hesitated to accuse legislators of having bad intentions without more evidence.

At first, *Mazurek* did not seem to be a major decision. States had long had the authority to stop non-physicians from performing abortions. But antiabortion leaders understood that *Mazurek* could have a major impact. First, *Mazurek* said something important about how *Casey*'s undue-burden test would work. The *Casey* test had two parts: a purpose prong and an effect prong. States could not have the intent to burden abortion access or introduce laws with that effect. The Center had tried to use the purpose prong to expose the antiabortion agenda of Montana lawmakers, but *Mazurek* seemed to shut down this strategy.

*Mazurek* also made a big difference to those hoping that medication abortion would eliminate the need for patients to go to abortion clinics. As a medical matter, RU 486 made it possible to imagine that patients could eventually get telehealth abortions in the privacy of their homes. But in *Mazurek*, the Supreme Court made clear that states could require all abortions, even those performed using a pill, to run through doctors. The FDA had yet to approve RU 486, but even after regulators took that step, antiabortion lawmakers could route any patient seeking the drug to an abortion clinic.

Right-to-lifers' battle to criminalize partial-birth abortion, by contrast, had stalled. As long as Bill Clinton was in office, a ban on partial-birth abortion seemed impossible for Congress to pass. The same was not true for states, many of which began passing restrictions on the procedure. Antiabortion leaders felt delighted by the progress of their campaign, no matter what had happened to the federal bill. Focusing on partial-birth abortion, right-to-lifers believed, would give more Americans second thoughts about *Roe*.

The antiabortion movement had more concern about the morning-after pill, a new form of **emergency contraception**. For decades, researchers had looked for a form of birth control that could be prescribed after sex but before a fertilized egg implanted in the uterus. In the 1960s, doctors had given rape victims very high doses of estrogen to block a pregnancy, but the regime had extreme side effects. **A. Albert Yuzpe**, a Canadian doctor, developed a related protocol using several different hormones in the 1970s. In 1998, Preven, a regime patterned on the Yuzpe regime, became available. The following year, the FDA approved Plan B as a form of emergency contraception.

When it came to new birth control technologies, organizations like National Right to Life Committee policed the line between birth control and abortion partly because of right-to-lifers' anxieties about RU 486. In the 1980s, when the drug first made headlines, some researchers suggested that mifepristone was actually a contraceptive, not an abortion pill. Antiabortion leaders recognized that there would be far less pushback to new birth control drugs than there would be to new abortion techniques and believed that their opponents would deny the abortifacient effects of a drug.

But pro-choice and pro-life advocates held competing definitions of birth control—and of when human life began. For years, most abortion foes believed that life began at fertilization—when sperm fertilized an egg. Some antiabortion activists asserted that the morning-after pill took effect after fertilization and counted as an abortion drug. Researchers disagreed and maintained that emergency contraception primarily operated by preventing or delaying ovulation.

Antiabortion groups did not succeed in derailing the approval of emergency contraception, but the battle taught them valuable lessons. Some lawmakers who would never have admitted to opposing birth control were happy to question the approval of Plan B or Preven if there was some doubt that it was an abortion drug. Creating uncertainty would prove to be an effective tactic when it came to partial-birth abortion too.

Antiabortion leaders had felt optimistic when Congress **impeached** Bill Clinton. The scandal began after **Paula Jones**, an Arkansas state employee, had accused Clinton of sexual harassment in 1994. Clinton also had troubles after the **Whitewater** controversy, which began with a failed real estate investment in Arkansas; the Clintons' partner in the venture, James McDougal, had headed a bank that collapsed during the **savings and loan** crisis, costing taxpayers millions of dollars; he was eventually convicted of fraud and conspiracy based on loans made to his former bank.

**Ken Starr**, the attorney named to investigate Clinton's involvement in the Whitewater controversy, got ahold of information about another woman that Clinton had reportedly harassed, **Monica Lewinsky**, a former White House intern. When Clinton got word that Lewinsky had been added to the witness list in Jones' lawsuit, he denied having a sexual relationship with Lewinsky. Republicans in Congress were sure he was lying, and in 1998, two years after he convincingly won reelection, the House of Representatives impeached Clinton for **perjury** and **obstruction of justice** for covering up his affair. But ultimately, the Senate voted to acquit Clinton, and antiabortion opponents turned their attention to the upcoming presidential election. They understood that a Republican president would sign a ban on partial-birth abortion into law and put new faces on the Supreme Court.

In the leadup to the 2000 election, antiabortion leaders deepened their involvement in the fight against **campaign-finance restrictions**. Ever since Watergate, Congress worried that unlimited election spending was corrupting democracy in the United States. Wealthy donors, corporations, and interest groups could buy influence even if most voters disagreed with the policies those entities favored. But in 1976, in ***Buckley v. Valeo***, the Supreme Court had placed constitutional limits on campaign-finance reform, but wealthy donors, parties, nonprofit corporations had found a way around existing limits. Antiabortion groups had been among the most vocal opponents of campaign-finance reform, and **Jim Bopp Jr.**, the general counsel of National Right to Life Committee, became one of the attorneys pushing constitutional challenges to campaign-finance rules.

Months before the 2000 presidential election, the Supreme Court put an abrupt halt to the progress of the partial-birth abortion campaign in a case called ***Stenberg v. Carhart***. *Stenberg* involved a Nebraska law that made it a felony to "deliver into the vagina a living unborn child, or a substantial portion thereof, for the purpose of performing a procedure that the [doctor] knows will kill the child and . . . does kill the child." Dr. LeRoy Carhart argued that the law was unconstitutionally vague because Nebraska had failed to carefully define the procedure it was outlawing and had effectively criminalized the much more common dilation and evacuation, the most safe and common procedure after the first trimester of pregnancy. Carhart further asserted that the law was unduly burdensome under *Casey* in part because it lacked a health exception.

In a five-to-four decision, the Court agreed with Carhart. Writing for the majority, Stephen Breyer began by noting that requiring women to endanger their health would violate the constitutional rule set by *Casey*. Nebraska responded that there was not enough reliable evidence that patients would be better off if doctors used the dilation and extraction technique rather than something else. The majority in *Stenberg* agreed that the question of the safety and importance of dilation and extraction was "strongly contested" but reasoned that most of the evidence supported the need for a health exception. Moreover, when the need for a health exception was unclear, *Stenberg* broke the tie in favor of patients because not requiring a health exception might put patients at unnecessary risk.

The *Stenberg* majority also believed that Nebraska had unduly burdened patients by criminalizing the dilation and evacuation procedure. Nebraska had made it a felony to perform an abortion after all or a substantial part of an unborn child or fetus had been drawn into the vagina. But this step happened in dilation and evacuation as well—the difference between the procedures was that doctors intended to remove a fetus or child intact in a dilation and extraction after collapsing the head whereas in a dilation and evacuation the doctor intended to dismember a fetus or child first. Dilation and evacuation was by far the safest and most widely used abortion procedure after the first twelve weeks of pregnancy, and criminalizing it struck the *Stenberg* majority as unduly burdensome.

It was no surprise that some of the dissenters in *Casey*—including Antonin Scalia, Clarence Thomas, and William Rehnquist—disagreed with the majority in *Stenberg* (the fourth dissenter in *Casey*, **Byron White**, had since retired from the Court).

Everyone paid more attention to the dissenting opinion of Anthony Kennedy, one of the architects of the *Casey* majority. Kennedy suggested that Nebraska had a legitimate interest in safeguarding public respect for the medical profession and encouraging respect for the dignity of life. Both interests, he reasoned, were advanced by passing a ban on dilation and extraction. In Kennedy's view, dilation and extraction was closer to infanticide, at least in appearance, and thus, Nebraska could legitimately single that procedure out for criminal censure.

Kennedy also saw no problem with the lack of a health exception in the bill. He stressed that dilation and extraction was a new procedure that was not part of standard medical practice. In Kennedy's view, *Casey* did not give doctors the right to choose the procedure that they found the most beneficial. Indeed, in Kennedy's view, when medical evidence was contested, the government should have more freedom to operate.

Surprisingly, with the 2000 presidential election looming, abortion foes did not change their minds about the value of a campaign against partial-birth abortion. Abortion foes understood that the composition of the Supreme Court could easily change; Harry Blackmun was older and had openly discussed the possibility of retirement; the same was true of other liberals on the Court.

As important, fights about partial-birth abortion were a winner for right-to-lifers even if the Court never reversed *Stenberg*. Antiabortion leaders had used the push against dilation and extraction to paint the opposition as extremist. This tactic seemed to have paid off: for the first time, in the 2000s, more Americans identified as pro-life than pro-choice. This did not seem to track a shift in what Americans thought about any specific abortion restriction or about the idea of abortion rights. Instead, when Americans thought about abortion, they focused on partial-birth abortion—an issue that favored the antiabortion movement. Antiabortion leaders believed that fighting for bans on partial-birth abortion would help their movement defeat Democrats and win over younger Americans.

After the 2000 presidential election, abortion foes also hoped for a reversal of *Stenberg*. **George W. Bush** won a historically close race—so close that, in the decisive state of Florida, the state supreme court ordered a recount. Bush sued, arguing that because the recount procedures varied from county to county, not every Florida voter's ballot carried the same weight. The Supreme Court concluded that the recount procedures denied Florida voters equal treatment under the law. More controversially, the Court's conservative members refused to give Florida an opportunity to remedy the problem. The Court's decision in ***Bush v. Gore*** had the effect of giving the election to Bush.

Bush was an evangelical Protestant who spoke openly of his conversion and his faith. Some of his positions worried antiabortion leaders: for example, Bush favored an exception to abortion bans in cases of rape and incest. But his election meant that it might be possible to pass a federal ban on partial-birth abortion and place conservative justices on the Supreme Court, bringing the reversal of *Roe* a step closer.

Not all antiabortion leaders approved of the emphasis put on the partial-birth abortion issue. Some absolutists believed that partial-birth abortion bans suggested that the value of unborn life was relative. As important, bans on dilation and extraction simply directed doctors to use one procedure rather than another instead of stopping abortions altogether. Absolutists vowed to oppose any law that allowed for any abortion.

Others, like attorneys **Harold Cassidy** and **Allan Parker**, thought that the partial-birth abortion strategy came from a playbook that had already failed. Cassidy, a trial attorney, had experience working with biological parents in adoption cases and **surrogates** in cases concerning **assisted reproductive technologies** (ART). Cassidy proposed an alternative legal strategy to the one championed by the National Right to Life Committee. First, Cassidy wanted to use what he saw as new evidence of fetal personhood—particularly, genetic research completed in recent decades. He also believed that abortion *denied* women their rights because women bonded with their unborn children during pregnancy and formed a full-fledged constitutional relationship with the fetuses they carried. By severing this bond, abortion denied women the right to continue a constitutionally protected relationship.

Cassidy began making this argument in the lawsuits brought by patients against abortion providers, maintaining that his clients had not known what abortion had really involved and had been denied the opportunity to give informed consent. In his new litigation effort, he received support from prominent conservative Christian organizations and caught the attention of Norma McCorvey, the "Jane Roe" of *Roe v. Wade*. McCorvey had spent years attending events hosted by the pro-choice movement, but in the mid-1990s she began talking with **Flip Benham**, a leader of Operation Rescue, became an evangelical Protestant Christian, and joined the antiabortion movement. She contacted Cassidy about representing her in a legal effort to overturn *Roe v. Wade*. Cassidy and a colleague, Allan Parker, helped McCorvey and **Sandra Cano**, the Doe in *Doe v. Bolton*, in an attempt to undo abortion rights; the two women argued that the Court had decided *Roe* without understanding the real facts about abortion. Although this effort failed, it inspired both Cassidy and Parker to develop a full-blown alternative to the work of the mainstream antiabortion movement; Parker created **Operation Outcry**, an organization that would collect statements from women who regretted their abortions.

Other antiabortion leaders decided to ask for more direct recognition for fetal personhood. Professor **Hadley Arkes** proposed a law preventing the abortion of children who were "born alive." In earlier decades, Arkes' proposal might have had a more significant effect. Some procedures, such as hysterotomy abortions and saline procedures, did sometimes result in the birth of a living fetus or child. But by the 2000s, such cases were vanishingly rare. Arkes, however, wanted to pass a law that at least implicitly recognized fetal personhood. His proposal was a success, and Congress passed the **Born-Alive Infants Protection Act** in 2002. The following year, Congress also passed the federal **Partial-Birth Abortion Ban Act**, and George W. Bush signed it into law. Bush won reelection in 2004.

From the standpoint of the abortion wars, the race turned out to be quite consequential. In 2004, Sandra Day O'Connor announced her retirement. Her husband was battling Alzheimer's disease, and O'Connor planned to take care of him. Bush selected **John Roberts** to replace her. Roberts had served in the Justice Department during the George H.W. Bush Administration and had worked on a **brief** asking for *Roe* to be overturned. But Roberts had a winning personality and charmed most members of Congress. While his nomination was pending, William Rehnquist died of cancer. Bush chose **Samuel Alito** to replace O'Connor and asked Roberts to replace Rehnquist as chief justice. As a lower court judge, Alito had voted to uphold the spousal notification law that the Court eventually struck down in *Planned Parenthood v. Casey*.

With new conservatives on the Court, it seemed possible that *Stenberg* would be overturned; O'Connor had cast the deciding vote to strike down Nebraska's ban on partial-birth abortion. Roberts and Alito might be willing to uphold such a restriction (as well as many more). Everything seemed to depend on Anthony Kennedy, a justice who had voted to save abortion rights in *Casey* while choosing to narrow them in *Stenberg*.

Lawyers for groups like Americans United for Life and the National Right to Life Committee tailored their strategies to please Kennedy, especially given his dissent in *Stenberg*. There, he seemed willing to recognize justifications for regulating abortion beyond those laid out in the Court's earlier precedents. Kennedy also concluded that states should have more liberty to restrict abortion when the science on a matter was uncertain. If right-to-lifers could effectively argue that a matter was scientifically uncertain, the Court might carve out more room for abortion restrictions, even in the context of medication abortion.

In 2000, at the conclusion of clinical trials, the Food and Drug Administration finally approved RU 486 for use in the first 49 days of pregnancy but designated it a drug used to treat a "serious or life-threatening condition"—which meant that restrictions applied to its distribution. First, pharmacists were not allowed to distribute mifepristone; only licensed physicians were allowed to do so. Second, doctors had to be physically present to distribute the pill, and it received a **black-box warning**, the most serious that could apply to a drug, which usually applied only to drugs that could cause serious injury or death, such as addictive narcotics. All of these regulations made it harder to access RU 486.

Antiabortion leaders justified restrictions on medication abortion by suggesting that the drug's safety was uncertain. Starting in 2004, states began introducing direct restrictions on medication abortion, again contesting the safety of RU 486. Some laws required adherence to the current FDA rules, regardless of whether future scientific advances changed the safety profile of the drug. Other states functionally outlawed **telehealth abortions**, procedures overseen by a physician remotely, using the Internet. These laws required a physician to be in person when a patient received abortion medication.

Arguments about scientific uncertainty helped to ensure that medication abortion did not revolutionize the abortion debate in the early 2000s. If anything, a relatively small number of patients even chose medical abortion in the years after RU 486 first became available. For most patients, abortion remained a surgical procedure performed at clinics.

Arguments about scientific uncertainty would become even more important after the Supreme Court agreed to hear a challenge to the federal Partial-Birth Abortion Ban Act in ***Gonzales v. Carhart*** [**Doc. 15**]. Dr. LeRoy Carhart argued that the federal statute was virtually identical to the one struck down in *Stenberg* and unconstitutional for the same reasons. Both pro-choice and pro-life lawyers retooled their strategies in *Gonzales*. Pro-choice groups stressed that dilation and extraction had become a more accepted part of medical practice in the years since 2000; the procedure appeared in some gynecology and obstetrics courses and textbooks. The **American College of Obstetricians and Gynecologists (ACOG)** had concluded that dilation and extraction was sometimes the safest procedure for patients.

But for pro-choice lawyers, winning the case was not just about better scientific evidence. Abortion-rights supporters also insisted that the opposition was politicizing science—ignoring elite medical opinion, manipulating data, and injecting the views of politicians into the private relationship between physicians and their patients. As pro-choice groups framed it, the best scientific evidence showed that bans on dilation and extraction required a health exception.

Together with antiabortion leaders, Congress responded that it was pro-choice groups who had politicized the medical establishment and the media. The National Right to Life Committee complained that the media gave unfairly positive coverage to the pro-choice movement when it came to partial-birth abortion, even when groups like the American Medical Association refused to recognize the procedure as safe or beneficial for patients.

Right-to-lifers already felt that the media was hopelessly biased. This conviction was increasingly widespread among conservative Americans as rightwing media flourished in the 2000s. In earlier decades, right-to-lifers had tried to create their own media ecosystem, putting out newsletters and films. Advocating for balanced coverage, conservatives sought to win a place in legacy media coverage.

Conservative media began to flourish in the 1990s with the spread of talk radio. Early that decade, however, radio host **Rush Limbaugh** was the only conservative media giant. By 1996, however, **Rupert Murdoch** launched **Fox News Channel**, a 24-hour news channel with a conservative bent. Conservative talk radio began to dominate the airwaves in the 2000s, with Limbaugh facing competition from a variety of hosts. **Newsmax** also launched a news site for conservatives. Conservative media outlets made the mainstream media part of the story, accusing journalists of concealing their political preferences, silencing those on the political right, and presenting slanted coverage. The more abortion foes distrusted the legacy media, the more prepared they were to accept alternative narratives from unconventional sources. There were few trusted arbiters of truth in US politics, both in the abortion debate and beyond it.

In *Gonzales*, Congress and antiabortion groups also insisted that the medical establishment was biased. Outside of court, they pointed to evidence that the American College of Obstetricians and Gynecologists was dominated by pro-choice doctors. In *Gonzales*, right-to-lifers focused on their own evidence—the hearings and findings made by Congress about dilation and extraction. Allan Parker submitted a brief on behalf of Operation Outcry arguing that there was no need for a health exception because abortion itself damaged women's health and citing women's personal stories as evidence.

Parker's argument seemed to resonate with the Supreme Court's new majority. In a five-to-four decision, the Court in *Gonzales* upheld the federal partial-birth abortion ban. Justice Anthony Kennedy opened with a graphic description of dilation and extraction. Right-to-lifers' efforts to frame the dilation and extraction procedure as disturbing seemed to pay dividends. Next, the majority concluded that Congress's law was not unconstitutionally vague and did not prohibit dilation and evacuation as well as dilation and extraction. Here, the Court emphasized the ways that Congress's definition of partial-birth abortion differed from the one adopted in *Stenberg*. Congress had added several new wrinkles: in a partial-birth abortion, the entire fetal body or trunk needed to be in the vagina while a fetus or unborn child was still alive; doctors had to intend to perform a partial-birth abortion and had to perform an overt act (other than delivery) that killed a fetus or child. As the *Gonzales* majority saw it, Congress had done enough to make clear what conduct was outlawed—and to ensure that only dilation and extraction, not dilation and evacuation, was prohibited.

*Gonzales* next asked whether the Partial-Birth Abortion Ban Act was unconstitutional under *Casey*. The Court suggested that there were several legitimate purposes served by Congress's ban. First, the law protected the dignity of fetal life—an interest distinct from preventing abortions. A ban on all abortions would protect fetal life by preventing a patient from ending a pregnancy. Prohibiting a specific technique would not stop anyone from getting an abortion. The majority suggested instead that partial-birth abortion affected the attitudes of bystanders about human life; leaving it legal would make people care less about the value of human life. If the law permitted a procedure that resembled infanticide, respect for life would suffer. As *Gonzales* explained, Congress could ban partial-birth abortion to encourage people to treat human life with more dignity.

*Gonzales* likewise concluded that Congress could try to protect the integrity of the medical profession. The majority suggested that doctors would damage their reputations by performing a procedure that, to some, resembled infanticide.

Finally, the majority relied heavily on Allan Parker's brief for Operation Outcry in recognizing an interest in preventing post-abortion regret.

At first, this argument seemed to be a bit convoluted. After all, Congress had not set out to inform women about anything; lawmakers had simply criminalized a single abortion technique. The Court nevertheless cited the Operation Outcry brief as proof that women had a bond with their unborn children and could sometimes regret their decision and suffer severe depression or trauma as a result of abortion—especially after choosing a technique that the majority found so gruesome. Eliminating this abortion method, the argument went, would protect women from regret.

*Gonzales* next considered whether the ban had the effect of unduly burdening women's decisions about abortion and rejected the need for a health exception. In *Stenberg*, the Court had held that if there was any uncertainty about the need for dilation and extraction, the Constitution required a health exception; anything less could put pregnant people in jeopardy. *Gonzales* reached the opposite conclusion. The Court noted that the need for such a health exception was contested; Congress had made findings suggesting that dilation and extraction was unnecessary and perhaps even unsafe, but some of these conclusions had obvious errors, and pro-choice experts disputed the rest. But the Court reasoned that when a matter was scientifically uncertain, lawmakers should have more room to regulate; anything else would unfairly tie lawmakers' hands. The Court upheld the statute.

Justice Ruth Bader Ginsburg wrote a biting dissent. She took issue with the idea that Congress had tried to protect women from regretting their abortions. In *Casey*, the Court had criticized the lawmakers who had passed a spousal notification for relying on outdated stereotypes of the roles of men and women. Yet, as Ginsburg saw it, *Gonzales* had written similar stereotypes into constitutional law—assuming that women were ignorant about abortion and needed to be stopped from responding to their own bad instincts.

Ginsburg's dissent aside, *Gonzales* upended the law and politics of abortion. The Court's decision confirmed that Anthony Kennedy, the author of the majority in *Gonzales*, would be the Court's swing vote on abortion. Future arguments about abortion rights would be made with Kennedy in mind. And Kennedy staked out a seemingly complex position on abortion: he had played a part in saving abortion rights but also seemed inclined to uphold a relatively wide range of restrictions.

As important, *Gonzales* gave antiabortion leaders a new roadmap for chipping away at abortion rights: groups like the National Right to Life Committee would argue that a whole host of issues were medically uncertain, starting with the safety of RU 486. In 2008, Congress amended federal food and drug law to create the **risk evaluation and mitigation strategy (REMS)** program for certain dangerous drugs. The REMS program applied to certain high-risk drugs to ensure that the benefits of access continued to outweigh the risks. The FDA not only issued a REMS for RU 486 but also added further restrictions through a specific type of REMS, an Elements to Ensure Safe Use.

Because of the REMS, RU 486 remained available primarily through abortion clinics. It ensured that patients could not get RU 486 from their pharmacy (emergency contraception, by contrast, was often available over the counter). As important, the REMS required physicians to be certified to prescribe RU 486. Some physicians hesitated to seek certification because doing so would identify them as abortion providers and possibly expose them to harassment or violence. Moreover, few physicians lacked the know-how to manage drug inventory themselves. Doctors did not wish to purchase a relatively expensive drug like RU 486 without knowing patient demand and did not have the time to make sure enough drug was in stock (or to prevent expired drugs from being prescribed to patients). A vanishingly small number of doctors prescribed RU 486, which remained mostly available through abortion clinics.

*Gonzales* seemed to open a new chapter in the abortion wars. Antiabortion leaders believed that the Court had watered down the undue burden rule, required significant deference to lawmakers, and made most (if not all) abortion restrictions constitutional. It was not clear exactly when the Court would be that deferential, but if legislators could claim that a matter was uncertain, *Gonzales* seemed to give them significant room to maneuver. Overturning *Roe* seemed less important if right-to-life legislators could do almost anything they liked under the undue burden test.

More cautious antiabortion leaders thought that *Gonzales* would help only when the movement made a credible scientific case—especially if a law prohibited a specific technique or kicked in later in pregnancy. In either case, the aftermath of *Gonzales* proved how far the abortion debate had moved beyond *Roe*. Neither movement was focused on whether the Constitution recognized a right to life or a right to choose. Instead, the conflict had moved into the trenches, with opposing lawyers, lobbyists, and grassroots activists battling about the safety profile of drugs and medical procedures—and debating who had the expertise to weigh in on these debates.

On the surface, of course, *Roe* still dominated debate. Right-to-life forces argued that because *Roe* had signed off on any abortion at any time, including partial-birth procedures, overruling the decision was imperative. Abortion-rights supporters again made *Roe* a symbol for concern about patient health. These debates only reinforced how *Roe* had come to mean different things to different activists (and in different contexts). While everyone seemed fixated on the fate of *Roe*, what they meant when they invoked the decision had changed dramatically.

# 6 Religious liberty and the intractable conflict

When **Barack Obama** won the race for the White House in 2008, arguments about religious liberty would not have struck many Americans as a flashpoint in the culture wars. When Obama, an Illinois Senator and former community organizer, ran for president, he emphasized his own religious beliefs and tried to express sympathy to religious Christians. Obama did win special plaudits from the pro-choice movement, which endorsed him early in his primary run over a better-known candidate, Hillary Clinton. His Republican opponent, John McCain, had a track record of voting with the antiabortion movement but defined himself as a maverick and was not always beloved by the Christian Right; during the Republican primary, right-to-lifers had supported several candidates, but McCain was not at the top of anyone's list.

Most Americans seemed too worried about a long and painful recession to prioritize the culture wars. Between 1997 and 2006, housing prices in the United States had increased substantially, and homeowners looked to refinance their mortgages at lower rates or took out second mortgages. Financial institutions fed a demand for mortgage-backed investment by enticing homeowners with below-market interest rates. These were riskier investments, and as housing prices began to fall in 2007, investment banks began to fail; others cut back on lending. Employers scaled back investments and laid off workers. Because voters laid responsibility on the doorstep of George W. Bush, the recession harmed McCain's chances. Fights about abortion—or religious liberty—seemed to have been pushed to the side.

If anything, for some time, Americans across the ideological spectrum had once seemed to agree on the importance of religious freedom. Constitutionally, Americans protecting their religious liberty relied on the **Free Exercise Clause** of the First Amendment. The Court had once found a violation of that clause if a law substantially burdened religious exercise—and if there was no compelling governmental purpose to justify that burden. For example, in one famous case, Adeil Sherbert, a Seventh-Day Adventist, lost her job after refusing to work on Saturdays, the Sabbath of her faith, and the state denied her unemployment insurance. In *Sherbert v. Verner*, the Supreme Court held that the government had severely burdened Sherbert's religious exercise without a compelling reason to do so.

DOI: 10.4324/9781003215936-9

But in 1990, in a decision by conservative justice Antonin Scalia, the Court made it far harder to bring a challenge based on the Free Exercise Clause. In *Employment Division, Department of Human Resources of Oregon v. Smith*, two Native American drug counselors lost their jobs after consuming the drug peyote during a religious ceremony. The law in Oregon, where the two men worked, treated peyote as a controlled substance. The two counselors were caught using the drug, lost their job, were unable to collect unemployment insurance, and brought suit. The Supreme Court found no constitutional issue with their inability to collect unemployment insurance. Scalia wrote an opinion holding that any law that applied to the general population without targeting religion would be constitutional under the Free Exercise Clause. Oregon's drug laws had nothing explicitly to do with religion and applied to everyone, not just believers. Therefore, the Court upheld it.

*Smith* alienated a wide variety of Americans. In 1993, with the support of a broad-based coalition, Congress passed the **Religious Freedom Restoration Act** (RFRA), a federal law which made it easier to establish that a law violated an individual's religious liberty. RFRA reinstated the old standard from *Sherbert*: any governmental action that substantially burdened religion would have to be justified by a compelling governmental purpose and would have to be the least restrictive means of achieving the government's objective. Progressive civil libertarians, conservative Christians, and members of a wide variety of faith communities supported more robust protections for religious freedom.

There had also historically been broad support for conscience-based protections in the abortion context as well. In the immediate aftermath of *Roe*, Congress passed the **Church Amendment**, which guaranteed protection for medical providers who did not wish to assist in abortions or sterilizations for religious or moral reasons. At the time, the Church Amendment received overwhelming bipartisan support. In the years since, other conscience protections were written into law. Although the abortion wars were as ugly as ever, few realized that conflicts about religious liberty would soon be almost as intense.

When Obama took office, the most intense political battles surrounded health care reform. Obama had vowed to create universal health care coverage during his run for the White House. With a Democratic majority in Congress, Obama planned to pass his **Affordable Care Act**. The reforms ordered by the act, also known as Obamacare, were far-ranging. Insurers could not exclude customers based on their preexisting conditions. States had to allow parents to keep their adult children on their insurance under certain circumstances, and all policies had to include coverage for certain essential benefits. The law mandated that individuals carry insurance or pay a penalty. Most consequentially, the bill massively expanded Medicaid. After a great deal of wrangling, the Affordable Care Act passed in March of 2010. Obama, the first Black American president, seemed off to an historic start.

The Affordable Care Act did spark a minor battle about abortion. Abortion foes contended that the bill would provide unlimited funding for abortions. Obama tried to defuse this argument (and win the votes of several antiabortion Democrats in Congress) by limiting abortion coverage. The Affordable Care Act prohibited federal funding for abortion and instituted administrative requirements for insurers to make sure that their plans did not use federal dollars to pay for abortion. Antiabortion groups were hardly satisfied and argued that the Affordable Care Act would increase funding to organizations like Planned Parenthood, which could then use federal dollars to offset the costs of abortion.

It was the backlash to the Affordable Care Act and other policies enacted by the Obama Administration that wrought a more lasting change in American politics. In 2009, Obama announced a foreclosure relief plan to help Americans hurt by a deep recession. On the CNBC network, commentator Rick Santelli called on angry Americans to stage a "tea party" to protest the move. Santelli and his followers were angry about what they saw as the unfair burden placed on financially responsible Americans by federal programs designed to help the poor, the young, and those who had immigrated to the United States. A series of protests began in cities across the United States.

Grassroots Tea Party organizations soon gained the backing of major Republican donors and lobbyists. FreedomWorks, a conservative advocacy group with ties to David and Charles Koch, the heads of Koch Industries, one of the largest private companies in the United States, helped endorse Tea Party candidates within the Republican Party, train volunteers, and get out the vote. Americans for Prosperity, another Koch-funded organization, also supported Tea Partiers. Tea Party Express, another organization, had ties to a well-established Republican lobbying firm.

The Tea Party attracted primarily white, older, conservative voters. Although organizations like FreedomWorks favored cutting most government entitlement programs, grassroots Tea Partiers had little interest in scaling back Social Security or Medicare. Instead, Tea Party voters tended to believe that their own benefits were slashed to help support undeserving groups, including immigrants, young people, immigrants, and the poor.

The 2010 election proved to be a coming-out party for the movement. Tea Partiers upset establishment Republicans in major primaries and gained seats in both the House and Senate. The Tea Party's effect on state legislatures was even more significant. Republicans made record gains, taking control of a majority of state legislatures. On the campaign trail, Tea Partiers had focused on fiscal issues, but in state legislatures Tea Party Republicans made a major impact on abortion policy, enacting a then-record 92 abortion restrictions in 2011.

Many of these new regulations targeted Planned Parenthood. **Lila Rose**, then a college student at the University of California-Los Angeles, made headlines after posting a viral video; Rose and a friend posted surreptitiously recorded videos filmed in clinics in six states that appeared to show Planned Parenthood workers failing to report statutory rapes. Rose became a hero to millennial right-to-lifers, and her videos supercharged the campaign to eliminate funding for Planned Parenthood.

Ever since 1976, the Hyde Amendment and related rules within the Title X program had ensured that no federal money paid for abortions. But abortion foes like Rose insisted that the more money Planned Parenthood received for other purposes, like family planning, the more costs would be offset, and the more abortions Planned Parenthood could perform. States began pushing laws that would deny *any* public funding for entities that performed abortions or advocated for abortion rights. Americans United for Life published what it framed as a comprehensive look at financial wrongdoing at Planned Parenthood, and Congress began considering a defunding proposal of its own.

Meanwhile, earlier consensus about religious liberty had broken down entirely. The cracks became most visible in fights about the **contraceptive mandate** of the Affordable Care Act. The mandate required insurers and group health plans to cover all female contraceptives approved by the Food and Drug Administration. Initially, exceptions applied to a limited subset of religious employers but did not cover secular businesses run by individuals or families with religious or moral objections to contraception. Eventually, the exemptions were broadened, but this was not enough for religious objectors.

In 2012, a variety of groups filed suit, including Hobby Lobby, a family-owned arts and crafts business. Hobby Lobby argued that the contraceptive mandate violated religious liberties protected by the Religious Freedom Restoration Act. The Greens, the family that ran Hobby Lobby, believed that several covered contraceptives were actually abortifacients, including emergency contraception and several forms of intrauterine device (IUD). The Greens, like some other right-to-lifers, believed that these drugs blocked implantation of a fertilized egg (and thereby caused an abortion). The American College of Obstetricians and Gynecologists (ACOG) responded that emergency contraception prevented ovulation, while IUDs either stopped fertilization or blocked implantation. In either case, ACOG maintained that a drug did not produce an abortion unless it acted *after* implantation had occurred.

The Greens certainly stood by their views of the effects of contraceptive drugs. But religious freedom arguments suggested that it did not matter who was right about the effects of certain contraceptives. If the Greens felt that these drugs produced an abortion—and believed that their religious liberty had been compromised—then nothing more had to be said.

The contraceptive mandate, together with ongoing struggles over same-sex marriage and abortion, crystallized conservatives' anxieties about religious liberty. In 2009, the press covered the wide dissemination of the ***Manhattan Declaration: A Call of Christian Conscience*** a statement of conservative Christian principles developed leaders like Princeton professor Robert George and Chuck Colson, a veteran of the Nixon Administration who had converted to evangelical Protestantism. The *Manhattan Declaration* proclaimed that unborn children had a right to life, that marriage was between one man and one woman, and that religious liberty deserved the upmost protection. It struck a nerve with a wide range of social conservatives and right-leaning Christians.

In part, conservative Christians reacted to growing support for same-sex marriage. In 1996, there seemed to be a bipartisan consensus against same-sex marriage. That year, Bill Clinton had signed the federal Defense of Marriage Act into law. Democrats and Republicans proclaimed themselves to be champions of traditional marriage.

By 2010, that consensus had frayed. State supreme courts in states like Massachusetts, Connecticut, New Jersey, Washington, and California continued to recognize a state constitutional right for same-sex couples to get married or enter into civil unions. Opponents of same-sex marriage fought back. In California, for example, after a fierce campaign, voters chose to amend the state constitution to explicitly ban same-sex marriage.

Nevertheless, the tide seemed to be turning against opponents of same-sex marriage. Each year, polls found more Americans favored allowing same-sex couples to marry, and by 2011, for the first time, a majority held that view. Some Christian conservatives worried that recognition of same-sex marriage would lead to the marginalization of Christians who disapproved of it. As important, arguments about religious liberty looked less politically risky for conservative Christians who recognized that a growing number of Americans favored access to same-sex marriage. Taking a stand against same-sex marriage was one thing. Arguing about religious liberty seemed far more strategically savvy.

Antiabortion groups also used religious liberty to stake out clearer opposition to the contraceptive mandate. For decades, abortion foes had steered clear of any discussion of birth control. The antiabortion movement had long faced accusations of being anti-woman and anti-sex rather than pro-life. But by framing their view on the contraceptive mandate as a vindication of religious liberty, more right-to-lifers felt comfortable voicing their opposition.

More right-leaning Americans worried about losing their religious liberty when Research by the Pew Forum did find significant decreases in the number of Americans who identified as Christian between 2007 and 2014, particularly among Catholics and mainline Protestants. The group of those who identified with no religious tradition, the so-called "nones," was getting substantially larger, growing from approximately 16 percent in 2007 to nearly 23 percent in the same time period.

When it came to abortion itself, the courts seemed to want to stay out of the conflict. Obama nominated two new justices to the Supreme Court. In 2009, David Souter announced his retirement. Obama selected **Sonia Sotomayor**, the first Latina woman to sit on the High Court, as his replacement. The following year, following the retirement of John Paul Stevens, Obama chose **Elena Kagan**, a former dean of Harvard Law School and the current Solicitor General of the United States, for the Court. Obama's picks did not change the balance of the Court, but Kagan and Sotomayor did shore up the Court's aging liberal wing, and Anthony Kennedy retained the deciding vote in most abortion cases.

Obama won reelection in 2012, but Republicans retained control of the House. For the time being, at least on the federal level, gridlock seemed likely. Abortion foes were not overly worried because Americans United for Life believed that the Court had already made the undue burden all but toothless in *Gonzales*. To these right-to-lifers, it seemed that *Gonzales* required almost unlimited deference to state legislatures.

Americans United for Life put together a strategy to clarify that the Court really would sign off on almost any abortion restriction. The group announced a package of model legislation, the **Woman's Health Projection Project**, consisting of restrictions claimed to protect women from the ravages of abortion. Some laws limited or banned later abortions; others regulated the operation or physical structure of abortion clinics, created waiting periods, or mandated that patients hear statements on what right-to-lifers called the risks of abortion.

When some of these laws came before the Supreme Court, Americans United for Life relied on *Gonzales* to argue that there was uncertainty about the safety of abortion for women—and that *Gonzales* required the courts to defer to legislatures on almost any question involving abortion. Texas became one of the states to adopt this strategy. In 2013, the state passed one AUL law requiring doctors to have admitting privileges at a clinic within 30 miles. A second AUL-inspired provision mandated that abortion clinics comply with the regulations governing out-patient surgical centers, some of which required pricey makeovers of existing facilities. These regulations would have the effect of closing down most abortion clinics.

The fight over the contraceptive mandate reached the Supreme Court first. In ***Burwell v. Hobby Lobby Stores*** (2014), the Court held that the contraceptive mandate violated the Religious Freedom Restoration Act. First, the Court had to address whether corporations could use federal law to protect their religious liberty. The Obama Department of Health and Human Services (HHS) contended that RFRA applied only to "persons," a term that the government said applied to human beings, not for-profit corporations. The department likewise reasoned that for-profit businesses could not truly exercise religion—and that language to that effect in RFRA was not intended to apply to for-profit businesses. In a majority opinion by Justice Samuel Alito, the Supreme Court disagreed. The Court reasoned that the law often maintained the fiction of treating corporations as "persons." Alito reasoned that RFRA offered broad protections for religious liberty, and there was no indication that lawmakers had intended to exclude merchants from those protections.

*Hobby Lobby* next addressed whether the contraceptive mandate violated RFRA. The majority had no trouble concluding that RFRA had created a substantial burden on religious exercise. If Hobby Lobby and other **closely held** for-profit businesses elected not to offer contraception, the company would have to pay a per-patient, per-day penalty of $100. It was not hard to see how these fines would pile up.

HHS replied that *complying* with the mandate would not impose much of a burden. True, lawmakers had long protected freedom of conscience.

But conscience protections had usually applied only to those the most directly involved with an abortion or sterilizations, such as the doctors or nurses who performed the procedures. By contrast, the Greens and other employers were several steps removed from an employee's decision to use contraception.

The Court saw the distinction between different levels of complicity as irrelevant. Instead, if a believer was sincere and felt pressure to act in contravention of those beliefs, the Court viewed a burden as substantial, full stop. *Hobby Lobby* assumed that even if the government had a compelling interest in ensuring that women had contraceptive access, the contraceptive mandate still failed under RFRA because it had not used the least restrictive means of achieving its objective. HHS could have broadened the exemptions from the contraceptive mandate to include certain for-profit businesses or could have just paid directly for patients' contraceptives.

*Hobby Lobby* put many on notice that the politics of religious freedom were changing. First, as the *Manhattan Declaration* suggested, conservative Christians had made religious liberty arguments a cornerstone of their agenda. To be sure, members of other faith communities at times relied on RFRA in advancing their own arguments about religion. But, increasingly, Americans began to associate religious liberty claims with the political right.

As important, those championing religious liberty asked courts and lawmakers to strike a different balance between the liberty of believers and the needs of the broader community. As Justice Scalia recognized in the *Smith* case, most religious liberty cases involved a request for an exemption from rules that applied to everyone else. Receiving an exemption, in turn, could burden those who were not part of that (or any) faith community. For example, when employers opted out of the contraceptive mandate, fewer employees might have contraceptive access. Another soldier would have to replace one with conscientious objections to fighting a war. To strike a fair balance, policymakers had always paid careful attention to the degree to which a believer felt complicit in an action that undercut her beliefs—and to the importance of the government's interest in regulating.

In *Hobby Lobby*, and cases after it, religious believers defined complicity more and more broadly—often to include those with no direct involvement in an offending activity. By extension, these arguments suggested that whatever policy objective was on the other side of the ledger—including contraceptive access—was not so important after all.

Arguments about religious liberty took on greater political symbolism after the Supreme Court recognized a federal right for same-sex couples to marry. A year before *Hobby Lobby*, the Court had held that the federal Defense of Marriage Act (DOMA) was unconstitutional. In that case, *United States v. Windsor*, the majority had emphasized that DOMA both denied same-sex couples and their children key monetary benefits and sent a message that their families were inferior. But, at the same time, *Windsor* stressed that the federal government had waded into an area almost always reserved for states to handle: the laws of marriage. So, after *Windsor*, no one could be sure how the Supreme Court would view *state* bans on same-sex marriage.

Over time, more states had voted to legalize same-sex marriage. Nevertheless, the Court's decision in ***Obergefell v. Hodges*** (2015) upended the law in many states. The Court heard a series of challenges to state laws denying access to marriage. The states, like many of the dissenting justices, argued that when figuring out the limits of constitutional rights, the Court often relied on history and tradition. And traditionally, in the United States, marriage had been between one man and one woman. The majority described the history of marriage in different terms: change, not continuity, had defined the history of marriage in the United States. At one point, for example, married women could not own property. Interracial couples could not marry. As the majority saw it, the meaning of marriage had changed over time as society understood constitutional liberty in different terms.

When it came to same-sex marriage, *Obergefell* believed that similar shifts had taken place. Whereas American law had once treated homosexuality as a crime or a form of mental illness, in recent years most had come to see sexual orientation as "a normal expression of human sexuality and immutable." Americans had become far more accepting of same-sex marriage, and some states had moved to protect it. For these reasons, the majority thought that history and tradition did not exclude recognition of same-sex marriage.

*Obergefell* set forth several principles that had governed the constitutional right to marry. First, marriage involved matters of "personal choice" central to "an individual's destiny." Marriage was a uniquely important social institution, one that helped to produce and shape citizens. And marriage safeguarded families and the children raised within them. The Court reasoned that all of these principles militated in favor of recognizing same-sex marriage.

*Obergefell* explicitly connected same-sex marriage both to the Due Process and Equal Protection Clauses. Same-sex marriage involved due process and autonomy because the choice of a marriage partner was a central part of a person's identity and lived experience. Equality interests came into play because of discrimination directed against same-sex couples as a group.

The majority was careful to say that its decision would not force those with religious objections to same-sex marriage to change their minds, much less act in contradiction of their beliefs. But that was precisely what some of the dissenting justices worried about. The dissenters, including Chief Justice John Roberts, accused the majority of judicial activism—of settling on a politically popular outcome regardless of what the Constitution had to say. Samuel Alito stressed that those who opposed same-sex marriage would be branded as bigots and ostracized for their most deeply held beliefs.

Alito's dissent reflected a much broader set of concerns on the right. Some conservative Christians compared *Obergefell* to *Roe*. Others proclaimed that the decision was not really about tolerance for same-sex couples but about intolerance of those who had religious objections to homosexuality. *Obergefell* deepened the sense of persecution and marginalization felt by many conservative Christians. Groups like the Alliance Defending Freedom (the former Alliance Defense Fund) stepped up their efforts to defend what they saw as the rights of Christians.

Many expected the Court to go in a far more conservative direction when it came to abortion. In 2016, the Supreme Court stood ready to hear a challenge to two woman-protective antiabortion laws in ***Whole Woman's Health v. Hellerstedt.*** While *Whole Woman's Health* was pending, Donald Trump had managed to upset his opponents to become the presumptive Republican nominee for president. A foul-mouthed, self-proclaimed billionaire, Trump had alienated many social conservatives, including abortion foes. Right-to-lifers did not trust the man, given his history of sexual harassment and his past support for legal abortion. But other GOP primary voters seemed to love Trump's anti-immigrant sentiment, racist comments, off-color jokes, and promises to use his business savvy to make Americans rich.

The Court's decision in *Whole Woman's Health* pushed right-to-lifers more firmly into Trump's camp. Texas had defended its regulations, an admitting-privilege regulation and an ambulatory surgical center provision, in part by arguing that the undue burden standard required almost complete deference to lawmakers. The state suggested that the admitting privileges requirement would improve continuity of care for patients who suffered complications after an abortion. Mandating that clinics comply with the rules governing ambulatory surgical centers would, the argument went, reduce the risks of abortions. In the wake of *Gonzales*, many expected the Supreme Court to agree.

But before the Court decided *Gonzales*, Antonin Scalia died during a Texas hunting trip, and the Court that rendered a decision in *Whole Woman's Health* had only eight members. To the surprise of many, the justices not only struck down both Texas regulations but also described a version of the undue burden test that was far more protective of abortion rights. The majority concluded that the undue burden test required courts to balance the benefits achieved by an abortion law against the burdens that the law placed on access to abortion. In practice, the Court suggested that laws might be unconstitutional if they served no purpose, even if they only placed modest burdens on abortion access.

The majority suggested that neither Texas requirement had any benefit. Texas had no evidence that requiring admitting privileges helped any patient. Besides, post-abortion complications were extremely rare—and when complications did occur, they tended to crop up well after a patient left an abortion clinic. The majority saw the ambulatory surgical center requirement as equally useless. Not all abortions were surgical, and many procedures with higher rates of complications did not need to meet the same requirements set for abortion clinics.

The Court saw both requirements as burdensome. Most abortion providers could not maintain admitting privileges because they did not admit enough patients to hospitals. That meant that many abortion clinics would have no choice but to close. The ambulatory surgical center requirement also would force the closure of clinics—Texas required clinics to undergo a costly overhaul that many could not afford. The Court invalidated both regulations.

*Whole Woman's Health* came as a shock to antiabortion leaders who believed that the Court would only defer further to legislators in the aftermath of *Gonzales*. Religious conservatives were also frustrated by a series of decisions on religious liberty. In *Zubik v. Burwell* (2016), the Court dealt with the latest round of challenges to the contraceptive mandate. The administration had revised its policy to allow religious employers to opt out of contraceptive coverage by filling out a form. Religious objectors argued that the act of filling out the form substantially burdened them (and made them complicit) under RFRA. The Court had largely sought to make the case go away. *Zubik* ordered the government and religious objectors to take more time to reach an accommodation that would please everyone.

No matter how distasteful or untrustworthy Trump seemed, he was the right-to-life movement's best opportunity to change the Court. His opponent, Hillary Clinton, had a long track record of supporting abortion rights, and she was running on the most pro-choice platform in decades. For some time, the Hyde Amendment, a ban on Medicaid reimbursement for abortion, had enjoyed bipartisan support. Clinton made its repeal a key campaign promise.

Moreover, the next president would have the chance to nominate at least one new Supreme Court justice (and probably more). Mitch McConnell, the Senate majority leader, had refused to hold a hearing on the judge Barack Obama selected to replace Scalia, Merrick Garland. McConnell argued that, with an election relatively close, it was more appropriate to let the next president fill Scalia's seat. Antiabortion leaders recognized that, as president, Trump could change the Court. In November 2016, Trump shocked many observers by defeating Clinton.

From the beginning, Trump battled historically low approval numbers. To stand a chance of reelection, he had to excite core GOP constituencies, including abortion foes, and he set out to do just that. He formed a new Conscience and Religious Freedom Division within HHS and issued regulations expanding the categories of employees who could refuse to participate in abortions, sterilizations, and other services. Aimed at Planned Parenthood, another regulation increased the number of faith-based Title X recipients and barred family planning organizations from Title X funding if they provided Title X services and abortion in the same physical location. He also named **Neil Gorsuch**, a judge from the Tenth Circuit Court of Appeals, to replace Scalia. Gorsuch had written a book on euthanasia that some read as signaling support for a right to life.

Conservative Christians were still often frustrated by the Court while Anthony Kennedy cast the deciding vote. This was true of *Masterpiece Cakeshop v. Colorado Civil Rights Commission* (2016), which began when a same-sex couple had sought to purchase a wedding cake from a conservative Christian baker. When he refused, citing his faith, the couple sought recourse from the state's civil rights commission. Colorado civil rights law prohibited discrimination on the basis of sexual orientation. The commission eventually penalized the baker, who appealed his case all the way to the Supreme Court. He argued that by forcing him to serve the same-sex couple, Colorado had violated his freedom of speech and freedom of religion.

*Masterpiece Cakeshop* seemed to be likely to be a major case: one that would settle the balance between protection for the rights of gay, lesbian, transgender, queer, and intersex persons and the religious liberty of those who objected to homosexuality. But the Court's ruling in the case was extremely narrow. The majority focused on the supposedly discriminatory comments made by members of the Colorado Civil Rights Commission. As the Court saw it, the commission had denied the baker the fair treatment required by the Free Exercise of the First Clause Amendment. The Court did not weigh in on how future disputes between gay rights and religious freedom would play out.

The Court may have been reticent to do anything major when Anthony Kennedy was planning to retire. In June 2018, he announced that he was leaving the Court. Kennedy had held the deciding vote on abortion in every case from *Casey* to *Whole Woman's Health*. With him gone, it seemed quite possible that the Court would overrule *Roe*.

Trump nominated **Brett Kavanaugh**, a judge from the DC Circuit Court of Appeals, to take Kennedy's place. Kavanaugh's hearings sparked controversy unseen since the nomination of Clarence Thomas in the 1990s. **Christine Blasey Ford**, a research psychologist and professor, claimed that Kavanaugh had sexually assaulted her at a party when the two were in high school. Kavanaugh denied the accusation, but other women came forward with stories of inappropriate and nonconsensual sexual behavior. After a brief FBI investigation, the Republican-majority Senate narrowly confirmed Kavanaugh.

Kavanaugh's arrival on the Court sparked a revolution in conservative legislatures. For the most part, even after the Tea Party swept into power in 2011, antiabortion lawmakers had followed the playbook used by groups like National Right to Life Committee and Americans United for Life, chipping away at *Roe* and passing incremental laws. But with Kavanaugh on the bench, it seemed possible that the Court would reverse *Roe* outright.

A growing number of states looked to a model forged by antiabortion activist **Janet Folger Porter**. Porter had been a member of an Ohio affiliate of NRLC before working in the Religious Right to oppose civil-rights legislation for gays and lesbians. In 2011, she had proposed a new strategy to reverse *Roe*: laws that banned abortion when a doctor could detect a fetal heartbeat or fetal cardiac activity—usually, somewhere between the sixth and eighth week of pregnancy.

Porter and her allies zeroed in on viability as a point of attack. *Casey* had retained viability as the point at which states could criminalize abortion outright. Porter suggested that the Supreme Court may find the heartbeat to be an attractive alternative—one that was scientifically "certain" and emotionally resonant.

At first, few states had acted on her idea. Following the elevation of Kavanaugh to the Court, that changed. In 2019, states began passing heartbeat bills in rapid succession. Most did not make exceptions for abortion in cases of rape and incest. Georgia's law also recognized fetal personhood when a heartbeat could be detected—and not just for the purpose of abortion [**Doc. 16**]. Alabama's law prohibited abortion from the moment of fertilization. With Kavanaugh on the Court, antiabortion legislatures believed that such sweeping laws might be upheld [**Doc. 17**].

The political calculus had also changed for Republican lawmakers. The spread of conservative media—by the 2010s the primary source of information for many right-leaning voters—meant that purist, even extremist, candidates often fared better in primaries than their establishment counterparts. **Gerrymandering**—the manipulation of election districts—had created more polarized districts that rewarded candidates who ran further to the right or left. Trump won in 2016 primarily by energizing and turning out supporters rather than appealing to voters in the middle. More Republican lawmakers believed they could hold on to office by exciting right-to-lifers in their base, regardless of what a majority of voters thought. And negative partisanship—hostility to people in the opposing political party—made Republican voters unwilling to vote for a Democrat even if they disapproved of steps taken by GOP lawmakers.

The new restrictions forced a new examination of what counted as an abortion in the first place. If *Roe* were overturned and laws like Alabama's went into effect, would they cover some forms of contraception? Those seeking fertility treatment raised similar questions. By 2018, a third of Americans had either had a fertility treatment or knew someone who had. But fertility treatments like **in vitro fertilization** (IVF) had relatively low success rates. Doctors often implanted multiple embryos and then terminated some pregnancies to maximize the chances of a successful pregnancy. Some worried that in a post-*Roe* world, antiabortion laws would make IVF far less effective.

The summer of 2020 offered the first look at what the new conservative majority would do to abortion law in the United States. The Court agreed to hear a challenge to a Louisiana law identical to the one recently struck down in *Whole Woman's Health*, a measure requiring hospitals to have admitting privileges at a nearby hospital. Louisiana lawmakers insisted that the reality in their state differed from the one the Court had evaluated in Texas: it was, the state claimed, far easier for abortion providers to get admitting privileges in Louisiana than Texas—and that these privileges conferred more tangible benefits on patients than had been the case in *Whole Woman's Health*.

Louisiana also raised an argument of its own, claiming that abortion providers should not be able sue on their patients' behalf. For the most part, the Supreme Court required people to vindicate their own rights, but the law made exceptions for certain third parties—those whose interests were closely aligned with the rights-holder—and those who could act when the rights-holder was not in a good position to protect her own interests. In 1976, in *Singleton v. Wulff*, the Court reasoned that abortion providers could represent their patients' interests. The Court stressed the confidentiality and closeness of the doctor–patient relationship. Moreover, the Court reasoned that pregnant people could not easily sue under their own names without risking stigma or worse. Besides, because pregnancy lasted only so long, cases could quickly become moot.

In ***June Medical Services v. Russo***, Louisiana framed this analysis as fundamentally flawed. The state suggested that abortion providers and patients had diametrically opposed interests when it came to safety regulations: whereas patients would want safer working conditions, doctors wanted less oversight and easier money.

The Court disappointed abortion foes when the justices voted five to four to invalidate Louisiana's law. Writing for four colleagues, Justice Stephen Breyer stressed that Louisiana's law provided patients with no benefits, all while making it difficult to access abortion in the state. John Roberts agreed that Louisiana's statute was unconstitutional but did not join Breyer's opinion and wrote one of his own—arguably the one that represented the law of the case. Roberts stressed the importance of precedent—*June Medical* and *Whole Woman's Health* dealt with exactly the same law. But Roberts believed that the plurality fundamentally misunderstood what the undue burden test was about. He concluded that there should be no balancing test and that the benefits of a law were irrelevant. If Roberts' understanding of the undue burden test prevailed, many more abortion restrictions would be constitutional.

In 2020, however, fewer people cared as much about what Roberts thought. Months before the 2020 presidential election, Ruth Bader Ginsburg died of cancer. Despite his earlier position on not confirming Supreme Court justices right before an election, Mitch McConnell rushed through the judge Trump picked to succeed Ginsburg, **Amy Coney Barrett**, who had served a brief time as an appellate judge after teaching law at Notre Dame. Unlike her predecessors, Barrett had personal (and seemingly profound) pro-life beliefs. The Senate quickly confirmed her, and many saw Barrett as the Court's sixth conservative justice.

Barrett's confirmation came at the height of a global pandemic sparked by the spread of coronavirus (COVID-19), a dangerous respiratory infection that quickly overwhelmed many health care systems. When some states implemented stay-at-home orders, governors designated abortion to be unessential and effectively barred access to it. Because it spread primarily through face-to-face contact, the pandemic prompted new interest in telehealth abortion. Some states responded by tightening limits on medication abortion. Led by the American College of Obstetricians and Gynecologists, physicians challenged the constitutionality of the FDA's requirement that physicians be physically present when a patient received abortion medication.

States forged ahead with ambitious abortion restrictions with the expectation that the Supreme Court would uphold them. Heartbeat bills, which had once made international headlines, came to seem anodyne. Texas introduced a unique version of the law that outsourced enforcement to private citizens, who could sue any doctor who performed an abortion after the detection of a fetal heartbeat, even if the person suing had no individual connection to the case.

Even after Donald Trump lost his bid for reelection (and failed in numerous attempts to get the courts or state legislatures to overturn the result), it seemed likely that *Roe* would soon be overturned. Trump alleged that massive election fraud in several key swing states had led to his defeat. He brought lawsuits, pressured state legislators to set aside the results, and urged members of Congress not to certify the election. All of these efforts came up short, but few right-to-lifers distanced themselves from Trump. He seemed to have forged a bullet-proof Supreme Court majority ready to reverse *Roe*.

A district court had blocked the FDA's in-person requirement, but in 2021 the Court voted to reinstate it. The Court was also considering whether to hear Mississippi's appeal in a major abortion case, *Dobbs v. Jackson Women's Health Center*, which involved a ban on abortion at 15 weeks. Like other states, Mississippi claimed its law banned abortion at the point that fetal pain was possible (most so-called pain-capable bills kicked in at 20 weeks rather than 15).The lower courts had all invalidated Mississippi's law because it banned abortions before viability; *Roe* and *Casey* allowed for states to ban abortion only when survival was possible outside the womb. Mississippi argued that the viability standard made no sense; it had received criticism from bioethicists and philosophers and seemed to be in constant flux as medical technology improved.

The Supreme Court sat on its hands before finally agreeing to hear *Dobbs* in the spring of 2021. The justices seemed poised to deal *Roe* a major blow. To uphold the law, as the Court was expected to do, the justices would have to either dismantle the viability standard or reverse *Roe* outright (a 15-week ban took effect a full 9 weeks before viability).

Nevertheless, whatever happened next with *Dobbs*, the abortion conflict seemed unlikely to end even if *Roe* were gone. Since the 1960s, abortion foes had defended the idea of a right to life that would require the outlawing of all abortions. Antiabortion leaders planned to wage battles in all 50 states to ensure that abortion was illegal. Others hoped that the conservative Supreme Court would decide to treat the fetus or unborn child as a rights-holding person and thereby criminalize all abortions. For right-to-lifers, reversing *Roe* would be only the beginning of a larger struggle.

Abortion-rights supporters were hardly going to give up if *Roe* were gone. Pro-choice leaders discussed the idea of a federal statute protecting abortion rights or prohibiting certain abortion restrictions. With *Roe* still on the books, Democrats could not find enough votes to pass such a bill, and if it passed some feared that the conservative Court would strike it down. But if the Court reversed *Roe*, the campaign for a federal bill would gain momentum. The same was true of the idea of adding justices to the Court. Progressive states strategized about how best to expand abortion access.

Of course, reversing *Roe* would at most mean that legislators would have a choice about whether to criminalize abortion. Battles would continue to reshape the Supreme Court and dictate policy in the states.

*Roe v. Wade* had preoccupied many in the abortion debate for some time, but the debate had moved well beyond it. Just the same, the decades after *Roe* offered powerful lessons about the intractability of the abortion conflict. All those years ago, Harry Blackmun had believed that the Supreme Court could help heal the nation's deep wounds when it came to abortion, but in the decades that followed many believed that the Court had made it worse. Of course, the problems did not begin and end with the justices. Party realignment, the spread of new contraceptive technology, negative partisanship, the politicization of science—all of these things deepened the nation's divide about abortion.

Abortion foes hungered so much for a win in *Roe* that they seemed to forget the greatest lessons of the past half century. Legal conflicts about abortion ran deep. *Roe v. Wade* had not launched the abortion wars in the United States, and reversing *Roe* would not bring them to an end.

# Part III

# Assessment

# 7 An abortion debate without end

For those outside the United States, the intractability of the abortion debate seems puzzling and uniquely American, and *Roe* is at the center of it all. As movements to legalize and criminalize abortion sprang up in other nations, *Roe* served as a touchstone for debate; high courts mentioned *Roe* in sketching the contours of their own constitutional abortion jurisprudence.

Because so much attention focused on *Roe*, it is easy for some to believe that its reversal will deescalate the abortion conflict. Republicans could no longer use *Roe* as a fundraising tool; perhaps single-issue voters would make decisions based on a wider variety of factors.

*Roe* certainly was significant. The decision produced a legal outcome that might not have been possible through democratic means, at least in the short term. The decision rewrote the nation's abortion laws; what had been a country where abortion was unavailable, heavily restricted, or outright criminal became a place where the procedure was legal in every state.

Scholars once argued that *Roe* created the antiabortion movement and the Religious Right. Surely, this is an exaggeration. *Roe* was a major rallying point for Christian conservatives but hardly the primary reason for their mobilization; other issues, from a constitutional Equal Rights Amendment to the rise of a movement for gay and lesbian rights, were just as crucial, as were the plans of New Right activists. The antiabortion movement was active well before *Roe* and did not change its principles or priorities after the decision.

But *Roe did* change the antiabortion movement. Having previously flourished as a flexible, state-by-state confederacy of organizations, the movement orchestrated a more coordinated national campaign against the idea of abortion rights after 1973. *Roe* did not guarantee any party alignment on abortion or even that abortion would become a major election issue. But by reaching a solution that appeared nationwide, the decision inspired both antiabortion and abortion-rights leaders to try harder to gain influence in national politics.

*Roe* also popularized the idea that the decision to have an abortion was a fundamental right. After the decision came down, the abortion-rights movement prioritized its defense over any other objective, at times giving short shrift to issues that primarily affected low-income people of color.

DOI: 10.4324/9781003215936-11

Because *Roe* described abortion as a matter of privacy and choice, related arguments gained far more attention (and in popular battles, sometimes displaced potentially promising arguments about equality or social justice).

But *Roe* alone explains only a small part of the US abortion wars. For decades, *Roe* did not represent the governing law on abortion; the *Casey* decision rejected a trimester framework in favor of an undue burden test that would dictate the result in abortion cases for decades.

Nor were many of the cultural changes around abortion attributable to *Roe*. Political party alignment around abortion that ratcheted up the conflict occurred the better part of a decade after the Court's decision and for reasons well beyond it. For Republicans, there was the rise of the New Right, the molding of evangelical Protestants into a political force, and the desire of Ronald Reagan to pick apart a coalition of New Deal voters. For Democrats, the growing influence of feminists and people of color changed the political calculus, as did the mainstreaming of the women's movement.

The terms of debate changed for reasons beyond political party realignment. The growing use of ultrasound and the spread of fetal images gave abortion foes a powerful new way of advocating their cause. Right-to-lifers recognized in the 1970s and 1980s that the Court would not recognize fetal rights soon and promoted laws intended to hollow out *Roe* and limit access. The more these laws became a priority, the more both sides focused on what abortion in America was really like, and areas of disagreement multiplied.

Broader cultural conflicts about deference to science—about who counted as an expert and whether public health or elite scientific institutions had been politicized—shaped the abortion battle, as clashing groups put forth their own experts and evidence. The growing influence of white evangelical Protestants in the GOP—and the embrace of a specific vision of America as a Christian nation—also made a difference. So did growing anxiety about the perceived secularization of the United States, together with conservative Christians' worries about same-sex marriage or birth control.

We think that *Roe* has mattered so much in part because so many players in the abortion wars have made it a symbol of other things. There is no reason to think that these symbolic meanings will lose power—or that *Roe* will cease to be a rallying cry—no matter what the Court says or does.

Conversely, it seems far-fetched to believe that reversing *Roe* will deescalate the conflict because the abortion wars have always reached well beyond it. Right-to-lifers will not be content with anything but the recognition of fetal personhood; pro-choice forces will not give up on reshaping the Court or enacting a broad reproductive justice agenda. Conflicts over abortion and contraception have already raged for hundreds of years in the United States, and they will not be stopping any time soon.

# Part IV

# Documents

## Document 1. Horatio Storer, *On Criminal Abortion in America* (1860)

*Storer, a leader of the American Medical Association, led a campaign to criminalize most abortions, including those performed early in pregnancy.*

. . . Too much zeal cannot be shown by physicians in relieving themselves from the weight of responsibility they may have incurred by innocently causing the increased destruction of human life. Let it not be supposed by the public that there is among us, either in theory or practice, any disregard of the unborn child. If such impression have already obtained, from our own negligence, the falsehoods of irregular practitioners, or otherwise, it should at once be removed. Fœtal life ever is, and ever has been, held sacred by all respectable physicians, and whenever criminal abortion has been known to have been advised, perpetrated or abetted by one claiming our honorable name, he has invariably and at once lost all professional standing.

We have seen that it is no trifling matter, this awful waste of human life. It is a subject that demands the best efforts of the whole profession as a body and as men. The crime, no longer practiced in secret, must be met boldly; and met with unanimity, it will be met successfully.

*Source*: Horatio Storer, *On Criminal Abortion in America* (Philadelphia: J.B. Lippincott & Co., 1860), 105.

## Document 2. Birth Control Review, November 1918

*Margaret Sanger's Birth Control Review portrayed women denied access to birth control as prisoners of "unwanted babies."*

*Source:* Wikimedia Commons, Birth Control Review, https://upload.wikimedia.org/wikipedia/commons/5/53/Birth_Con_Rev_1918.jpg, accessed August 30, 2021

DOI: 10.4324/9781003215936-13

## Document 3. *Buck v. Bell*, 274 U.S. 200, May 2, 1927

*In this notorious decision, the Supreme Court upheld laws compelling the sterilization of people deemed to be genetically unfit.*

. . . Carrie Buck is a feeble minded white woman who was committed to the State Colony above mentioned in due form. She is the daughter of a feeble minded mother in the same institution, and the mother of an illegitimate feeble minded child. She was eighteen years old at the time of the trial of her case in the Circuit Court, in the latter part of 1924. An Act of Virginia, approved March 20, 1924, recites that the health of the patient and the welfare of society may be promoted in certain cases by the sterilization of mental defectives . . .

The attack is not upon the procedure, but upon the substantive law. It seems to be contended that in no circumstances could such an order be justified. It certainly is contended that the order cannot be justified upon the existing grounds. The judgment finds the facts that have been recited, and that Carrie Buck "is the probable potential parent of socially inadequate offspring, likewise afflicted, that she may be sexually sterilized without detriment to her general health, and that her welfare and that of society will be promoted by her sterilization," and thereupon makes the order.

. . . We have seen more than once that the public welfare may call upon the best citizens for their lives. It would be strange if it could not call upon those who already sap the strength of the State for these lesser sacrifices, often not felt to be such by those concerned, in order to prevent our being swamped with incompetence. It is better for all the world if, instead of waiting to execute degenerate offspring for crime or to let them starve for their imbecility, society can prevent those who are manifestly unfit from continuing their kind. The principle that sustains compulsory vaccination is broad enough to cover cutting the Fallopian tubes. . . . Three generations of imbeciles are enough. . . .

*Source*: Cornell Law School Legal Information Institute, *Buck v. Bell*, https://www.law.cornell.edu/supremecourt/text/274/200, accessed August 30, 2021

## Document 4. *Griswold v. Connecticut*, 381 U.S.479 (1965)

*In this landmark decision, the Supreme Court held that the Constitution protects an implied right to privacy that covered married couples' right to use contraception.*

The statutes whose constitutionality is involved in this appeal are §§ 53–32 and 54–196 of the General Statutes of Connecticut (1958 rev.). The former provides:

> "Any person who uses any drug, medicinal article or instrument for the purpose of preventing conception shall be fined not less than fifty dollars or imprisoned not less than sixty days nor more than one year or be both fined and imprisoned."

Section 54–196 provides:

> "Any person who assists, abets, counsels, causes, hires or commands another to commit any offense may be prosecuted and punished as if he were the principal offender."

The appellants were found guilty as accessories and fined $100 each, against the claim that the accessory statute, as so applied, violated the Fourteenth Amendment. . . .

The association of people is not mentioned in the Constitution nor in the Bill of Rights. The right to educate a child in a school of the parents' choice—whether public or private or parochial—is also not mentioned. Nor is the right to study any particular subject or any foreign language. Yet the First Amendment has been construed to include certain of those rights. . . .

The foregoing cases suggest that specific guarantees in the Bill of Rights have penumbras, formed by emanations from those guarantees that help give them life and substance. Various guarantees create zones of privacy. The right of association contained in the penumbra of the First Amendment is one, as we have seen. The Third Amendment, in its prohibition against the quartering of soldiers "in any house" in time of peace without the consent of the owner, is another facet of that privacy. The Fourth Amendment explicitly affirms the "right of the people to be secure in their persons, houses, papers, and effects, against unreasonable searches and seizures." The Fifth Amendment, in its Self-Incrimination Clause, enables the citizen to create a zone of privacy which government may not force him to surrender to his detriment. The Ninth Amendment provides: "The enumeration in the Constitution, of certain rights, shall not be construed to deny or disparage others retained by the people."

. . . The present case, then, concerns a relationship lying within the zone of privacy created by several fundamental constitutional guarantees. And it concerns a law which, in forbidding the use of contraceptives, rather than regulating their manufacture or sale, seeks to achieve its goals by means having a maximum destructive impact upon that relationship. . . . Would we allow the police to search the sacred precincts of marital bedrooms for telltale signs of the use of contraceptives? The very idea is repulsive to the notions of privacy surrounding the marriage relationship.

We deal with a right of privacy older than the Bill of Rights—older than our political parties, older than our school system. Marriage is a coming together for better or for worse, hopefully enduring, and intimate to the degree of being sacred. It is an association that promotes a way of life, not causes; a harmony in living, not political faiths; a bilateral loyalty, not commercial or social projects. Yet it is an association for as noble a purpose as any involved in our prior decisions. . . .

*Source*: Cornell Law School Legal Information Institute, *Griswold v. Connecticut*, https://www.law.cornell.edu/supremecourt/text/381/479, accessed August 30, 2021

## Document 5. Hugh Moore, *The Population Bomb* (1954)

*Hugh Moore, a magnate and leading population controller, argued that without drastic new limits, the world's growing population would cause a surge in crime, international instability, and environmental degradation.*

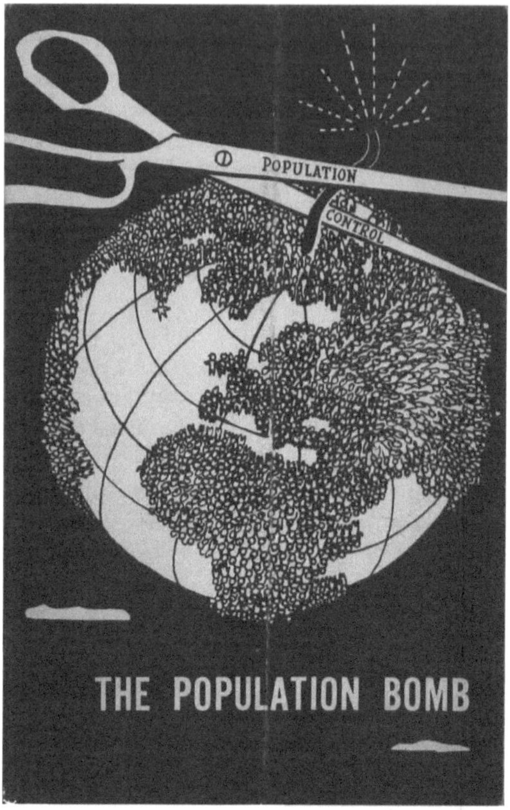


*Source*: Wikimedia Commons, *The Population Bomb*, https://commons.wikimedia.org/wiki/File:Population_Bomb_cover_1954_by_Hugh_Moore_Fund.png, accessed August 30, 2021

## Document 6. *Byrn v. New York Health and Hospitals Corporation*, 31 N.Y.2d 194 (N.Y. App. 1972)

*In this case, the New York courts temporarily recognized fetal personhood and named Robert Byrn, a law professor, to act as guardian ad litem for unborn children scheduled for abortion. New York's highest state court, the Court of Appeals, ultimately reversed this outcome in the below decision.*

. . . The issue, a novel one in the courts of law, is whether children in embryo are and must be recognized as legal persons or entities entitled under the State and Federal Constitutions to a right to life. It is not effectively contradicted, if it is contradicted at all, that modern biological disciplines accept that upon conception a fetus has an independent genetic "package" with the potential to become a full-fledged human being and that it has an autonomy of development and character although it is for the period of gestation dependent upon the mother. It is human, if only because it may not be characterized as not human, and it is unquestionably alive.

The issue has been debated below and in this court on two levels. The first level turns on the legal history of the concept of persons in the law and of the act of abortion. . . . The answer is clear enough. Unborn, and even unconceived, children have been recognized as acquiring rights or interests in narrow legal categories involving the inheritance or devolution of property . . . Fetuses, if they are born alive, have been entitled in modern times to recover in tort for injuries sustained through the host mother . . . Indeed, unconceived children have been represented in proceedings affecting property by guardians ad litem . . .

But unborn children have never been recognized as persons in the law in the whole sense. . . . As for abortion, when the act has been made criminal or otherwise unlawful in the law, the direct design was evidently to protect the mother from injury and dangerous practices (Means, The Phoenix of Abortional Freedom, 17 New York Law Forum 335). It has been argued, of course, that anti-abortion laws were also designed to protect the fetus; but the argument is hard to sustain so long as there have been provisions that limited unlawful abortions to pregnancies after "quickening" and abortions have been justified to protect the mother even though it meant destruction of the fetus.

In any event, the historical analysis is interesting, not determinative, and only of limited influence. . . .

The second level of debate is the real one, and that turns on whether a human entity, conceived but not yet born, is and must be recognized as a person in the law. If so, it is argued that the person is immediately subsumed under the class entitled to constitutional protection, it being assumed that an entity if treated anywhere in the law as a person must be so treated for all purposes. Issue is never really joined at this level because the antagonists are talking about different things although they use the same terminology. Conceptually, whether in philosophy or in religious doctrine, and the doctrine is not confined to any one religion, a conceived child may be regarded as a person, albeit at a fetal stage. It is not true, however, that the legal order necessarily corresponds to the natural order. . . .

Whether the law should accord legal personality is a policy question which in most instances devolves on the Legislature, subject again of course to the Constitution as it has been "legally" endered. That the legislative action may be wise or unwise, even unjust and violative of principles beyond the law, does not change the legal issue or how it is to be resolved. The point is that it is a policy determination whether legal personality should attach and not a question of biological or "natural" correspondence. . . .

Moreover, plaintiff of necessity occupies a less than completely consistent position. He agrees that abortion is justified to save the mother's life because it is one life for another. But that is not satisfactory. Necessity may justify in the law every kind of harm to save one's life, except to take the life of an innocent. Before the law one life is as good as another, saint or sinner, genius or imbecile, child or adult. Besides, if the contrary were true, should not the one to lose his life be entitled to notice and hearing through a guardian ad litem, as would be done with any child's property rights, born or unborn?

There are, then, real issues in this litigation, but they are not legal or justiciable. They are issues outside the law unless the Legislature should provide otherwise. The Constitution does not confer or require legal personality for the unborn; the Legislature may, or it may do something less, as it does in limited abortion statutes, and provide some protection far short of conferring legal personality.

Accordingly, the order of the Appellate Division should be affirmed without costs.

*Source*: Google Scholar, *Byrn v. New York City Health and Hospital Corporation*, https://scholar.google.com/scholar_case?case=12689090639378096121&q=byrn+v.+new+york&hl=en&as_sdt=40006, accessed August 30, 2021

## Document 7. Richard Nixon, Statement about policy on abortions at military bases in the United States, April 3, 1971

*In this speech, Nixon reversed his earlier, implicit support for some abortions and began using the abortion issue to peel away antiabortion voters from the Democratic coalition.*

HISTORICALLY, laws regulating abortion in the United States have been the province of States, not the Federal Government. That remains the situation today, as one State after another takes up this question, debates it, and decides it. That is where the decisions should be made.

Partly for that reason, I have directed that the policy on abortions at American military bases in the United States be made to correspond with the laws of the States where those bases are located. If the laws in a particular State restrict abortions, the rules at the military base hospitals are to correspond to that law.

The effect of this directive is to reverse service regulations issued last summer, which had liberalized the rules on abortions at military hospitals. The new ruling supersedes this—and has been put into effect by the Secretary of Defense.

But while this matter is being debated in State capitals and weighed by various courts, the country has a right to know my personal views.

From personal and religious beliefs I consider abortion an unacceptable form of population control. Further, unrestricted abortion policies, or abortion on demand, I cannot square with my personal belief in the sanctity of human life—including the life of the yet unborn. For, surely, the unborn have rights also, recognized in law, recognized even in principles expounded by the United Nations.

Ours is a nation with a Judeo-Christian heritage. It is also a nation with serious social problems—problems of malnutrition, of broken homes, of poverty, and of delinquency. But none of these problems justifies such a solution.

A good and generous people will not opt, in my view, for this kind of alternative to its social dilemmas. Rather, it will open its hearts and homes to the unwanted children of its own, as it has done for the unwanted millions of other lands.

*Source*: University of California Santa Barbara, The Presidency Project, https://www.presidency.ucsb.edu/documents/statement-about-policy-abortions-military-base-hospitals-the-united-states, accessed August 30, 2021

## Document 8. *United States v. Vuitch*, 402 U.S. 62, April 21, 1971

*In this case, the Supreme Court upheld an antiabortion ordinance from Washington, DC, but defined a quite broad category of abortions that could be justified on the basis of health.* Vuitch *sparked considerable debate about what the Court would do next about abortion.*

Appellee Milan Vuitch was indicted for producing and attempting to produce abortions in violation of D. C. Code Ann. § 22–201. That Act provides in part:

> "Whoever, by means of any instrument, medicine, drug or other means whatever, procures or produces, or attempts to procure or produce an abortion or miscarriage on any woman, unless the same were done as necessary for the preservation of the mother's life or health and under the direction of a competent licensed practitioner of medicine, shall be imprisoned in the penitentiary not less than one year or not more than ten years . . ."

Without waiting for trial, the District Judge dismissed the indictments on the ground that the abortion statute was unconstitutionally vague. . . .

. . . The trial court apparently felt that the term was vague because there "is no indication whether it includes varying degrees of mental as well as physical health." . . . It is true that the legislative history of the statute gives no guidance as to whether "health" refers to both a patient's mental and physical state. The term "health" was introduced into the law in 1901 when the statute was enacted in substantially its present form. The House Report on the bill contains no discussion of the term "health" and there was no Senate report. Nor have we found any District of Columbia cases prior to this District Court decision that shed any light on the question. Since that decision, however, the issue has been considered in *Doe* v. *General Hospital of the District of Columbia*, 313 F. Supp. 1170 (DC 1970). There District Judge Waddy construed the statute to permit abortions "for mental health reasons whether or not the patient had a previous history of mental defects."

. . . We see no reason why this interpretation of the statute should not be followed. Certainly this construction accords with the general usage and modern understanding of the word "health," which includes psychological as well as physical well-being. Indeed *Webster's Dictionary*, in accord with that common usage, properly defines health as the "[s]tate of being . . . sound in body [or] mind." Viewed in this light, the term "health" presents no problem of vagueness. Indeed, whether a particular operation is necessary for a patient's physical or mental health is a judgment that physicians are obviously called upon to make routinely whenever surgery is considered.

We therefore hold that properly construed the District of Columbia abortion law is not unconstitutionally vague, and that the trial court erred in dismissing the indictments on that ground. Appellee has suggested that there are other reasons why the dismissal of the indictments should be affirmed. Essentially, these arguments are based on this Court's decision in *Griswold v. Connecticut*, 381 U. S. 479 (1965). Although there was some reference to these arguments in the opinion of the court below, we read it as holding simply that the statute was void for vagueness. . . . Since that question of vagueness was the only issue passed upon by the District Court it is the only issue we reach here. . . .

*Source*: Google Scholar, *United States v. Vuitch*, https://scholar.google.com/scholar_case?case=10998638112293258776&hl=en&as_sdt=6&as_vis=1&oi=scholarr, accessed August 30, 2021

## Document 9. *Eisenstadt v. Baird*, 405 U.S. 438, March 22, 1972

*In this decision, the Supreme Court extended the right to use birth control to all individuals.*

MR. JUSTICE BRENNAN delivered the opinion of the Court.

Appellee William Baird was convicted at a bench trial in the Massachusetts Superior Court under Massachusetts General Laws Ann., c. 272, § 21, first, for exhibiting contraceptive articles in the course of delivering a lecture on contraception to a group of students at Boston University and, second, for giving a young woman a package of Emko vaginal foam at the close of his address.

. . . Massachusetts General Laws Ann., c. 272, § 21, under which Baird was convicted, provides a maximum five-year term of imprisonment for "whoever . . . gives away . . . any drug, medicine, instrument or article whatever for the prevention of conception," except as authorized in § 21A. . . . The statutory scheme distinguishes among three distinct classes of distributees—*first*, married persons may obtain contraceptives to prevent pregnancy, but only from doctors or druggists on prescription; *second*, single persons may not obtain contraceptives from anyone to prevent pregnancy; and, *third*, married or single persons may obtain contraceptives from anyone to prevent, not pregnancy, but the spread of disease. . . .

The basic principles governing application of the Equal Protection Clause of the Fourteenth Amendment are familiar. . . . A classification "must be reasonable, not arbitrary, and must rest upon some ground of difference having a fair and substantial relation to the object of the legislation, so that all persons similarly circumstanced shall be treated alike." . . .

It would be plainly unreasonable to assume that Massachusetts has prescribed pregnancy and the birth of an unwanted child as punishment for fornication, which is a misdemeanor under Massachusetts General Laws Ann., c. 272, § 18. Aside from the scheme of values that assumption would attribute to the State, it is abundantly clear that the effect of the ban on distribution of contraceptives to unmarried persons has at best a marginal relation to the proffered objective.

. . . Even conceding the legislature a full measure of discretion in fashioning means to prevent fornication, and recognizing that the State may seek to deter prohibited conduct by punishing more severely those who facilitate than those who actually engage in its commission, we, like the Court of Appeals, cannot believe that in this instance Massachusetts has chosen to expose the aider and abetter who simply *gives away* a contraceptive to *20* times the *90-day* sentence of the offender himself. The very terms of the State's criminal statutes, coupled with the *de minimis* effect of §§ 21 and 21A in deterring fornication, thus compel the conclusion that such deterrence cannot reasonably be taken as the purpose of the ban on distribution of contraceptives to unmarried persons.

*Second.* Section 21A was added to the Massachusetts General Laws by Stat. 1966, c. 265, § 1. The Supreme Judicial Court . . . held that the purpose of the amendment was to serve the health needs of the community by regulating the distribution of potentially harmful articles. . . . If health were the rationale of § 21A, the statute would be both discriminatory and overbroad. . . . [I]t would not only invidiously discriminate against the unmarried, but also be overbroad with respect to the married. . . .

*Third.* If the Massachusetts statute cannot be upheld as a deterrent to fornication or as a health measure, may it, nevertheless, be sustained simply as a prohibition on contraception? . . .

If under *Griswold* the distribution of contraceptives to married persons cannot be prohibited, a ban on distribution to unmarried persons would be equally impermissible. It is true that in *Griswold* the right of privacy in question inhered in the marital relationship. Yet the marital couple is not an independent entity with a mind and heart of its own, but an association of two individuals each with a separate intellectual and emotional makeup.

If the right of privacy means anything, it is the right of the *individual,* married or single, to be free from unwarranted governmental intrusion into matters so fundamentally affecting a person as the decision whether to bear or beget a child. . . .

*Source*: Google Scholar, *Eisenstadt v. Baird*, https://scholar.google.com/scholar_case?case=14131534241682283357&q=eisenstadt+v+baird&hl=en&as_sdt=40006, accessed August 30, 2021.

## Document 10. *Roe v. Wade*, 410 U.S. 113, January 22, 1973

*In this blockbuster opinion, the Supreme Court recognized a right to choose abortion.*

Mr. Justice BLACKMUN delivered the opinion of the Court.

This Texas federal appeal and its Georgia companion, *Doe v. Bolton*, . . . present constitutional challenges to state criminal abortion legislation. The Texas statutes under attack here are typical of those that have been in effect in many States for approximately a century. The Georgia statutes, in contrast, have a modern cast and are a legislative product that, to an extent at least, obviously reflects the influences of recent attitudinal change, of advancing medical knowledge and techniques, and of new thinking about an old issue.

We forthwith acknowledge our awareness of the sensitive and emotional nature of the abortion controversy, of the vigorous opposing views, even among physicians, and of the deep and seemingly absolute convictions that the subject inspires. One's philosophy, one's experiences, one's exposure to the raw edges of human existence, one's religious training, one's attitudes toward life and family and their values, and the moral standards one establishes and seeks to observe, are all likely to influence and to color one's thinking and conclusions about abortion.

In addition, population growth, pollution, poverty, and racial overtones tend to complicate and not to simplify the problem.

Our task, of course, is to resolve the issue by constitutional measurement, free of emotion and of predilection. We seek earnestly to do this, and, because we do, we have inquired into, and in this opinion place some emphasis upon, medical and medical-legal history and what that history reveals about man's attitudes toward the abortion procedure over the centuries. . . .

It perhaps is not generally appreciated that the restrictive criminal abortion laws in effect in a majority of States today are of relatively recent vintage. Those laws, generally proscribing abortion or its attempt at any time during pregnancy except when necessary to preserve the pregnant woman's life, are not of ancient or even of common-law origin. Instead, they derive from statutory changes effected, for the most part, in the latter half of the 19th century.

1. Ancient attitudes. These are not capable of precise determination. We are told that at the time of the Persian Empire abortifacients were known and that criminal abortions were severely punished. We are also told, however, that abortion was practiced in Greek times as well as in the Roman Era, and that "it was resorted to without scruple." . . . Ancient religion did not bar abortion.
2. The Hippocratic Oath. What then of the famous Oath that has stood so long as the ethical guide of the medical profession and that bears the name of the great Greek (460(?)–377(?) B.C.), who has been described as the Father of Medicine, the "wisest and the greatest practitioner of his art," and the "most important and most complete medical personality of antiquity," who dominated the medical schools of his time, and who typified the sum of the medical knowledge of the past? The Oath varies somewhat according to the particular translation, but in any translation the content is clear: "I will give no deadly medicine to anyone if asked, nor suggest any such counsel; and in like manner I will not give to a woman a pessary to produce abortion," or "I will neither give a deadly drug to anybody if asked for it, nor will I make a suggestion to this effect. Similarly, I will not give to a woman an abortive remedy."

   . . . The Oath was not uncontested even in Hippocrates' day; only the Pythagorean school of philosophers frowned upon the related act of suicide. Most Greek thinkers, on the other hand, commended abortion, at least prior to viability. . . .

   Dr. Edelstein then concludes that the Oath originated in a group representing only a small segment of Greek opinion and that it certainly was not accepted by all ancient physicians. He points out that medical writings down to Galen (A.D. 130–200) "give evidence of the violation of almost every one of its injunctions." But with the end of antiquity a decided change took place. Resistance against suicide and against abortion became common. The Oath came to be popular. The emerging teachings of Christianity were in agreement with the Pythagorean ethic. The Oath "became the nucleus of all medical ethics" and "was applauded as the embodiment of truth." Thus, suggests Dr. Edelstein, it is "a Pythagorean manifesto and not the expression of an absolute standard of medical conduct."

   This, it seems to us, is a satisfactory and acceptable explanation of the Hippocratic Oath's apparent rigidity. It enables us to understand, in historical context, a long-accepted and reversed statement of medical ethics.
3. The common law. It is undisputed that at common law, abortion performed before "quickening"—the first recognizable movement of the fetus in utero, appearing usually from the 16th to the 18th week of pregnancy was not an indictable offense. The absence of a common-law crime for pre-quickening abortion appears to have developed from a confluence of earlier philosophical, theological, and civil and canon law concepts of when life begins. These disciplines variously approached the question in terms of the point at which the embryo or fetus became

"formed" or recognizably human, or in terms of when a "person" came into being, that is, infused with a "soul" or "animated." A loose consensus evolved in early English law that these events occurred at some point between conception and live birth. . . .

5. The American law. . . . By 1840, when Texas had received the common law, only eight American States had statutes dealing with abortion. It was not until after the War Between the States that legislation began generally to replace the common law. Most of these initial statutes dealt severely with abortion after quickening but were lenient with it before quickening. . . .

   Gradually, in the middle and late 19th century the quickening distinction disappeared from the statutory law of most States and the degree of the offense and the penalties were increased. By the end of the 1950's a large majority of the jurisdictions banned abortion, however and whenever performed, unless done to save or preserve the life of the mother. . . . In the past several years, however, a trend toward liberalization of abortion statutes has resulted in adoption, by about one-third of the States, of less stringent laws, most of them patterned after the ALI Model Penal Code, § 230. . . .

6. The position of the American Medical Association. The anti-abortion mood prevalent in this country in the late 19th century was shared by the medical profession. Indeed, the attitude of the profession may have played a significant role in the enactment of stringent criminal abortion legislation during that period.

. . . Except for periodic condemnation of the criminal abortionist, no further formal AMA action took place until 1967. In that year, the Committee on Human Reproduction urged the adoption of a stated policy of opposition to induced abortion, except when there is "documented medical evidence" of a threat to the health or life of the mother, or that the child "may be born with incapacitating physical deformity or mental deficiency," or that a pregnancy "resulting from legally established statutory or forcible rape or incest may constitute a threat to the mental or physical health of the patient," two other physicians "chosen because of their recognized professional competency have examined the patient and have concurred in writing," and the procedure "is performed in a hospital accredited by the Joint Commission on Accreditation of Hospitals."

. . . On June 25, 1970, the House of Delegates adopted preambles and most of the resolutions proposed by the reference committee. The preambles emphasized "the best interests of the patient," "sound clinical judgment," and "informed patient consent," in contrast to "mere acquiescence to the patient's demand."

. . . Three reasons have been advanced to explain historically the enactment of criminal abortion laws in the 19th century and to justify their continued existence.

It has been argued occasionally that these laws were the product of a Victorian social concern to discourage illicit sexual conduct. Texas, however, does not advance this justification in the present case, and it appears that no court or commentator has taken the argument seriously. . . .

A second reason is concerned with abortion as a medical procedure. When most criminal abortion laws were first enacted, the procedure was a hazardous one for the woman. This was particularly true prior to the development of antisepsis. . . .

Modern medical techniques have altered this situation. Appellants and various amici refer to medical data indicating that abortion in early pregnancy, that is, prior to the end of the first trimester, although not without its risk, is now relatively safe. . . . Moreover, the risk to the woman increases as her pregnancy continues. Thus, the State retains a definite interest in protecting the woman's own health and safety when an abortion is proposed at a late stage of pregnancy,

. . . The third reason is the State's interest-some phrase it in terms of duty-in protecting prenatal life. . . .

The Constitution does not explicitly mention any right of privacy. In a line of decisions, however, . . . the Court has recognized that a right of personal privacy, or a guarantee of certain areas or zones of privacy, does exist under the Constitution . . .

This right of privacy, whether it be founded in the Fourteenth Amendment's concept of personal liberty and restrictions upon state action, as we feel it is, or, as the District Court determined, in the Ninth Amendment's reservation of rights to the people, is broad enough to encompass a woman's decision whether or not to terminate her pregnancy. The detriment that the State would impose upon the pregnant woman by denying this choice altogether is apparent. Specific and direct harm medically diagnosable even in early pregnancy may be involved. Maternity, or additional offspring, may force upon the woman a distressful life and future. Psychological harm may be imminent. Mental and physical health may be taxed by childcare. There is also the distress, for all concerned, associated with the unwanted child, and there is the problem of bringing a child into a family already unable, psychologically and otherwise, to care for it. In other cases, as in this one, the additional difficulties and continuing stigma of unwed motherhood may be involved. All these are factors the woman and her responsible physician necessarily will consider in consultation.

On the basis of elements such as these, appellant and some amici argue that the woman's right is absolute and that she is entitled to terminate her pregnancy at whatever time, in whatever way, and for whatever reason she alone chooses. With this we do not agree. Appellant's arguments that Texas either has no valid interest at all in regulating the abortion decision, or no interest strong enough to support any limitation upon the woman's sole determination, are unpersuasive. The Court's decisions recognizing a right of privacy also acknowledge that some state regulation in areas protected by that right is appropriate. As noted above, a State may properly assert important interests in safeguarding health, in maintaining medical standards, and in protecting potential life. At some point in pregnancy, these respective interests become sufficiently compelling to sustain regulation of the factors that govern the abortion decision. The privacy right involved, therefore, cannot be said to be absolute. In fact, it is not clear to us that the claim asserted by some amici that one has an unlimited right to do with one's body as one pleases bears a close relationship to the right of privacy previously articulated in the Court's decisions. . . .

The appellee and certain amici argue that the fetus is a "person" within the language and meaning of the Fourteenth Amendment. In support of this, they outline at length and in detail the well-known facts of fetal development. If this suggestion of personhood is established, the appellant's case, of course, collapses, for the fetus' right to life would then be guaranteed specifically by the Amendment. The appellant conceded as much on reargument. On the other hand, the appellee conceded on reargument that no case could be cited that holds that a fetus is a person within the meaning of the Fourteenth Amendment.

The Constitution does not define "person" in so many words. Section 1 of the Fourteenth Amendment contains three references to "person." The first, in defining "citizens," speaks of "persons born or naturalized in the United States." The word also appears both in the Due Process Clause and in the Equal Protection Clause. "Person" is used in other places in the Constitution: in the listing of qualifications for Representatives and Senators, Art, I, § 2, cl. 2, and § 3, cl. 3; in the Apportionment Clause, Art. I, § 2, cl. 3; in the Migration and Importation provision, Art. I, § 9, cl. 1; in the Emoluments Clause, Art, I, § 9, cl. 8; in the Electors provisions, Art. II, § 1, cl. 2, and the superseded cl. 3; in the provision outlining qualifications for the office of President, Art. II, § 1, cl. 5; in the Extradition provisions, Art. IV, § 2, cl. 2, and the superseded Fugitive Slave Clause 3; and in the Fifth, Twelfth, and Twenty-second Amendments, as well as in §§ 2 and 3 of the Fourteenth Amendment. But in nearly all these instances, the use of the word is such that it has application only postnatally. None indicates, with any assurance, that it has any possible prenatal application.

All this, together with our observation, supra, that throughout the major portion of the 19th century prevailing legal abortion practices were far freer than they are today, persuades us that the word "person," as used in the Fourteenth Amendment, does not include the unborn.

. . . Texas urges that, apart from the Fourteenth Amendment, life begins at conception and is present throughout pregnancy, and that, therefore, the State has a compelling interest in protecting that life from and after conception. We need not resolve the difficult question of when life begins. When those trained in the respective disciplines of medicine, philosophy, and theology are unable to arrive at any consensus, the judiciary, at this point in the development of man's knowledge, is not in a position to speculate as to the answer.

It should be sufficient to note briefly the wide divergence of thinking on this most sensitive and difficult question. There has always been strong support for the view that life does not begin until live birth. This was the belief of the Stoics. It appears to be the predominant, though not the unanimous, attitude of the Jewish faith. It may be taken to represent also the position of a large segment of the Protestant community, insofar as that can be ascertained; organized groups that have taken a formal position on the abortion issue have generally regarded abortion as a matter for the conscience of the individual and her family. As we have noted, the common law found greater significance in quickening. Physicians and their scientific colleagues have regarded that event with less interest and have tended to focus either upon conception, upon live birth, or upon the interim point at which the fetus becomes "viable," that is, potentially able to live outside the mother's womb, albeit with artificial aid. Viability is usually placed at about seven months (28 weeks) but may occur earlier, even at 24 weeks. The Aristotelian theory of "mediate animation," that held sway throughout the Middle Ages and the Renaissance in Europe, continued to be official Roman Catholic dogma until the 19th century, despite opposition to this "ensoulment" theory from those in the Church who would recognize the existence of life from the moment of conception. The latter is now, of course, the official belief of the Catholic Church. As one brief amicus discloses, this is a view strongly held by many non-Catholics as well, and by many physicians. Substantial problems for precise definition of this view are posed, however, by new embryological data that purport to indicate that conception is a "process" over time, rather than an event, and by new medical techniques such as menstrual extraction, the "morning-after" pill, implantation of embryos, artificial insemination, and even artificial wombs.

In areas other than criminal abortion, the law has been reluctant to endorse any theory that life, as we recognize it, begins before life birth or to accord legal rights to the unborn except in narrowly defined situations and except when the rights are contingent upon life birth. . . .

In view of all this, we do not agree that, by adopting one theory of life, Texas may override the rights of the pregnant woman that are at stake. . . .

With respect to the State's important and legitimate interest in the health of the mother, the "compelling" point, in the light of present medical knowledge, is at approximately the end of the first trimester. This is so because of the now-established medical fact, referred to above at 149, that until the end of the first trimester mortality in abortion may be less than mortality in normal childbirth. It follows that, from and after this point, a State may regulate the abortion procedure to the extent that the regulation reasonably relates to the preservation and protection of maternal health. Examples of permissible state regulation in this area are requirements as to the qualifications of the person who is to perform the abortion; as to the licensure of that person; as to the facility in which the procedure is to be performed, that is, whether it must be a hospital or may be a clinic or some other place of less-than-hospital status; as to the licensing of the facility; and the like.

This means, on the other hand, that, for the period of pregnancy prior to this "compelling" point, the attending physician, in consultation with his patient, is free to determine, without regulation by the State, that, in his medical judgment, the patient's pregnancy should be terminated. If that decision is reached, the judgment may be effectuated by an abortion free of interference by the State. . . .

*Source*: Google Scholar, *Roe v. Wade*, https://scholar.google.com/scholar_case?case=12334123945835207673&q=roe+v.+wade&hl=en&as_sdt=40006, accessed August 30, 2021

## Document 11. *Maher v. Roe*, 434 U.S. 464, June 20, 1977

*In this major decision, the Supreme Court held that states could refuse to pay or reimburse for abortions for low-income patients.*

A regulation of the Connecticut Welfare Department limits state Medicaid benefits for first trimester abortions to those that are "medically necessary," a term defined to include psychiatric necessity. . . . Connecticut enforces this limitation through a system of prior authorization from its Department of Social Services. In order to obtain authorization for a first trimester abortion, the hospital or clinic where the abortion is to be performed must submit, among other things, a certificate from the patient's attending physician stating that the abortion is medically necessary.

This attack on the validity of the Connecticut regulation was brought against appellant Maher, the Commissioner of Social Services, by appellees Poe and Roe, two indigent women who were unable to obtain a physician's certificate of medical necessity.

. . . The Constitution imposes no obligation on the States to pay the pregnancy-related medical expenses of indigent women, or indeed to pay any of the medical expenses of indigents. But when a State decides to alleviate some of the hardships of poverty by providing medical care, the manner in which it dispenses benefits is subject to constitutional limitations. Appellees' claim is that Connecticut must accord equal treatment to both abortion and childbirth, and may not evidence a policy preference by funding only the medical expenses incident to childbirth. This challenge to the classifications established by the Connecticut regulation presents a question arising under the Equal Protection Clause of the Fourteenth Amendment. . . .

The District Court read our decisions in *Roe* . . ., and the subsequent cases applying it, as establishing a fundamental right to abortion and therefore concluded that nothing less than a compelling state interest would justify Connecticut's different treatment of abortion and childbirth. We think the District Court misconceived the nature and scope of the fundamental right recognized in *Roe*.

At issue in *Roe* was the constitutionality of a Texas law making it a crime to procure or attempt to procure an abortion, except on medical advice for the purpose of saving the life of the mother. . . . The Texas statute imposed severe criminal sanctions on the physicians and other medical personnel who performed abortions, thus drastically limiting the availability and safety of the desired service. . . .

. . . The Connecticut regulation before us is different in kind from the laws invalidated in our previous abortion decisions. The Connecticut regulation places no obstacles—absolute or otherwise—in the pregnant woman's path to an abortion. An indigent woman who desires an abortion suffers no disadvantage as a consequence of Connecticut's decision to fund childbirth; she continues as before to be dependent on private sources for the service she desires. The State may have made childbirth a more attractive alternative, thereby influencing the woman's decision, but it has imposed no restriction on access to abortions that was not already there. The indigency that may make it difficult—and in some cases, perhaps, impossible—for some women to have abortions is neither created nor in any way affected by the Connecticut regulation. We conclude that the Connecticut regulation does not impinge upon the fundamental right recognized in *Roe*. . . .

*Source*: Google Scholar, *Maher v. Roe*, https://scholar.google.com/scholar_case?case=10803349459097846233&hl=en&as_sdt=6&as_vis=1&oi=scholarr, accessed August 30, 2021

## Document 12. "Jerry Falwell Talks About His First Time," Parody interview, *Hustler Magazine*, November 1983

*In this parody interview*, Hustler, *an adult magazine, mocked Jerry Falwell, the leader of the Moral Majority. Falwell brought a defamation lawsuit that ultimately failed, with the Supreme Court finding that the First Amendment protected* Hustler's *satire.*

*Source*: Wikimedia Commons, https://commons.wikimedia.org/wiki/File:Jerry_Falwell_Parody_Interview_in_Hustler_Magazine.jpg, accessed August 30, 2021

## Document 13. Ronald Reagan, remarks announcing the nomination of Robert H. Bork to be associate justice of the Supreme Court of the United States, July 1, 1987

*In this speech, Reagan tried to frame the battle over Robert Bork's ultimately failed confirmation as a debate about the value of judicial restraint versus judicial activism—the latter of which Republicans often tied to* Roe.

. . . Judge Bork, widely regarded as the most prominent and intellectually powerful advocate of judicial restraint, shares my view that judges' personal preferences and values should not be part of their constitutional interpretations. The guiding principle of judicial restraint recognizes that under the Constitution it is the exclusive province of the legislatures to enact laws and the role of the courts to interpret them. We're fortunate to be able to draw upon such an impressive legal mind, an experienced judge and a man who already has devoted so much of his life to public service. He'll bring credit to the Court and his colleagues, as well as to his country and the Constitution. . . .

*Source:* Ronald Reagan Presidential Library and Museum Digital Archive, https://www.reaganlibrary.gov/archives/speech/remarks-announcing-nomination-robert-h-bork-be-associate-justice-supreme-court, accessed August 30, 2021

## Document 14. *Planned Parenthood of Southeastern Pennsylvania v. Casey*, 505 U.S. 833, June 29, 1992

*In this pathbreaking decision, the Supreme Court preserved what it called the "essential" holding of* Roe v. Wade*—that there was a right to choose abortion before viability—while making it substantially easier for states to restrict access to abortion.*

Liberty finds no refuge in a jurisprudence of doubt. Yet 19 years after our holding that the Constitution protects a woman's right to terminate her pregnancy in its early stages, *Roe v. Wade* . . ., that definition of liberty is still questioned. . . .

At issue in these cases are five provisions of the Pennsylvania Abortion Control Act of 1982 as amended in 1988 and 1989 . . . . The Act requires that a woman seeking an abortion give her informed consent prior to the abortion procedure, and specifies that she be provided with certain information at least 24 hours before the abortion is performed. § 3205. For a minor to obtain an abortion, the Act requires the informed consent of one of her parents, but provides for a judicial bypass option if the minor does not wish to or cannot obtain a parent's consent. § 3206. Another provision of the Act requires that, unless certain exceptions apply, a married woman seeking an abortion must sign a statement indicating that she has notified her husband of her intended abortion. § 3209. The Act exempts compliance with these three requirements in the event of a "medical emergency," which is defined in § 3203 of the Act. See §§ 3203, 3205(a), 3206(a), 3209(c). . . .

. . . Our law affords constitutional protection to personal decisions relating to marriage, procreation, contraception, family relationships, child rearing, and education. . . . At the heart of liberty is the right to define one's own concept of existence, of meaning, of the universe, and of the mystery of human life. Beliefs about these matters could not define the attributes of personhood were they formed under compulsion of the State. . . . These considerations begin our analysis of the woman's interest in terminating her pregnancy but cannot end it, for this reason: though the abortion decision may originate within the zone of conscience and belief, it is more than a philosophic exercise. Abortion is a unique act. It is an act fraught with consequences for others: for the woman who must live with the implications of her decision; for the persons who perform and assist in the procedure; for the spouse, family, and society which must confront the knowledge that these procedures exist, procedures some deem nothing short of an act of violence against innocent human life; and, depending on one's beliefs, for the life or potential life that is aborted. Though abortion is conduct, it does not follow that the State is entitled to proscribe it in all instances. That is because the liberty of the woman is at stake in a sense unique to the human condition and so unique to the law. The mother who carries a child to full term is subject to anxieties, to physical constraints, to pain that only she must bear. That these sacrifices have from the beginning of the human race been endured by woman with a pride that ennobles her in the eyes of others and gives to the infant a bond of love cannot alone be grounds for the State to insist she make the sacrifice. Her suffering is too intimate and personal for the State to insist, without more, upon its own vision of the woman's role, however dominant that vision has been in the course of our history and our culture. The destiny of the woman must be shaped to a large extent on her own conception of her spiritual imperatives and her place in society.

. . . While we appreciate the weight of the arguments made on behalf of the State in the case before us, arguments which in their ultimate formulation conclude that *Roe* should be overruled, the reservations any of us may have in reaffirming the central holding of *Roe* are outweighed by the explication of individual liberty we have given combined with the force of *stare decisis*. We turn now to that doctrine. . . .

So in this case we may inquire whether *Roe*'s central rule has been found unworkable; whether the rule's limitation on state power could be removed without serious inequity to those who have relied upon it or significant damage to the stability of the society governed by the rule in question; whether the law's growth in the intervening years has left *Roe*'s central rule a doctrinal anachronism discounted by society; and whether *Roe*'s premises of fact have so far changed in the ensuing two decades as to render its central holding somehow irrelevant or unjustifiable in dealing with the issue it addressed. . . .

Although *Roe* has engendered opposition, it has in no sense proven "unworkable.". . . While *Roe* has, of course, required judicial assessment of state laws affecting the exercise of the choice guaranteed against government infringement, and although the need for such review will remain as a consequence of today's decision, the required determinations fall within judicial competence. . . .

The inquiry into reliance counts the cost of a rule's repudiation as it would fall on those who have relied reasonably on the rule's continued application.

. . . Abortion is customarily chosen as an unplanned response to the consequence of unplanned activity or to the failure of conventional birth control, and except on the assumption that no intercourse would have occurred but for *Roe's* holding, such behavior may appear to justify no reliance claim. . . .

To eliminate the issue of reliance that easily, however, one would need to limit cognizable reliance to specific instances of sexual activity. But to do this would be simply to refuse to face the fact that for two decades of economic and social developments, people have organized intimate relationships and made choices that define their views of themselves and their places in society, in reliance on the availability of abortion in the event that contraception should fail. The ability of women to participate equally in the economic and social life of the Nation has been facilitated by their ability to control their reproductive lives. See, *e.g.*, R. Petchesky, Abortion and Woman's Choice 109, 133, n. 7 (rev. ed. 1990). The Constitution serves human values, and while the effect of reliance on *Roe* cannot be exactly measured, neither can the certain cost of overruling *Roe* for people who have ordered their thinking and living around that case be dismissed.

No evolution of legal principle has left *Roe*'s doctrinal footings weaker than they were in 1973. No development of constitutional law since the case was decided has implicitly or explicitly left *Roe* behind as a mere survivor of obsolete constitutional thinking.

. . . Our analysis would not be complete, however, without explaining why overruling *Roe*'s central holding would not only reach an unjustifiable result under principles of *stare decisis*, but would seriously weaken the Court's capacity to exercise the judicial power and to function as the Supreme Court of a Nation dedicated to the rule of law.

. . . The Court's power lies, rather, in its legitimacy, a product of substance and perception that shows itself in the people's acceptance of the Judiciary as fit to determine what the Nation's law means and to declare what it demands.

. . . The underlying substance of this legitimacy is of course the warrant for the Court's decisions in the Constitution and the lesser sources of legal principle on which the Court draws.

. . . Where, in the performance of its judicial duties, the Court decides a case in such a way as to resolve the sort of intensely divisive controversy reflected in *Roe* and those rare, comparable cases, its decision has a dimension that the resolution of the normal case does not carry. It is the dimension present whenever the Court's interpretation of the Constitution calls the contending sides of a national controversy to end their national division by accepting a common mandate rooted in the Constitution.

The Court is not asked to do this very often. . . . But when the Court does act in this way, its decision requires an equally rare precedential force to counter the inevitable efforts to overturn it and to thwart its implementation. . . . So to overrule under fire in the absence of the most compelling reason to reexamine a watershed decision would subvert the Court's legitimacy beyond any serious question. . . .

That brings us, of course, to the point where much criticism has been directed at *Roe*, a criticism that always inheres when the Court draws a specific rule from what in the Constitution is but a general standard. We conclude, however, that the urgent claims of the woman to retain the ultimate control over her destiny and her body, claims implicit in the meaning of liberty, require us to perform that function. Liberty must not be extinguished for want of a line that is clear. And it falls to us to give some real substance to the woman's liberty to determine whether to carry her pregnancy to full term. . . .

We conclude the line should be drawn at viability, so that before that time the woman has a right to choose to terminate her pregnancy. We adhere to this principle for two reasons. First, as we have said, is the doctrine of *stare decisis*. Any judicial act of line-drawing may seem somewhat arbitrary, but *Roe* was a reasoned statement, elaborated with great care. . . .

The second reason is that the concept of viability, as we noted in *Roe*, is the time at which there is a realistic possibility of maintaining and nourishing a life outside the womb, so that the independent existence of the second life can in reason and all fairness be the object of state protection that now overrides the rights of the woman.

. . . We reject the trimester framework, which we do not consider to be part of the essential holding of *Roe*. . . . As our jurisprudence relating to all liberties save perhaps abortion has recognized, not every law which makes a right more difficult to exercise is, *ipso facto*, an infringement of that right.

. . . The trimester framework, however, does not fulfill *Roe*'s own promise that the State has an interest in protecting fetal life or potential life. . . . Before viability, *Roe* and subsequent cases treat all governmental attempts to influence a woman's decision on behalf of the potential life within her as unwarranted. This treatment is, in our judgment, incompatible with the recognition that there is a substantial state interest in potential life throughout pregnancy. . . .

The very notion that the State has a substantial interest in potential life leads to the conclusion that not all regulations must be deemed unwarranted.

Not all burdens on the right to decide whether to terminate a pregnancy will be undue. In our view, the undue burden standard is the appropriate means of reconciling the State's interest with the woman's constitutionally protected liberty.

. . . A finding of an undue burden is a shorthand for the conclusion that a state regulation has the purpose or effect of placing a substantial obstacle in the path of a woman seeking an abortion of a nonviable fetus. A statute with this purpose is invalid because the means chosen by the State to further the interest in potential life must be calculated to inform the woman's free choice, not hinder it. And a statute which, while furthering the interest in potential life or some other valid state interest, has the effect of placing a substantial obstacle in the path of a woman's choice cannot be considered a permissible means of serving its legitimate ends. . . .

[Scalia, J., dissenting]

The Court's description of the place of *Roe* in the social history of the United States is unrecognizable. Not only did *Roe* not, as the Court suggests, *resolve* the deeply divisive issue of abortion; it did more than anything else to nourish it, by elevating it to the national level where it is infinitely more difficult to resolve. National politics were not plagued by abortion protests, national abortion lobbying, or abortion marches on Congress, before *Roe v. Wade* was decided. Profound disagreement existed among our citizens over the issue—as it does over other issues, such as the death penalty—but that disagreement was being worked out at the state level. As with many other issues, the division of sentiment within each State was not as closely balanced as it was among the population of the Nation as a whole, meaning not only that more people would be satisfied with the results of state-by-state resolution, but also that those results would be more stable. Pre-*Roe*, moreover, political compromise was possible.

*Roe*'s mandate for abortion-on-demand destroyed the compromises of the past, rendered compromise impossible for the future, and required the entire issue to be resolved uniformly, at the national level. At the same time, *Roe* created a vast new class of abortion consumers and abortion proponents by eliminating the moral opprobrium that had attached to the act. ("If the Constitution *guarantees* abortion, how can it be bad?"—not an accurate line of thought, but a natural one.) Many favor all of those developments, and it is not for me to say that they are wrong. But to portray *Roe* as the statesmanlike "settlement" of a divisive issue, a jurisprudential Peace of Westphalia that is worth preserving, is nothing less than Orwellian. *Roe* fanned into life an issue that has inflamed our national politics in general, and has obscured with its smoke the selection of Justices to this Court in particular, ever since. . . .

*Source:* Google Scholar, *Planned Parenthood v. Casey*, https://scholar.google.com/scholar_case?case=6298856056242550994&q=planned+parenthood+of+southeastern+pa+v+casey&hl=en&as_sdt=40006, accessed August 30, 2021

## Document 15. *Gonzales v. Carhart*, 550 U.S. 124, April 21, 2007

The Act proscribes a particular manner of ending fetal life, so it is necessary here, as it was in *Stenberg*, to discuss abortion procedures in some detail. . . .

Abortion methods vary depending to some extent on the preferences of the physician and, of course, on the term of the pregnancy and the resulting stage of the unborn child's development. Between 85 and 90 percent of the approximately 1.3 million abortions performed each year in the United States take place in the first three months of pregnancy, which is to say in the first trimester. . . .

Of the remaining abortions that take place each year, most occur in the second trimester. The surgical procedure referred to as "dilation and evacuation" or "D & E" is the usual abortion method in this trimester. . . . Although individual techniques for performing D & E differ, the general steps are the same.

A doctor must first dilate the cervix at least to the extent needed to insert surgical instruments into the uterus and to maneuver them to evacuate the fetus. . . . A doctor often begins the dilation process by inserting osmotic dilators, such as laminaria (sticks of seaweed), into the cervix. The dilators can be used in combination with drugs, such as misoprostol, that increase dilation. . . .

After sufficient dilation the surgical operation can commence. The woman is placed under general anesthesia or conscious sedation. The doctor, often guided by ultrasound, inserts grasping forceps through the woman's cervix and into the uterus to grab the fetus. The doctor grips a fetal part with the forceps and pulls it back through the cervix and vagina, continuing to pull even after meeting resistance from the cervix. The friction causes the fetus to tear apart. For example, a leg might be ripped off the fetus as it is pulled through the cervix and out of the woman. The process of evacuating the fetus piece by piece continues until it has been completely removed. . . .

The abortion procedure that was the impetus for the numerous bans on "partial birth abortion," including the Act, is a variation of this standard D & E. . . . In an intact D & E procedure the doctor extracts the fetus in a way conducive to pulling out its entire body, instead of ripping it apart. . . .

. . . Under the principles accepted as controlling here, the Act, as we have interpreted it, would be unconstitutional "if its purpose or effect is to place a substantial obstacle in the path of a woman seeking an abortion before the fetus attains viability." . . .

The Act's purposes are set forth in recitals preceding its operative provisions. A description of the prohibited abortion procedure demonstrates the rationale for the congressional enactment. The Act proscribes a method of abortion in which a fetus is killed just inches before completion of the birth process. Congress stated as follows: "Implicitly approving such a brutal and inhumane procedure by choosing not to prohibit it will further coarsen society to the humanity of not only newborns, but all vulnerable and innocent human life, making it increasingly difficult to protect such life." Congressional Findings ¶ (14)(N). The Act expresses respect for the dignity of human life.

Congress was concerned, furthermore, with the effects on the medical community and on its reputation caused by the practice of partial-birth abortion. The findings in the Act explain:

> "Partial-birth abortion . . . confuses the medical, legal, and ethical duties of physicians to preserve and promote life, as the physician acts directly against the physical life of a child, whom he or she had just delivered, all but the head, out of the womb, in order to end that life." *Id.,* ¶ (14)(J).

There can be no doubt the government "has an interest in protecting the integrity and ethics of the medical profession." . . .

Respect for human life finds an ultimate expression in the bond of love the mother has for her child. . . . While we find no reliable data to measure the phenomenon, it seems unexceptionable to conclude some women come to regret their choice to abort the infant life they once created and sustained. See Brief for Sandra Cano et al. as *Amici Curiae* in No. 05-380, pp. 22–24. Severe depression and loss of esteem can follow. See *ibid.*

In a decision so fraught with emotional consequence some doctors may prefer not to disclose precise details of the means that will be used, confining themselves to the required statement of risks the procedure entails. From one standpoint this ought not to be surprising. Any number of patients facing imminent surgical procedures would prefer not to hear all details, lest the usual anxiety preceding invasive medical procedures become the more intense. This is likely the case with the abortion procedures here in issue. . . .

The State has an interest in ensuring so grave a choice is well informed. It is self-evident that a mother who comes to regret her choice to abort must struggle with grief more anguished and sorrow more profound when she learns, only after the event, what she once did not know: that she allowed a doctor to pierce the skull and vacuum the fast-developing brain of her unborn child, a child assuming the human form.

It is a reasonable inference that a necessary effect of the regulation and the knowledge it conveys will be to encourage some women to carry the infant to full term, thus reducing the absolute number of late-term abortions. . . .

The Act's furtherance of legitimate government interests bears upon, but does not resolve, the next question: whether the Act has the effect of imposing an unconstitutional burden on the abortion right because it does not allow use of the barred procedure where "necessary, in appropriate medical judgment, for the preservation of the . . . health of the mother."

. . . There is documented medical disagreement whether the Act's prohibition would ever impose significant health risks on women. . . .

The question becomes whether the Act can stand when this medical uncertainty persists. The Court's precedents instruct that the Act can survive this facial attack. The Court has given state and federal legislatures wide discretion to pass legislation in areas where there is medical and scientific uncertainty . . .

*Source:* Google Scholar, *Gonzales v. Carhart*, https://scholar.google.com/scholar_case?case=5971780753882938659&hl=en&as_sdt=6&as_vis=1&oi=scholarr, accessed August 30, 2021

## Document 16. *SisterSong Reproductive Justice Collective v. Kemp*, Verified Complaint for Declaratory and Injunctive Relief, Case 1:19-cv-02973-SCJ, June 28, 2019

*This was a constitutional challenge to Georgia's heartbeat law, which bans abortion and recognizes fetal personhood at six weeks.*

1. This is a constitutional challenge to House Bill 481 ("H.B. 481"), attached as Exhibit A, which bans practically all abortions. This law is an affront to the dignity and health of Georgians. It is in particular an attack on low-income Georgians, Georgians of color, and rural Georgians, who are least able to access medical care and least able to overcome the cruelties of this law. Georgians face a critical shortage of reproductive health care providers, including obstetrician-gynecologists, and the rate at which Georgians, particularly Black Georgians, die from pregnancy-related causes is among the highest in the nation.
2. Rather than working to end those preventable deaths, and rather than honoring Georgians' reproductive health care decisions, the Legislature has instead chosen to criminalize abortion from the earliest stages of pregnancy. H.B. 481 criminalizes pre-viability abortions in direct conflict with *Roe v. Wade*. . . . Specifically, it criminalizes abortion after embryonic cardiac activity is detectable, which generally occurs around six weeks in pregnancy, when many people are unaware they are pregnant. The law undermines a woman's "ability . . . to participate equally in the economic and social life of the Nation," which "has been facilitated by their ability to control their reproductive lives." *Planned Parenthood v. Casey*, 505 U.S. 833, 856 (1992).
3. In addition, this law threatens a vast array of medical care critical for the health of Georgia's women of reproductive age. Its vague language threatens clinicians with prosecution for any medical care they provide to pregnant patients that could harm an embryo/fetus.2 The threat of criminal liability is likely to have a chilling effect on health care providers across Georgia, shaping provider and patient decisions about a wide range of health conditions and restricting treatment options for people who are pregnant or perceived to be capable of pregnancy.

. . .

45. Georgians who seek clinical abortion care will struggle and suffer under H.B. 481. Those who can will travel of out of state, though for

many, such travel will delay care and impose other hardships; others will remain pregnant and give birth against their will; still others will end their own pregnancies or seek care outside the regulated clinical setting, which will expose some women to increased risk of harm. H.B. 481 will be particularly devastating for low-income Georgians, Georgians of color, and rural Georgians, who are already least able to access medical care, and who have the least resources to navigate the law's cruelties.

46. Women seek abortions for a variety of deeply personal reasons, including familial, medical, and financial. Some women have abortions because they conclude that it is not the right time in their lives to have a child or to add to their families. For example, some decide to end a pregnancy because they want to pursue their education; some because they feel they lack the economic resources or level of partner support or stability they want to raise children; some because they are concerned that if they increase their family size, they will be unable to provide and care adequately for their existing children and/or for their ill or dying parents. Others end a pregnancy in order to be able to leave an abusive partner. Some women seek abortions to preserve their life or health by reducing their risk of injury or death; some because they have become pregnant as a result of rape or incest; and others because they decide not to have children at all. Some women decide to have an abortion because of a diagnosed fetal medical condition. Some families feel they do not have the societal or personal resources—financial, medical, educational, or emotional—to care for a child with physical or intellectual disabilities, or to do so and simultaneously provide for their existing children. The decision to terminate a pregnancy is motivated by a constellation of diverse, complex, and interrelated factors, intimately related to the individual's core religious beliefs, values, and family circumstances.
47. Approximately one in four women in this country will have an abortion by age forty-five. A majority of women having abortions (61%) already have at least one child, while most (66%) also plan to have a child or additional children in the future.5

. . .

61. As between maintaining a pregnancy or having an abortion, H.B. 481 would mandate the medically far riskier course, regardless of whether it is contrary to an individual patient's will. Forcing a woman to continue a pregnancy against her will can pose a risk to her physical, mental, and emotional health, and even her life, as well as to the stability and wellbeing of her family, including her existing children.
62. Even those able to overcome the obstacles to accessing care outside Georgia would be delayed, which would increase the risks of the care: although abortion is extremely safe, the risks associated with pregnancy increase as pregnancy advances.
63. H.B. 481's three narrow exceptions provide little relief from its near complete ban on abortions.

64. First, H.B. 481 will force women pregnant as a result of sexual assault to continue their pregnancies against their will. H.B. 481's exception for sexual assault survivors applies only before 20 weeks post-fertilization, and only when "an official police report has been filed alleging the offense of rape or incest." § 4(b)(2). Many survivors of these crimes are never able to file a police report for many reasons, including that they fear violent retaliation by the rapist, that they are coping with trauma, or that filing a report would deepen their trauma. Many more are unable to file a police report within the timeframe that H.B. 481 requires to abort a pregnancy resulting from those crimes. Plaintiffs' abortion patients include survivors of rape or incest who have not filed police reports.
65. Second, there are severe and potentially lethal fetal conditions that lead women to decide to have an abortion, but that would not satisfy H.B. 481's narrow exception for "medically futile" pregnancies, which is limited to the presence of "a profound and irremediable congenital or chromosomal anomaly that is incompatible with sustaining life after birth." H.B. 481 § 4 (amending O.C.G.A. § 16-12-141(a)(4)). For example, in the condition severe diaphragmatic hernia, the fetal intestines impinge on the lungs and prevent their development, which can result in a stillbirth. If a baby is born with this condition, surgeries may allow breathing, or such surgeries may fail, resulting in death. Yet, these and many other similarly severe conditions would not qualify as "medically futile" under H.B. 481.
66. Third, H.B. 481's "medical emergency" exception is so limited that the ban would block care even for many women who desperately need abortions to protect their health, including some of Plaintiffs' patients. A patient who was not in, or who had not yet deteriorated to the point that she was in, a medical emergency as narrowly defined would have to remain pregnant, regardless of the harm to her health.
    a. In one of many examples, high blood pressure can worsen as pregnancy advances. In some patients, this leads to serious conditions during pregnancy including pre-eclampsia, eclampsia, cardiac hypertrophy, heart attack, and stroke; for some patients, remaining pregnant with high blood pressure can lead to heart or kidney damage well after pregnancy. Some patients with this profile seek abortion care to avoid these serious risks; others remain pregnant and have their physicians manage the risk as best as possible; and of those, some later decide that the risk has passed the point that they deem acceptable, and they have an abortion. But unless such a patient had deteriorated to the point of a "medical emergency" as defined in H.B. 481, she would have to remain pregnant and be exposed to those near-term and long-term medical risks.

. . .

*Source*: American Civil Liberties Union, Complaint: *SisterSong v. Kemp*, https://www.aclu.org/legal-document/sistersong-v-kemp-complaint, accessed August 30, 2021

## Document 17. *Testimony of Janet Folger Porter, Ohio House Health Committee, in favor of S.B. 23, The Heartbeat Bill,* March 19, 2019

*In this legislative testimony, Janet Porter, the architect of the heartbeat campaign, laid out her strategy for passing six-week prohibitions.*

. . . With the appointments of Justices Gorsuch and Kavanaugh to the Supreme Court, there is a pro-life majority, expected to increase next year. I can tell you what the Eighth Circuit Court of Appeals said, but all we really need to do is count to five—the number of pro-life judges already on the Supreme Court, with more expected soon.

While the Eighth Circuit Court was bound by precedent to turn down the Arkansas and North Dakota Heartbeat Laws, they asked the Supreme Court to take up the case, arguing that it should be the states who decide. The Eighth Circuit Court rightly declared that "heartbeat" is a "more certain and consistent" indicator of life than the one the Supreme Court is currently using: viability. The Supreme Court has said the states can protect human life if there's a likelihood of survival to live birth. But the indicator they're using now is a lousy one. In "Life, Heartbeat, Birth: A Medical basis for Reform," Constitutional Law Professor David Forte points out that the determination of viability can be as much as 90 percent wrong.

On the other hand, an unborn child with a detectable heartbeat has a 95–98 percent likelihood of survival to live birth. Heartbeat is the most accurate indicator of whether a child in the womb will survive to live birth. That means the court can simply move the line of allowable legal protection to a place that is more in keeping with its intent—heartbeat. We now have what the Eighth Circuit called a "more consistent and certain marker" than viability, the Supreme Court's current arbitrary and unscientific standard to allow legal protection. We are simply handing them a more accurate yardstick. Once a heartbeat is detected in an unborn child, that child is not only shown to be currently alive, he or she is virtually certain to be born. That is precisely what the Supreme Court is looking for, and with the Heartbeat Bill, they will have it with scientific certainty. After nearly a decade of hearings and debate, you know the Heartbeat Bill will do. It will legally protect unborn children whose heartbeats can be detected by a doctor except to save the life or physical health of the mother.

*Source*: Ohio State Digital Archive, https://search-prod.lis.state.oh.us, accessed August 30, 2021

# Glossary

**Affordable Care Act:** Passed in 2010, the Affordable Care Act vastly expanded Medicaid coverage, created state insurance exchanges, blocked insurers from excluding those with preexisting conditions, and created an individual mandate that required Americans to carry insurance or pay a penalty. The law changed health care coverage and sparked a political backlash that helped to bring the Tea Party movement to the forefront of US politics.

**Alliance Defending Freedom:** Formerly known as the Alliance Defense Fund, the Alliance Defending Freedom was founded in 1993 to expand the rights of conservative Christians. A wealthy organization with vast reach, the group primarily works to train lawyers and fund public interest litigation involving opposition to same-sex marriage or abortion and the freedom of speech and religion of conservative Christians.

**American Birth Control League:** Started in 1921 by Margaret Sanger, the league advocated for contraceptive access both as a matter of rights for women and a eugenic tool. The league lobbied for changes to birth control laws and helped to open birth control clinics across the United States. In 1942, it merged with other birth control organizations to become the Planned Parenthood Federation of America.

**American Center for Law and Justice:** Founded in 1990 by televangelist Pat Robertson and Jay Sekulow, the American Center for Law and Justice is a conservative Christian public interest law firm headquartered at Robertson's Regent University School of Law.

**American Civil Liberties Union:** Founded in 1920, a civil liberties organization best known for its free speech advocacy that joined the fight for reproductive rights and women's rights in the 1970s.

**American College of Obstetricians and Gynecologists (ACOG):** A professional association of obstetricians and gynecologists, the College often serves as the standard setter for specialists in its field. ACOG has been involved in several abortion cases and takes the position that abortion should be legal.

**American Law Institute:** A research and advocacy group of lawyers, law professors, and judges that advocated for legal reforms. The American Law Institute proposed a reform of abortion laws in 1959 that would serve as a model for legislators in the 1960s.

**American Medical Association:** A professional association for doctors, the American Medical Association led the fight to criminalize abortion in the nineteenth century. Later, in the 1960s and 1970s, the organization helped pave the way for the reform of criminal abortion laws and continues to participate in fights about the regulation of medicine in the abortion context.

**Americans United for Life:** Founded in the early 1970s, Americans United for Life is a right-to-life public interest law firm. Lawyers with the group have led incremental attacks on abortion rights since the late 1970s.

**Assisted reproductive technologies:** Medical procedures used to address infertility and other issues, including surrogacy, in vitro fertilization, and artificial insemination.

**Association for the Study of Abortion:** A New York-based organization that led early efforts to reform abortion laws. The Association for the Study of Abortion was small but was home to many of the figures who would lead efforts to legalize abortion, including Larry Lader and Alan Guttmacher.

**Association for Voluntary Sterilization (AVS):** Originally founded as the Sterilization League of New Jersey in 1937, AVS embraced sterilization as a method of birth control. While distancing their organization from eugenics, AVS leaders suggested that sterilization was a superior contraceptive method and did not advocate for the legalization of abortion. In 2001, the group again renamed itself EngenderHealth and continues work on reproductive and sexual issues.

**Bill of Rights:** The first ten amendments to the Constitution, the Bill of Rights sets out individual rights and liberties, including freedoms of speech, religion, and the right to bear arms. At first, the Bill of Rights applied only to the federal government, which meant that individuals could not sue states for violating their rights. In the second half of the twentieth century, the Court gradually "incorporated" the Bill of Rights, which now represents a key source of constitutional protection.

**Birth control pill:** Developed by biologists John Rock and Gregory Pincus, the pill was tested on patients in a state mental hospital and on patients in Puerto Rico. Approved in the United States in 1960, the pill quickly became a popular, if controversial, contraceptive.

**Black genocide:** In the abortion context, an argument that the legalization of abortion reflected racist motives and would lead to the elimination of Black children, especially in low-income communities.

**Black-box warning:** The most serious warning issued by the Food and Drug Administration, often for drugs that can lead to serious injury or death.

**Born-Alive Infants Protection Act:** A 2002 statute criminalizing abortions performed if a child or fetus is born alive.

***Bray v. Alexandria Women's Health Clinic*:** A 1993 decision, *Bray* rejected the use of the Ku Klux Klan Act to prevent clinic blockades.

*Bray* also firmed up the argument that denying access to or opposing abortion did not count as sex discrimination.

**Brief:** A written legal document that provides arguments as to why one party should prevail.

**Bubble zone law:** Alternatively known as buffer zones, these laws create a perimeter around abortion providers, patients, and clinics that antiabortion picketers cannot enter. Antiabortion protestors have challenged the constitutionality of such laws as violating the Free Speech Clause of the First Amendment, but with varying success.

***Buckley v. Valeo*:** A 1976 Supreme Court decision striking down parts of the Federal Election Campaign Act while upholding others. *Buckley* upheld certain campaign finance limits, such as those on direct contributions to candidates and ads that expressly endorsed a candidate, while striking down those on expenditures (which covered most other forms of election spending). *Buckley* set the terms of later fights about campaign finance.

***Burwell v. Hobby Lobby Stores*:** A 2014 decision holding that a federal contraceptive mandate, requiring employer plans to cover all approved birth control methods, violated the federal Religious Freedom Restoration Act.

***Bush v. Gore*:** A 2000 decision holding that Florida's recount methods violated the Constitution, *Bush v. Gore* had the effect of placing George W. Bush in office.

**Campaign finance:** A term covering the rules that govern election spending.

**Center for Reproductive Rights (formerly, the Center for Reproductive Law and Policy):** A public interest law firm focusing on reproductive rights and justice founded 1992, the Center spearheads litigation around the world.

**Church Amendment:** A series of legislative modifications, the Church Amendments extend conscience protections to doctors and others who directly perform abortions and sterilizations. Originally passed with strong bipartisan support, the Church Amendment began a much longer conversation about the limits of conscientious objection.

**Cisgender:** A term applied to those who identify with their genetic sex at birth.

***City of Akron v. Akron Center for Reproductive Health*:** A 1983 decision striking down an Akron ordinance that required informed consent, among other things. Sandra Day O'Connor wrote a provocative dissent questioning the workability of *Roe*.

**Clergy Consultation Service:** Started by primarily Jewish and Protestant clergy in 1967, the Clergy Counseling Service provided referrals for safe abortion services in the years when abortion was a crime.

**Climate change:** Global warming driven by human emissions of greenhouse gasses and resulting shifts in weather patterns.

**Closely held corporation:** Also known as a private or privately held corporation, any company owned by a relatively small group of shareholders.

**Cold War:** A period of geopolitical tension between the United States and the Soviet Union, the Cold War lasted roughly from the end of World War II to the formal dissolution of the Soviet Union in 1991.

**Committee to End Sterilization Abuse (CESA):** Founded in 1974 by Dr. Helen Rodríguez-Trías, Dr. Raymond Rakow, and Maritza Arrastia, CESA campaigned against involuntary sterilizations, particularly those involving low-income people of color.

**Compulsory sterilization laws:** State policies forcing the sterilization of those thought unfit to have children. Over 30 states passed such laws, which purported to deal with perceived aggression, criminality, and poverty of men and the supposed sexual misconduct of women by blocking them from having children.

**Concurring opinion:** In the United States, concurring opinions agree with the legal outcome reached by a majority of judges but offer different reasons for supporting that result.

**Contraceptive mandate:** A part of the Affordable Care Act, the contraceptive mandate required employer insurance plans to cover all female contraceptives approved by the federal Food and Drug Administration. The mandate sparked considerable controversy, and its exemptions have broadened over time. Conflicts continue about the balance between the religious objections of some employers and contraceptive access for workers.

**Crisis pregnancy center:** An antiabortion facility designed to discourage patients from having abortions and to provide pregnancy tests, religious instruction, ultrasounds, or supportive services. The first crisis pregnancy centers opened in the 1960s, and by the 2000s enjoyed significant governmental funding.

***Declaration of Sentiments*:** Patterned on the Declaration of Independence, this document, which emerged from the Seneca Falls Convention of 1848, set forth a vision of rights, including suffrage and equal treatment in property ownership, government participation, employment opportunities, and divorce. Primarily written by feminist Elizabeth Cady Stanton, the *Declaration* became a cornerstone of early feminism.

**Dissenting opinion:** In the United States, a dissenting opinion disagrees with the result reached by a majority on a court.

**Dilation and evacuation:** The most common and safe abortion procedure after the first trimester of pregnancy, dilation and evacuation involves the dilation of the cervix and the removal of a fetus or fetal tissue in parts.

**Dilation and extraction:** An abortion procedure often performed later in pregnancy, dilation and extraction requires the dilation of the cervix and the removal of an intact fetus. Viewed as akin to infanticide by abortion foes, dilation and extraction was prohibited by the federal Partial-Birth Abortion Ban Act.

***Doe v. Bolton*:** The companion case of *Roe v. Wade*, *Doe* was a 1973 case striking down a Georgia law that allowed abortion only to patients who cleared certain medical hurdles. *Doe* also embraced a broad definition of "health"—one that included a patient's mental wellbeing.

**Domestic violence:** Violence committed in a family or relational setting, including marriage, dating, or cohabitation.

**Draft:** A lottery system, the Vietnam draft determined the order that young men would be called to serve in Vietnam. The draft proved to be highly unpopular and served as a catalyst for the antiwar movement in the United States.

**Due Process of Law:** Based on the Due Process Clause of the Fourteenth Amendment, due process in the United States has two components. First, courts interpreting the Due Process Clause have defined a procedural guarantee of fairness before an individual loses life, liberty, or property. Second, the courts have developed a doctrine of substantive due process, looking to the clause as a source of new rights at most implied by the text of the Constitution.

**Dying declarations:** A rule that allowed the statements of a dying person to be admitted as evidence, even if those statements were hearsay and made by someone who could not be cross-examined in court.

**Earth Day:** An annual event, Earth Day calls for more environmental protection. Begun by population controller Hugh Moore in 1970, Earth Day has grown to become a touchstone of international environmental advocacy.

***Eisenstadt v. Baird*:** A 1972 decision striking down Massachusetts's contraception law, *Eisenstadt* suggested that the right to use birth control belonged to individuals—and involved autonomy and self-determination.

**Emergency contraception:** Medication that can be used after sexual intercourse to block a pregnancy, most forms of emergency contraception are available without a prescription.

**Equal Protection:** Based on the Equal Protection Clause of the Fourteenth Amendment of the US Constitution, a doctrine that guarantees equal treatment under the law. The courts scrutinize laws especially carefully when they classify individuals on an insidious basis, such as race, or when they deny individuals access to fundamental rights.

**Eugenics:** Doctrine that provided that the government should intervene to improve a nation's genetic stock. In the United States, proponents of negative eugenics—the idea that the wrong people should not be allowed to reproduce—passed laws requiring a blood test before marriage, mandating compulsory sterilization, or limiting immigration.

**Evangelical Protestant:** A worldwide, Christian, trans-denominational movement, evangelical Protestantism holds that salvation is through God's grace alone. Evangelicals also tended to privilege experience of conversion, or being born again, and defer heavily to Biblical authority, which some evangelicals view as inerrant. Evangelical denominations differ from one another and include Baptists, Methodists, Pentecostals, as well as some Lutherans and Anglicans.

**Federalist Society:** An organization of conservatives and libertarians that seek to influence legal doctrine, legal education, the legal elites, and the composition of the federal courts.

**First-wave feminists:** A term referring to activists who battled for women's rights in the nineteenth and early twentieth centuries. First-wave feminism focused on reforming the property rights of married women and the ability of women to participate in the nation's political life, especially by voting. Persistent racism limited its impact for women of color.

**Fornication:** A term applied to sex outside of marriage, fornication was treated as a crime in most states for much of US history, even after prosecutors had stopped enforcing state laws.

**Fox News Channel:** Founded in 1996, Fox News Channel takes a conservative stance on the news of the day and has faced criticism for inaccurate coverage. As more Americans relied on Fox News Channel as an exclusive source of news, the network revolutionized media consumption in the United States.

**Free love:** A nineteenth-century worldview that called for the freedom to marry, divorce, and bear children without governmental interference.

**Freedom of Access to Clinic Entrances Act (FACE Act):** A statute passed in 1994, FACE protected access to clinic entrances, imposing prison time and fines on those who obstructed clinic access.

**Freedom of Choice Act:** A proposed federal law that would have codified a right to choose abortion and invalidated many state restrictions on abortion, the Freedom of Choice Act divided the pro-choice coalition and never passed.

**Free Exercise Clause:** Part of the First Amendment of the Constitution, the Free Exercise Clause protects religious exercise from some forms of governmental interference.

**Full Faith and Credit Clause:** Article VI, Section 1 of the Constitution, the Full Faith and Credit Clause requires that all judicial decisions, public records, and acts be respected by other states. During early battles about same-sex marriage, the Full Faith and Credit Clause fueled anxiety in conservative states and inspired the spread of state laws and constitutional amendments banning same-sex marriage.

**Gerrymandering:** The manipulation of electoral boundaries to achieve an unfair advantage for one party.

***Gonzales v. Carhart*:** A 2007 Supreme Court decision, *Gonzales* upheld the federal Partial-Birth Abortion Act and gave states more latitude to regulate in cases of claimed scientific uncertainty.

**Great Depression:** The worst international economic crisis in the history of the industrialized world, the Great Depression lasted from roughly 1929 to the late 1930s. In the United States, at the lowest point of the Depression, some 15 million Americans were unemployed, and nearly half the banks in the nation had failed.

***Griswold v. Connecticut*:** A 1965 Supreme Court decision, *Griswold* recognized an implied right for married couples to use birth control.

*Griswold* served as the foundation for other privacy rights in the United States, including the right to abortion.

***Harris v. McRae*:** A 1980 Supreme Court decision upholding the Hyde Amendment.

**Hearsay:** Statements made by someone else and reported by a witness in court. Judges often did not allow the admission of hearsay evidence at trial, subject to certain exceptions.

**HIV/AIDS crisis:** Human Immunodeficiency Virus (HIV) is a disease transmitted through the blood or through sexual fluids that attacks the immune system. Acquired Immune Deficiency Syndrome (AIDS) is the most advanced stage of HIV. The disease disproportionately affects communities of color and men who sleep with men. While there is no cure for HIV, it can be managed through treatment. By contrast, at the height of the HIV/AIDS crisis, the disease was one of the leading causes of worldwide mortality.

**Holocaust:** The genocide of European Jews during World War II, the Holocaust killed some 6 million Jews, roughly two-thirds of the European population of Jews at the time.

***Humanae Vitae*:** A 1968 encyclical that restated the Catholic Church's opposition to birth control.

**Hyde Amendment:** A rider to a bill funding the Department of Health, Education, and Welfare, the Hyde Amendment prohibits reimbursement under the federal Medicaid program for abortions.

**Hysterotomy abortion:** A surgical abortion procedure, a hysterotomy removes an intact fetus from the uterus in a process similar to a Cesarean section.

**Immigration Restriction Act of 1924:** Eugenic-inspired law that changed immigration quotas to favor immigrants from the British Isles and Western Europe over those from Eastern or Southern Europe. The statute also excluded any immigrant barred from achieving citizenship—a rule that blocked many Asian migrants, particularly the Japanese, from the United States.

**Impeachment:** The process by which a legislative body, such as the House of Representatives in the United States, initiates charges of wrongdoing against a public official.

**Intrauterine device:** A form of contraception placed in the uterus to act as birth control.

**In vitro fertilization:** A fertility treatment in which a doctor creates embryos in a laboratory and then implants them into a gestational carrier, who may or may not be the genetic parent of the embryos.

**Jane Collective:** An underground abortion service operated by the Chicago Women's Liberation Collective from 1969 to 1973, Jane directed women to abortion providers with good safety records and eventually began offering abortion services, ultimately performing as many as 11,000 abortions.

***June Medical Services v. Russo*:** A 2020 decision, *June Medical* invalidated a Louisiana law requiring abortion doctors to have admitting privileges at a nearby hospital. In a concurring opinion, Chief Justice John Roberts set out a new version of the undue burden standard, one that would allow for more state regulation of abortion. Lawyers and lower courts subsequently battled about whether the Roberts opinion was controlling law.

**Ku Klux Klan Act:** A statute passed in the aftermath of the Civil War, the law was initially used to stop atrocities committed by the Ku Klux Klan. Over time, attorneys began relying on the law to address other conspiracies to deprive protected groups of civil rights.

**LSD:** Also known as acid, LSD was a potent hallucinogenic drug popular in the 1960s and 1970s.

***Madsen v. Women's Health Center*:** A 1994 decision upholding limits on antiabortion protests outside of abortion clinics.

***Maher v. Roe*:** A 1977 decision holding that the right to choose abortion did not conflict with a regulation banning the public funding of elective abortions.

**Majority opinion:** An opinion agreed to by more than half of a court, a majority opinion sets forth the law of the case.

**Malpractice insurance:** A type of insurance carried by medical professionals to deal with personal injury lawsuits.

***Manhattan Declaration*:** A 2009 statement of principles intended to unite social conservatives and outline agenda priorities, including protection of the right to life, opposition to same-sex marriage, and defense of religious liberty.

***Mazurek v. Armstrong*:** A 1997 Supreme Court decision, *Mazurek* held that states could require that all abortions be performed by a licensed physician.

**Menstrual extraction:** A manual aspiration abortion method, menstrual extraction was popularized by feminists Lorraine Rothman and Carol Downer before 1973. To avoid criminal liability, Rothman and Downer advertised the procedure as a way to remove all menstrual blood and tissue at once. Menstrual extraction enjoyed a revival starting in the 1990s as abortion restrictions cut down access to the procedure.

**Moral Majority:** Founded in 1979, the Moral Majority became one of the best-known and most powerful groups in the Religious Right. The organization came together through the work of veteran conservative operative Paul Weyrich and Jerry Falwell, a televangelist and minister of the largest independent Baptist church in the United States. The Moral Majority opposed legal abortion, gay and lesbian rights, sex education in school, and a constitutional amendment prohibiting sex discrimination. Following financial struggles in the 1980s, the organization disbanded in 1989.

**National Abortion Federation (NAF):** Founded in 1977, NAF is a professional association of abortion providers. NAF members include private clinics, feminist women's health centers, Planned Parenthood affiliates, doctors' offices, and other professionals who offer abortion services.

The organization sets quality standards for abortion and hosts conferences where providers exchange information.

**National Abortion Rights Action League (NARAL):** Formerly known as the National Association for the Repeal of Abortion Laws, NARAL formed in 1969 to advocate for abortion rights. The group continued fighting abortion restrictions in the post-*Roe* era and became NARAL Pro-Choice America in in 2003.

**National Organization for Women:** Co-founded by Betty Friedan in 1966, the National Organization for Women was a leading feminist organization that worked on issues from employment equality for women to abortion. In recent years, the organization has taken a more intersectional approach to feminism, analyzing the relationship between discrimination on the basis of sex, race, sexual orientation, class, age, and disability.

**National Right to Life Committee (NRLC):** The oldest and largest national antiabortion organization, the National Right to Life Committee was founded by the National Conference of Catholic Bishops to lead a secular antiabortion movement. The organization has spearheaded major campaigns, including efforts to keep abortion pills off the market and to criminalize so-called partial-birth abortion.

**Natural selection:** Evolutionary principle that species better adapted to their environment are better able to survive and reproduce.

**Nazi Party:** A far-right political party active in Germany from the 1920s to 1945, the Nazis promoted a racist ideology and oversaw the Holocaust.

**Negative partisanship:** The tendency of voters to make decisions based primarily on hatred of the opposing political party. Negative partisanship tends to increase voters' loyalty to the party with which they identify and to nationalize even the most local of races.

**Negro Project:** An initiative launched by Margaret Sanger's Birth Control Federation of America, the Negro Project was intended to expand birth control usage in the Black community, particularly across the US South.

**Newsmax:** Launched by Christopher Ruddy in 1998, Newsmax began as a conservative news and opinion site. In 2014, Ruddy launched Newsmax TV, a cable news channel known to tack further to the right than competitors like the Fox News Channel.

**New Right:** A term coined during the 1964 presidential campaign of Barry Goldwater, the New Right applied to an ultraconservative, openly populist wing of the Republican Party.

**Ninth Amendment:** The ninth amendment to the Constitution, this provision explicitly states that the spelling out of rights in the Constitution did not exhaust the liberties that the document protected. At times, courts have used the Ninth Amendment as a source of implied fundamental rights.

**Nineteenth Amendment:** Ratified in 1920, prohibited Congress and the states from denying the right to vote based on sex. The Nineteenth

Amendment gave women the vote but was rarely enforced by the courts in the decades after ratification, and racism, together with segregation and racist violence, ensured that many of women of color were unable to vote until the 1960s.

***Obergefell v. Hodges*:** A 2015 decision, *Obergefell* recognized a constitutional right for same sex couples to marry, one based on both equality under the law and due process interests in self-determination.

**Obstruction of justice:** Crimes that prevent the impartial proceedings of the criminal justice system, obstruction of justice under federal law can include tampering with witnesses, informants, or jurors, destruction of records or evidence, or retaliation against witnesses or jurors. Most states punish obstruction of justice, as does federal law.

**Operation Outcry:** A project launched by antiabortion attorney Allan Parker, Operation Outcry is an effort to collect and publicize the testimonials of women who regretted or felt injured by past abortions.

**Oral argument:** Spoken presentations by lawyers to a judge or court, oral arguments offer reasons that one side or another should prevail in a legal matter.

**Originalism:** A method of judicial interpretation of a Constitution that aims to discern the original public meaning of the Constitution or the intentions of the framers.

**Partial-birth abortion:** Otherwise known as intact dilation and extraction, partial-birth abortion is a procedure that removes an intact fetus from the uterus. Physicians use dilation and extraction after a miscarriage or stillbirth or in second or third trimester abortions.

**Partial-Birth Abortion Ban Act:** Signed into law by George W. Bush in 2003, the Partial-Birth Abortion Ban Act prohibited dilation and extraction procedures. The Supreme Court upheld the ban in 2007.

***People of the State of New York v. Margaret Sanger*:** Criminal trial and appeal of Margaret Sanger for distributing birth control in violation of New York state law. Although the trial judge and appellate courts affirmed Sanger's conviction, the case established that doctors could not be prosecuted for distributing birth control under New York law and made possible the opening of a network of birth control clinics.

**Perjury:** A criminal offense, perjury involves willfully lying under oath.

**Planned Parenthood Federation of America:** Founded in 1942, Planned Parenthood helped legitimize family planning in the United States. The organization went on to become one of the nation's leading advocates for abortion rights and the largest abortion provider in the United States.

***Planned Parenthood v. Casey*:** A 1992 Supreme Court decision, *Casey* rejected invitations to dismantle a right to choose abortion but did put in place a less protective test for abortion restrictions, the undue burden test.

**Plurality decision:** A decision in which no single opinion commands the votes of a majority of the court. The plurality, the decision receiving the most attention thereafter, is the opinion that received the most votes while falling short of a majority.

**Political action committee:** A political committee organized for the purpose of raising and spending money on political campaigns.

**Population control movement:** Formed after World War II, the population control movement tried to curb demographic growth. Population controllers had a variety of motives: some eugenic, some focused on the environment, others focused on Cold War politics. The movement revolutionized international and domestic family planning policy, all while triggering powerful accusations of racism and classism.

**Population Council:** Started in 1952 by former eugenicist Frederick Osborn, the Population Council focuses on research on family planning, particularly abroad. The organization helped to legitimize population control in the United States in the 1950s and 1960s.

**Population Crisis Committee:** Founded by Hugh Moore in 1965, the Population Crisis Committee took an alarmist approach to population control, at times adopting racist rhetoric about welfare rates and illegitimacy. The group fought to establish the United Nations Population Fund and funded the International Planned Parenthood Federation. Today, the organization operates as Population Action International.

**Privileges and Immunities Clause:** Part of the Fourteenth Amendment to the United States Constitution, this provision guarantees privileges and immunities to "citizens of the several states." Once viewed as a potential source of implied fundamental rights, the clause was narrowly interpreted by the Supreme Court in the *Slaughterhouse Cases* (1873) and is rarely used in constitutional litigation.

**Prostaglandins:** Prostaglandins were a hormone used as an abortion drug in the 1970s. Prostaglandins worked by inducing uterine contractions and the expulsion of a fetus.

**Quickening doctrine:** Legal principle that abortion was criminal only after the point at which fetal movement could be detected, usually in the second trimester of pregnancy.

**Religious Freedom Restoration Act:** Passed in 1993, the Religious Freedom Restoration Act prevents government actors from substantially burdening the exercise of religion unless the government's actions have a compelling purpose and count as the least restrictive means of achieving the government's objectives.

**Religious Right:** The Religious Right or Christian Right is a coalition of Christian groups united around a socially conservative political agenda. The power of the first generation of Religious Right groups declined after the 1980s, but the Religious Right continued to exercise power in areas from abortion to same-sex marriage.

**Repeal:** Repeal was the term applied to the fight in the late 1960s and early 1970s to remove all legal restrictions on abortion.

**Reproductive justice:** A comprehensive agenda that includes the right to personal autonomy, the right to have children, the right not to have children, and the right to safely raise children, reproductive justice became a focal point for organizing in the late 1990s. Often led by people of color, reproductive justice organizing has become important to the broader pro-choice movement since the 2010s.

**Republicans for Choice:** Founded in 1989 by Ann Stone, a direct mail fundraiser, on the advice of Republican consultant Lee Atwater, Republicans for Choice is a political action committee supporting pro-choice Republicans. Although it never achieved significant influence, Republicans for Choice still supports a handful of pro-choice members of the congressional GOP.

**Risk Evaluation and Mitigation Strategy (REMS):** A drug safety program, REMS apply to a limited set of drugs with specific safety concerns to ensure safe use. Despite a lack of evidence that abortion drugs are dangerous, mifepristone (RU 486) had been long been subject to a REMS that limited access to it.

**Rockefeller Foundation:** Established by the wealthy Rockefeller Family, the foundation is a philanthropic body that supports a variety of causes, from scientific research to food security. The Foundation was one of the leading funders of the population control movement in the United States.

***Roe v. Wade*:** Seven-to-two Supreme Court decision, *Roe* recognized a right to choose abortion, reasoned that fetuses or unborn children were not rights-holding persons, and denied the existence of a compelling interest in protecting life from the moment of conception.

**RU 486:** Another name for mifepristone, RU 486 is a drug that is used in combination with misoprostol to produce abortions in the first or second trimester of pregnancy. RU 486 works by blocking the effects of progesterone, a hormone needed to continue a healthy pregnancy.

**Saline abortions:** A rarely used abortion method, these procedures involved the injection of urea, a saline solution, or prostaglandin into the uterus. Saline abortions involved considerable discomfort and occasionally produced live births and for these reasons, have since fallen out of use.

**Savings and loan crisis:** Savings and loans, or thrifts, were financial institutions that accepted deposits and made personal loans for mortgages, cars, and the like. When thrifts began to struggle, the Reagan Administration loosened the regulations limiting the risks taken by savings and loans. A combination of risky investing and fraud led to the failure of hundreds of thrifts in the 1980s. The crisis led to a renewed push for regulatory and campaign-finance reform—many thrifts had contributed to candidates and urged them to oppose regulation.

**Second-wave feminism:** Lasting roughly from the 1960s and 1980s, second-wave feminism declared that the personal is political. While first-wave feminists often focused on voting and political participation, second-wave feminists committed to ending discrimination at work and the family. Led by activists like Gloria Steinem and Betty

Friedan, second-wave feminists tried to reform divorce, expand reproductive rights, undermine gender stereotypes, eliminate sexual harassment and marital rape, and champion an equal rights amendment to the Constitution.

**Sexual revolution:** A social movement that challenged traditional attitudes and practices around sex, the sexual revolution lasted roughly from the 1960s to the 1980s, challenging prohibitions on heterosexual sex outside of marriage and homosexuality.

**SisterSong Reproductive Justice Collective:** Formed in 1997, a leading organization in the reproductive justice movement that organizes people of color to pursue social justice and a more comprehensive approach to reproductive health.

***Slaughterhouse Cases*:** Decided in 1873, the *Slaughterhouse Cases* involved a challenge made by butchers to a monopoly granted to a specific slaughterhouse. The Supreme Court rejected the idea the Privileges and Immunities Clause protected the right to freedom of contract. By interpreting the clause so narrowly, *Slaughterhouse Cases* closed the door on use of the Privileges and Immunities Clause for future litigants.

**Socialism:** In the early twentieth-century United States, socialism focused on fighting monopolies and trusts and the concentration of wealth and power in the hands of businesses and employers. It also advocated for broader rights for workers.

***Stare decisis*:** The legal principle of respecting precedent and determining points in litigation based on what precedent has held.

***Stenberg v. Carhart*:** A 2000 Supreme Court decision, *Stenberg* struck down a Nebraska ban on partial-birth abortion because it lacked a health exception and because it swept in dilation and evacuation, the most commonly used procedure after the first trimester of pregnancy.

**Sterilization abuse:** Sterilization procedures in which is a patient is coerced or deceived, sterilization abuse made headlines in the 1970s following the exposure of a pattern of abuse directed against women and girls of color.

**Surrogacy:** An arrangement where a gestational carrier agrees to bear a child for other persons, surrogacy can occur in cases in which the gestational carrier is or is not a genetic parent. The legal status of surrogacy in the United States varies from state to state, although most jurisdictions are more likely to treat surrogacy as legal if a surrogate is not genetically related to the child she is carrying.

**Telehealth abortion:** The use of electronic communications and technology to deliver and supervise abortion services. Telehealth abortion is often limited by statute but hailed by its proponents as a way of expanding care, especially for those in rural communities or those far away from a provider.

***The Feminine Mystique*:** A 1963 book by Betty Friedan, *The Feminine Mystique* argued that stereotypes about the roles of men and women had crippled and demoralized both sexes. Some credit the book with helping to inspire second-wave feminism.

***The Woman Rebel*:** Published in eight issues starting in 1914, a magazine overseen by Margaret Sanger that discussed birth control and education, focusing on working-class women.

**Therapeutic abortion committees:** Launched in the 1940s and 1950s, therapeutic committees had to approve an abortion before one could be performed at a specific hospital. Intended to bring down the total number of abortions, the committees eventually produced more debate about when abortions should be permitted and launched the abortion reform movement.

***Thornburgh v. American College of Obstetricians and Gynecologists*:** A 1986 Supreme Court ruling striking down several Pennsylvania restrictions, *Thornburgh* was notable because the majority in favor of abortion rights in the case had shrunk to five justices, suggesting that a few more nominations could mean the reversal of *Roe v. Wade.*

**Title X of the Public Health Service Act:** First enacted in 1970, Title X provides grants as a way of providing comprehensive family planning access to low-income Americans.

**Transgender:** A term for persons whose identity and gender does not correspond with their birth sex.

**TRAP law:** Shorthand for Targeted Regulation of Abortion Providers, TRAP laws apply onerous and often unique restrictions to abortion clinics. While abortion foes claim these laws intend to guarantee the basic safety of abortion, critics argue that that TRAP laws serve primarily to force clinics to close.

**Trimester framework:** The rule created in the 1973 *Roe* decision, the trimester framework limited regulation in the first trimester, allowed restrictions only to protect patient health in the second trimester, and found the state's interest in protecting fetal life to be compelling only after viability, the point at which survival was possible outside the womb. In 1992, in *Planned Parenthood v. Casey*, the Court undid the trimester framework in favor of a new rule, the undue burden test.

**Undue burden test:** The undue burden test, created by *Planned Parenthood v. Casey*, holds abortion regulations unconstitutional when they have the purpose or effect of creating a substantial obstacle for someone seeking abortion. The precise application and meaning of the test have been contested since its creation in 1992.

***United States v. Vuitch*:** A 1971 decision, *Vuitch* upheld a Washington, DC, abortion ordinance and rejected the argument that the law's definition of "health" was too vague to be constitutional.

**Unworkability:** An opinion or legal rule is considered unworkable when courts cannot successfully put it into effect. Courts will consider whether a precedent is workable as one of the factors bearing on the decision to overrule past decisions.

**Vacuum aspiration abortion:** An abortion technique that removes a fetus through a vacuum, vacuum aspiration is commonly used from the fifth to the twelfth week of pregnancy.

**Veto:** The power to unilaterally stop an official action, especially legislation. Executive branch officials, including presidents and governors, exercise veto power when overturning laws passed by legislatures.

**Viability:** Fetal viability is the point at which survival without significant morbidity outside the womb is possible. At the time of writing, most physicians date viability to 24 weeks of pregnancy, but the time of viability can shift depending on available technology and medical standards.

**Vietnam War:** Also known as the Second Indochina War, the Vietnam War was a conflict that lasted from 1955 to 1975, pitting Communist North Vietnam against South Vietnam, a capitalist regime backed by the United States. The Vietnam draft produced considerable controversy and became a major political issue before the war's end. Media coverage of the war—much of which contradicted the official narrative—also contributed to declining faith in the federal government.

**Voluntary motherhood:** Ideal articulated by feminists in the nineteenth century that motherhood was a choice, not an obligation. Voluntary motherhood often focused not on birth control but on the right of married women to refuse sex with their spouses.

**Watergate:** A political scandal that unfolded during and immediately after the 1972 presidential election, Watergate began when former covert agents broke into the offices of the Democratic National Committee, stole confidential papers, and tried to bug phone calls. A subsequent investigation exposed the involvement of Richard Nixon's presidential administration and led to his resignation in 1974.

**Wedge issue:** A divisive political issue used by a political candidate to attract or alienate the supporters of a rival politician.

**Whitewater:** A 1990s political controversy, Whitewater involved failed real estate investments by Bill and Hillary Clinton in Arkansas. The Clintons' associates in the scheme, Jim and Susan McDougal, had become involved in the savings and loan crisis and faced criminal liability for fraudulent loans tied to their bank. Although the Clintons never faced criminal charges, the scandal prompted a federal investigation that led to revelations of Clinton's sexual wrongdoing and eventual impeachment.

***Whole Woman's Health v. Hellerstedt*:** A 2016 decision, *Whole Woman's Health* struck down two Texas abortion regulations and held that the undue burden test required the balancing of the benefits of a regulation and the burden it imposed on abortion access.

**Woman's Health Projection Project:** An ongoing initiative of Americans United for Life, the Woman's Health Protect Project is composed of legislation said to protect women from abortion. Related laws regulate abortion clinics, provide contested information about abortion, and limit access later in pregnancy.

**Zero Population Growth, Inc. (ZPG):** A population control organization founded in 1968, ZPG was popular on college campuses. Embracing the goal of small families and environmental preservation, ZPG was also one of a small number of population control organizations to embrace the legalization of abortion. In 2002, the organization became known as the Population Connection.

# Further reading

The US abortion debate has generated a rich body of scholarship, and so the list of studies here is hardly exhaustive. The earliest writings on abortion focused on the origins of criminal bans on abortion in the nineteenth century. Then, in the 1990s, as more scholars turned to studies of abortion and contraception, scholars mined several important veins. Some penned careful studies of key activists in the movements fighting for contraception or abortion. Others explored the connections between the two issues. Many put the Supreme Court at the center of the story, explaining the forces that led up to the *Roe* decision. Later, scholars began looking at the history of abortion and the law "from the bottom up," focusing on the experiences of patients with criminal abortion laws and the social movements fighting to change the legal status quo. Studies explored the role of race or religion in abortion politics. Historians compared the trajectory of abortion law in the United States and other countries. Some shone a light on the work of the antiabortion movement and its role in rightwing politics. Still others wove together the legal histories of abortion, sterilization, and even immigration.

## Origins of abortion bans

In chronicling the history of abortion and the law, some key histories begin with birth control (and its relationship to the termination of pregnancy). Linda Gordon's *The Moral Property of Women: A History of Birth Control Politics in America* (2002) offers a sweeping history of contraception from the colonial era to modern times. Other studies tell the stories of those who led the fight for or against birth control access, including Ellen Chesler's *Woman of Valor: Margaret Sanger and the Birth Control Movement in America* (1992), Nicola Kay Beisel's *Imperiled Innocents: Anthony Comstock and Family Reproduction in Victorian America* (1998), and Amy Werbel's *Lust on Trial: Censorship and the Rise of Obscenity in the Age of Anthony Comstock* (2018). Janet Farrell Brodie's *Abortion and Contraception in Nineteenth-Century America* (1994) homes in on the period in which states criminalized many forms of abortion and birth control.

James Mohr's *Abortion in America: The Origins and Evolution of National Policy* (1979) has long been considered the canonical account of the origins of nineteenth-century bans on abortion. Recently, some scholars have questioned Mohr's account, including Joseph Dellapenna in *Dispelling the Myths of Abortion History* (2006).

## From criminal abortions to reform

Leslie Reagan's *When Abortion Was a Crime: Women, Medicine, and Law in the United States, 1867–1973* (1997) offers an in-depth look at the shifting uses of criminal abortion laws. Rickie Solinger has studied the politics of unwed motherhood and abortion in the pre-*Roe* years, including in *Wake Up, Little Susie: Single Pregnancy and Race Before* Roe v. Wade (1992) and *Beggars and Choosers: How the Politics of Choice Shape Adoption, Abortion, and Welfare in the United States* (2001). Scholars have also produced in-depth studies of the networks used by patients seeking illegal abortions, including Laura Kaplan's *The Story of Jane: The Legendary Feminist Underground Abortion Service* (1995), Alicia Gutierrez-Romine's *From the Back Alley to the Border: Criminal Abortion in California, 1920–1969* (2020), and Kelly S. O'Donnell's "Reproducing Jane: Abortion Stories and Women's Political Histories," *Signs: Journal of Women in Culture and Society* 43 (2017): 77–96.

## Eugenics and population control

Scholars have studied the influence of eugenics on science, politics, and constitutional law in the United States. Scholarship focused on the courts and the law include Paul Lombardo's *Three Generations, No Imbeciles: Eugenics, the Supreme Court, and* Buck v. Bell (2008), Adam Cohen's *Imbeciles: The Supreme Court, American Eugenics, and the Sterilization of Carrie Buck* (2016), Randall Hansen and Desmond King's *Sterilized by the State: Eugenics, Race, and the Population Scare in North America* (2013), and Stefan Kuhl's *The Nazi Connection: Eugenics, American Racism, and German National Socialism* (1994).

Key overviews of the influence of eugenics law and policy in the United States include Alexandra Stern's *Eugenic Nation: Faults and Frontiers of Better Breeding in Modern America* (2005), Wendy Kline's *Building a Better Race: Gender, Sexuality, and Eugenics from the Turn of the Century to the Baby Boom* (2005), and Daniel Kevles' *In the Name of Eugenics: Genetics and the Uses of Human Heredity* (1985). Melissa Wilde's *Birth Control Battles: How Race and Class Divided American Religion* (2019) studies how American religious traditions that embraced eugenics embraced birth control.

Some studies have taken a broad view of the connections between birth control, abortion, and population control, including Donald Critchlow's *Intended Consequences: Birth Control, Abortion, and the Federal Government in Modern America* (1999). Matthew Connelly's *Fatal Misconception: The Struggle to Control World Population* (2008) offers an international perspective on population control. Others zero in on the role of sterilization in population politics, including Ian Dowbiggin's *The Sterilization Movement and Global Fertility in the Twentieth Century* (2008) and Rebecca Kluchin's *Fit to Be Tied: Sterilization and Reproductive Rights in America, 1950–1980* (2009). Laura Briggs' excellent *Reproducing Empire: Race, Sex, Science, and US Imperialism in Puerto Rico* (2003) helps make sense of how eugenics and population policy intersected with questions of race in Puerto Rico. Johanna Schoen's *Choice and Coercion: Birth Control, Sterilization, and Abortion in Public Health and Welfare* (2005) zeroes in on the experiences of Southern women of color with the state and reproductive decisions in the decades immediately after the Second World War.

## From reform to repeal

Reva Siegel and Linda Greenhouse have created an indispensable collection of primary resources for students of the abortion debate in *Before* Roe v. Wade: *Voices That Shaped Debate Before the Supreme Court Decision* (2010). David Garrow's *Liberty and Sexuality: The Right to Privacy and the Making of* Roe v. Wade (1998) offers an authoritative look at the litigation strategies that produced *Roe* and decisions like it. Sara Dubow's *Ourselves Unborn: A History of the Fetus in Modern America* (2010) historicizes attitudes toward fetal life in the United States. Other books place the rise of *Roe* in the history of broader efforts to change law and public attitudes toward sex and sexuality, including Geoffrey Stone's *Sex and the Constitution: Sex, Religion, and the Law from America's Origins to the Twenty-First Century* (2017) and Leigh Ann Wheeler's *How Sex Became a Civil Liberty* (2013). Suzanne Staggenborg's *The Pro-Choice Movement: Organization and Activism in the Abortion Conflict* (1991) offers an excellent look at the groups and strategies defining early abortion-rights work. Kristin Luker's *Abortion and the Politics of Motherhood* (1984) is a crucial sociological resource for understanding the movements on either side of the abortion question.

## Opposition to abortion

Daniel K. Williams' *Defenders of the Unborn: The Pro-Life Movement Before* Roe v. Wade (2016) evaluates the origins of the antiabortion movement and its journey to partnering with the Republican Party. Several historians have questioned aspects of Williams' account, especially those related to civil rights and race. Key works in this vein include Jennifer Holland's *Tiny You: A Western History of the Anti-Abortion Movement* (2020) and Gil Frank's "The Colour of the Unborn: Anti-Abortion and Anti-Bussing Politics in Michigan, United States, 1967–1973," *Gender and History* 26 (2014). Karissa Hausberg's *Women Against Abortion: Inside the Largest Moral Reform Movement of the Twentieth Century* (2017) focuses on female leaders of the antiabortion movement—and provides particularly valuable insight on the work of crisis pregnancy centers. In *Kitchen Table Politics: Conservative Women and Family Values in New York* (2017), Stacie Taranto tells the story of female abortion foes who helped to reshape US conservatism. Michelle Nickerson's *Mothers of Conservatism: Women and the Postwar Right* (2012) also provides helpful guidance on the role of women in the antiabortion movement.

There is a rich body of study on the history of the Religious Right and its work against abortion, with foundational books including Neil Young's *We Gather Together: The Religious Right and the Problem of Interfaith Politics* (2015), Daniel K. Williams' *God's Own Party: The Making of the Christian Right* (2010), Darren Dochuk's *From the Bible Belt to the Sunbelt: Plain-Folk Religion, Grassroots Politics, and the Rise of Evangelical Conservatism* (2011).

Joshua C. Wilson's *The Street Politics of Abortion: Speech, Violence, and America's Culture Wars* (2013) focuses on protests outside of abortion clinics—and the free speech issues they have raised. With Amanda Hollis-Brusky, Wilson has also explored the role played by conservative Christian schools in *Separate But Faithful: The Christian Right's Radical Struggle to Transform Law and Culture* (2020).

## Law, medicine, and politics in the post-*Roe* era

In *Abortion After* Roe (2015), Joanna Schoen has studied how the law has reshaped the medical practice of abortion. Historians have explored the emergence of the reproductive justice movement and the intersecting politics of race and abortion. Key works include Jennifer Nelson's *Women of Color and the Reproductive Rights Movement* (2003) and Jael Silliman, Marlene Gerber Fried, Loretta Ross, and Elena Gutiérrez's *Undivided Rights: Women of Color Organizing for Reproductive Justice* (2004). Mary Ziegler's *Beyond Abortion:* Roe v. Wade *and the Fight for Privacy* (2018) looks at the ways that *Roe* became a symbol for autonomy in fights about everything from consumer rights to the end-of-life decision-making.

For in-depth looks at the figures who shaped the abortion debate of the 1980s and 1990s, important works include Faye Ginsburg's *Contested Lives: The Abortion Debate in an American Community* (1989), Cynthia Gorney's *Articles of Faith: A Frontline History of the Abortion Wars* (1998), and James Risen and Judy Thomas' *Wrath of Angels: The American Abortion War* (1998). Mary Ziegler's *After* Roe: *The Lost History of the Abortion Debate* (2015) studies the pivotal decade after *Roe*, debunking many of the myths surrounding the decision and showing how abortion politics only gradually became more polarized. Some social movement studies of the players in the struggle include Ziad Munson's *The Making of Pro-Life Activists: How Social Movement Mobilization Works* (2010), Carol Mason's *Killing for Life: The Apocalyptic Narrative of Pro-Life Politics* (2002), and Andrew Lewis' *The Rights Turn in Conservative Christian Politics: How Abortion Transformed the Culture Wars* (2017).

## Equal protection, originalism, and abortion

The legal literature on abortion is extensive and complex, and so the suggestions here necessarily do not cover all the work in this area. Scholars have considered different doctrinal foundations for abortion rights. Several studies explore the possible role of equal protection of the law as a foundation for abortion rights, including Ruth Bader Ginsburg's "Some Thoughts on Autonomy and Equality in Relation to *Roe v. Wade*," *North Carolina Law Review* 63 (1985): 375–384, Sylvia Law's "Rethinking Sex and the Constitution," *University of Pennsylvania Law Review* (1984): 955–980, and Reva B. Siegel's "Reasoning from the Body: A Historical Perspective on Abortion and Equal Protection," *Stanford Law Review* 44 (1992): 261–380. Scholars opposed to abortion rights have published studies questioning the power of an equal protection rationale, including Erika Bachiochi's "Embodied Equality: Debunking Equal Protection Arguments for Abortion Rights," *Harvard Journal of Law and Policy* 34 (2011): 896–940.

Some critics of the *Roe* decision argue that it lacks any foundation in the text or history of the Constitution. Notable examples include John Hart Ely's "The Wages of Crying Wolf: A Commentary on *Roe v. Wade*," *Yale Law Journal* 82 (1973): 920–949. More recently, others have argued that *Roe* is consistent with the original public meaning of the Equal Protection Clause of the Fourteenth Amendment, including Jack Balkin's "Abortion and Public Meaning," *Constitutional Commentary* 24 (2007): 291–302. Mark Graber's *Rethinking Abortion: Equal Choice, the Constitution, and Reproductive Politics* (1996) argues that abortion jurisprudence should focus on affording all pregnant people an equal choice about abortion. Laurence Tribe's *Abortion: The Clash of Absolutes* (1992) also proposes thought-provoking solutions to the abortion wars.

## Bodily integrity, trauma, and abortion

Some scholars have explored the possibility that abortion rights rely on the notion of sovereignty over one's body. Key studies include Judith Jarvis Thompson's "A Defense of Abortion," *Philosophy and Public Affairs* 1 (1971): 47–66 and Eileen McDonagh's *From Choice to Consent: Breaking the Abortion Deadlock* (1996). Arguments about trauma and the body again gained attention during debates about partial-birth abortion and post-abortion regret. Foundational scholarship on trauma discourse includes Reva B. Siegel's "Dignity and the Politics of Protection: Abortion Restrictions under *Casey/Carhart*," *Yale Law Journal* 117 (2008): 1696–1796, Jeannie Suk-Gersen's "The Trajectory of Trauma: Bodies and Minds of Abortion Discourse," *Columbia Law Review* 110 (2010): 1193–1252, and David Garrow's "Significant Risks: *Gonzales v. Carhart* and the Future of Abortion Law," *Supreme Court Review* (2007): 1–50.

## Backlash and abortion

Commentators have debated whether *Roe* produced a damaging backlash. Discussions of backlash and *Roe* include Gerald Rosenberg's *The Hollow Hope: Can Courts Bring About Social Change?* (2008) and William N. Eskridge's "Pluralism and Distrust: How Courts Can Support Democracy by Lowering the Stakes of Politics," *Yale Law Journal* 114 (2005): 1312. Other commentators have questioned the backlash narrative, including Gene Burns in *The Moral Veto: Contraception, Abortion, and Cultural Pluralism in the United States* (2005) and Reva B. Siegel and Linda Greenhouse in "Before (and After) *Roe v. Wade*: New Questions About Backlash," *Yale Law Journal* 120 (2011): 2028–2087.

## Arguments for reversing *Roe* or recognizing a right to life

Scholars have also made the case that *Roe* was wrongly decided or that the Constitution recognizes fetal personhood. Early key work in this vein includes Robert Byrn's "An American Tragedy: The Supreme Court on Abortion," *Fordham Law Review* 41 (1973): 807–841 and John T. Noonan's "Root and Branch of *Roe v. Wade*," *Nebraska Law Review* 63 (1984): 668–679. More recent work has proposed a natural law framework for recognition of a life or fetal personhood, including Francis J. Beckwith's *Defending Life: A Moral and Legal Case for Abortion Choice* (2007) and Hadley Arkes, *Natural Rights and the Right to Choose* (2004). Recently, John Finnis and Joshua Craddock have made the case that the authors of the Fourteenth Amendment intended to include unborn children as rights-holding persons. Finnis' most recent work on this issue is "Abortion Is Unconstitutional," *First Things*, April 2021. Craddock's best-known work on the question is "Protecting Prenatal Persons: Does the Fourteenth Amendment Prohibit Abortion?" *Harvard Journal of Law and Public Policy* 40 (2021): 539–571. Clarke Forsythe's "A Draft Opinion Overruling *Roe v. Wade*," *Georgetown Journal of Law and Public Policy* 16 (2018): 446–491 offers one possible path that the Court could take to overturning *Roe*.

## Today

Several works showcase the central role played by state legislatures in the post-*Roe* era, including Joshua C. Wilson's *The New States of Abortion Politics* (2016) and David Cohen and Carole Joffe's *Obstacle Course: The Everyday Struggle to Get an Abortion in America* (2020).

Michele Goodwin's Policing the Womb: Invisible Women and the Criminalization of Motherhood (2020) positions abortion in a longer history of punishing pregnant people of color. Carol Sanger's About Abortion: Terminating Pregnancy in Twenty-First Century America (2017) explores the origins of the stigma surrounding abortion and evaluates how the debate might change if conversations about abortion were more open. Melissa Murray's "Race-ing Roe: Reproductive Justice, Racial Justice, and the Battle for Roe v. Wade," Harvard Law Review 134 (2021): 2027–2101 explores how arguments about racism and eugenics serve as a new basis for attacks on abortion rights.

*Reproductive Rights and Justice Stories* (2019), edited by Melissa Murray, Kate Shaw, and Reva Siegel digs into the backstories of key cases on reproduction. Mary Ziegler's *Abortion and the Law in America:* Roe v. Wade *to the Present* (2020) provides a comprehensive legal history of the years between *Roe* and the late 2010s.

# Index